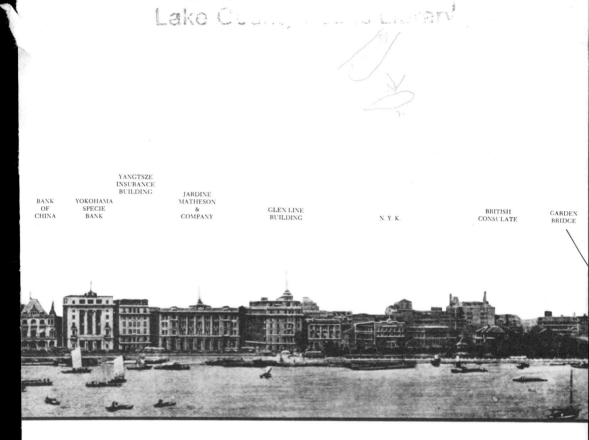

BANK
OF
CHINA

YOKOHAMA
SPECIE
BANK

YANGTSZE
INSURANCE
BUILDING

JARDINE
MATHESON
&
COMPANY

GLEN LINE
BUILDING

N. Y. K.

BRITISH
CONSULATE

GARDEN
BRIDGE

WATERFRONT OF SHANGHAI

by Noel Barber

THE FALL OF
SHANGHAI

NOEL BARBER

Coward, McCann & Geoghegan
New York

First American Edition 1979
Copyright © 1979 by Noel Barber

Library of Congress Cataloging in Publication Data

Barber, Noël.
  The fall of Shanghai.

  1. Shanghai—History. 2. China—History—Civil
War, 1945-1949. I. Title.
DS796.S257B37 1979   951′.132′042   79-17523
ISBN 0-698-10996-1

Printed in the United States of America

For Hope and Julian Bach

Contents

Maps

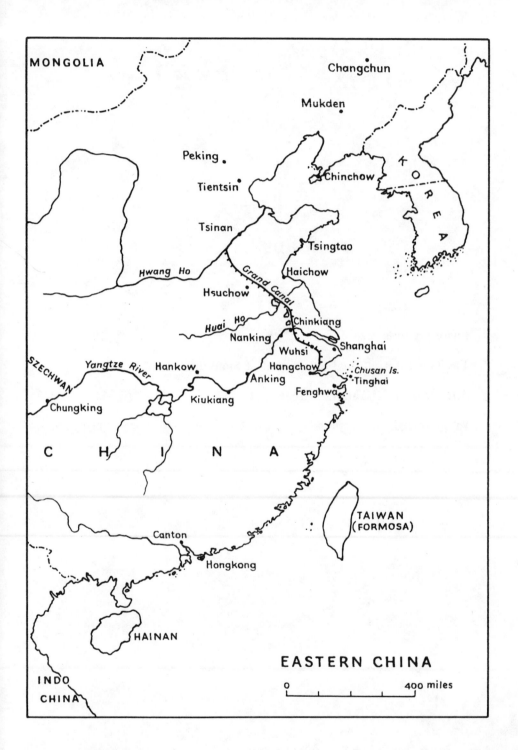

MONGOLIA

Changchun

Mukden

Peking

Tientsin

Tsinan

Hwang Ho

Hsuchow

Huai Ho

Nanking

Yangtze River

SZECHWAN

Chungking

Hankow

Kiukiang

Anking

C   H   I   N   A

Canton

Hongkong

HAINAN

INDO
CHINA

KOREA

Chinchow

Tsingtao

Haichow

Grand Canal

Chinkiang

Wuhsi

Hangchow

Shanghai

Chusan Is.
Tinghai

Fenghwa

TAIWAN
(FORMOSA)

EASTERN CHINA

0   400 miles

Introduction

Before the Second World War, Shanghai was a unique International City which continued to function under its Western leaders even when the Japanese invaded China and surrounded it. After Pearl Harbor, however, the Japanese occupied Shanghai until VJ-Day in 1945, by which time Shanghai had changed its status and become a Chinese city.

Even so, it sprang to life again and, despite the struggle for power in China between Chiang Kai-shek and Mao Tse-tung, the city, with its foreign residents, continued to prosper – until 1949, when the Communists crossed the Yangtze and Shanghai fell to Mao Tse-tung. This book deals with that period – the Communist take-over of Asia's greatest city; and it could never have been written without the kind co-operation of scores of men and women in many lands, for it is a book about people – the inhabitants of Shanghai, and their experiences prior to, during and after the Communist take-over. I have visited them in places as far apart as Britain, Hongkong, Australia, the east and west coasts of America. I had met many of them previously on my visits to Shanghai, the first of which was in 1939. All have been most generous with their time and the loan of private papers or diaries.

I would like to thank Sir Robert Urquhart of Edinburgh and John Cabot of Washington, DC, respectively the British and American Consuls-General in Shanghai in 1949, for allowing me to study their papers and diaries.

My thanks, too, to Mrs Tommy Lucy for entrusting to me for nearly two years the massive collection of letters and memorabilia of her father and mother, Billy and Gladys Hawkings. Others who lent me their papers include Mrs Gertrude Bryan, David Middleditch, Norman Watts and many more who contributed in smaller degree, not forgetting three old friends, John Proud, George Vine and Theodore H. White. My thanks to them all. I should make it clear that those who have helped do not necessarily share any views that I have expressed, or conclusions that I have drawn.

I am also grateful to the British Foreign Office, the School of Oriental and African Studies of the University of London, and to the Council on Foreign Relations in New York for unstinting help. And finally my thanks to Donald Dinsley and Anthony Davis whose painstaking research has been of major assistance to me.

For the sake of convenience, I have simplified the spelling of a few Chinese names, merely by the omission of the apostrophe, e.g. General Chen Yi instead of Ch'en Yi. I have throughout referred to Taiwan (the name meaning 'terraced bay'), the name which is always used by the Chinese and Japanese, rather than the Western name of Formosa. To make for easier reading I have throughout referred to Chiang Kai-shek's government as Nationalist rather than Kuomintang or KMT.

London, 1979   N.B.

1

The City

Summer 1948

Even by the summer of 1948, when the Communists were surging
south towards the Yangtze, Shanghai remained unique. Asia's
greatest city, the fourth largest port in the world, it stood alone –
not courageously, no bastion of stubborn defiance, but in a
strange way aloof, flaunting its unconcern for the future, as
though its six million inhabitants had closed a collective eye to the
civil war around them and were determined that, until the enemy
reached the gates, the city would remain in all its glory, a last oasis
of yesterday in the China of tomorrow.

If the Parisians regarded their city as peerless in the West, the
Shanghailanders considered the city they had adopted as queen
of the East; so that every foreigner who played a part in its frenetic
life thought of it as unique. To be a Shanghailander – whether
British or American, whether stateless Jew or Russian refugee –
had always seemed an honoured privilege. Shanghai was a city of
homes, not a city of transients. Young people might in the first
instance be posted by a trading house to work there for a few
years, but often as the moment of transfer approached, they
begged to stay. People of every nationality settled there, married,
raised children. Though originally developed by the British, the
city had escaped the taint of colonialism, for it had been run by its
own businessmen – 'men like us', as one Shanghailander described
them – and not by stuffy governors decked out with cockaded
hats and jingling swords.

And yet, though Shanghai had been an important Chinese
centre, achieving the dignity of a district city as early as 1360,
Western traders had for a long time ignored its possibilities. The

13

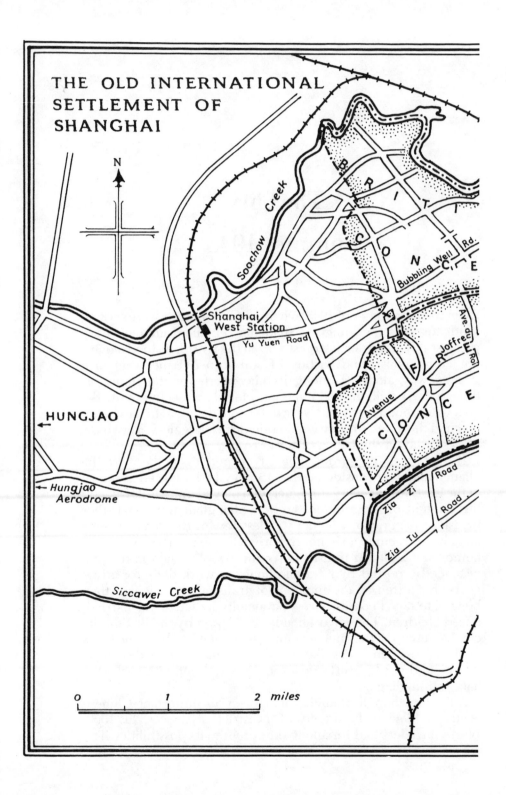

THE OLD INTERNATIONAL
SETTLEMENT OF
SHANGHAI

N

Soochow Creek

BRITISH CONCE

Bubbling Well Rd.

Shanghai
West Station

Yu Yuen Road

Ave. du Roi

Joffre

HUNGJAO

Avenue

FR

CONCE

← Hungjao
Aerodrome

Zia Zi Road

Zia Tu Road

Siccawei Creek

0   1   2 *miles*

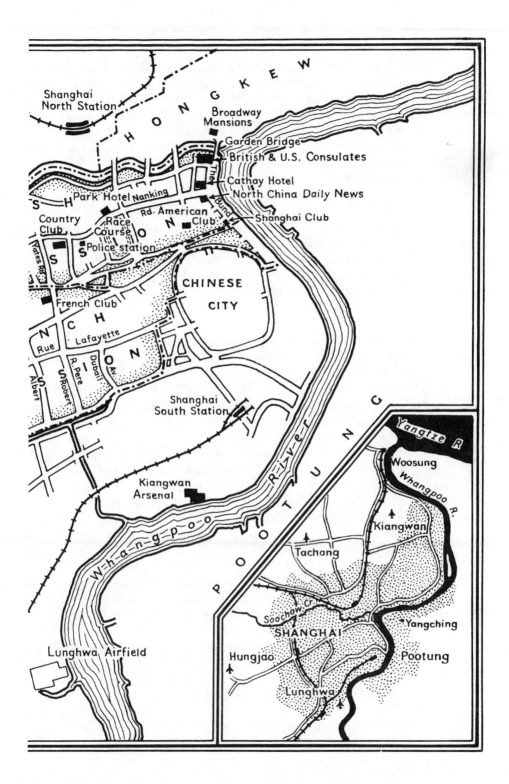

East India Company had founded a settlement in Amoy in 1625, and another in Canton two years later, but not for 130 years did the Company appreciate the advantages of establishing a post at Shanghai. Even then nearly a century passed before, in 1843, British merchant adventurers settled there, after being given permission to do so following the Treaty of Nanking which ended the Opium Wars.

Under the treaty the British were granted the right to trade in several ports, including the swamp and mud between the Soochow Creek and the walled Chinese city. The French and the Americans followed, and eventually the original tract of land became the unique International Settlement, a Western oasis in China – a city governed by its own municipal council, with its own police force, its own customs authorities, its own volunteer force to protect the traders.

Not until the first traders landed – originally ninety Britons, including seven ladies – did the West realise the unique geographical location of Shanghai. Here was no small trading post in which to exchange a few trinkets for silk or tea; this mosquito-infested township drew its strength from an unseen giant, the greatest river in Asia, the Yangtze-Kiang. Not only did its rich silt and mud deposits nourish the soil along its banks but it was itself a mighty route along which the riches of the East could be carried to the new city.

Because the estuary of the Yangtze was wide and unprotected, Shanghai itself grew ten miles inland on the banks of a tributary, the Whangpoo, which flows into the Yangtze near its mouth.

Life in Shanghai has been bound up with the river ever since. Its length, 3400 miles, is greater than the distance from New York to Los Angeles. Before it reaches the sea, it has cut its way through a land of mountain and plain, of snow and desert. From where it rises, surrounded by blue poppies, from 18,000 feet above sea level in Tibet, it has tumbled and foamed downwards in a gigantic funnel through the deep gorges of Szechwan, twisting past the rocky promontory of Chungking until its last giant waterfall spills into a sudden stillness, with all the magic of a lake, where the lowlands begin. From there the Yangtze flows majestically, a king of rivers, across eleven hundred miles of rich, fertile plains dotted with farms, villages, towns and cities, until finally, coffee-coloured and turbid, it reaches the open sea.

For a century Shanghai had grown, but by the end of the Second

World War, a change of great significance had taken place. In January 1943 Britain and America had signed a treaty with Chiang Kai-shek abrogating their extraterritorial rights. The French followed suit. Thus the International Settlement ended; within a week of VJ-Day Chiang's troops and Chiang's politicians took control, while those who had been interned by the Japanese trooped out of their camps to become aliens in what had been their own city. Yet they hoped that nothing would change. China now needed Western expertise more than ever.

Indeed by 1948 Shanghai was the most prosperous city in Asia. Britain alone had £400 million invested in China, most of it in Shanghai, and despite the Japanese occupation in the Second World War, the city was still thriving; though British and American factories suffered, hundreds of business concerns run by neutrals such as the Swiss and the Swedes had flourished, keeping Shanghai busy and prosperous until the war ended.

It was a city of contrasts, in which nothing, it seemed, could be done in moderation. If it was rich beyond man's wildest dreams, the wealthy who went shopping had to pick their way carefully between corpses in the streets; it had the tallest skyscrapers in Asia – their plate-glass windows overlooking the Orient's most scrofulous slums; it had the grandest boulevards, laid out with care and pride – and jutting off them narrow alleys with only open drains to carry away human excrement. It had Chinese courtesans who were maintained in the style of princesses – and penniless prostitutes at every corner.

Even the climate was extreme. In winter sleet and snow whistled round every corner, and thin fogs, drifting in from the sea, chilled you to the bone. Only the youngsters enjoyed it, making their way out of the city to the frozen rice fields which had been flooded by the farmers after the harvest – the rich to skate, the poor to slide; for most people winter was a season to be endured. The rich cocooned themselves in furs – in a city where sables were cheap enough to be used as car rugs – while the poor, huddled in unheated tenements, died in their thousands.

Yet if the winter was long and cruel, the summer was even worse; for then came the heat, pressing like a blanket over the panting city, each day wrapped in steamy sunshine and dripping humidity which no quivering ceiling fan could hope to alleviate; and each night a torment in which limp bodies, tired by the day's exertions, tossed and turned before waking soaked with sweat to

17

face another leaden-footed day. It was a city in which, by 1948, a worker earning $3 million Chinese a week (which would have made him a millionaire ten years previously) now starved, but where a foreigner dining at Kafka's, the best Russian restaurant in town, could have his fill of caviare and vodka for $1.50 American. To the foreigners – including 4000 British and 2000 Americans – who were paid in their own coin, it was a cut-price paradise.

The Bund was the heart of the great, ugly attractive city, perhaps the single most famous street in the East in those days. It curved along the river bank for nearly a mile from the Shanghai Club at the corner of the avenue Edouard VII to the British Consulate, its manicured lawns and compound protected by forbidding walls, its gates guarded by turbaned Sikhs for decades recruited by the British as police and guards.

Between these two points stood the banks and the offices of the great trading houses, each name evocative of the city's earliest settlers – Jardine Matheson, Sassoon, Butterfield & Swire, the Glen Line, the Chartered Bank, the *North China Daily News*, itself almost a hundred years old. To walk up the Bund was like turning over a page in a history book with each building.

Most of the trading houses had their own godowns, or warehouses, towering over pavements thronged with pedestrians, messengers, businessmen, typists, hawkers, all casting around for something to buy or sell, the hawkers beseeching you with guttural cries to accept a cold drink, examine a pair of Chinese slippers, or try their fountain pens. Dozens of tiny stalls held mysterious cooking implements, and as you walked past you could smell noodles cooking, or the sharper whiff of Szechwan food laced with chillis. One Chinese wit insisted that he could smell his way across every province of China each time he walked the length of the Bund.

Silk hawkers carried their rolls in deep bags slung round their necks; bearded professional letter-writers, each with his minuscule desk and pots of ink and flourish of brushes, peered over spectacles; boot-black boys pointed scornfully at your shoes, however highly polished. Silver dollars were surreptitiously on sale at almost every corner, the black marketeers jingling a stream of coins in their pockets to proclaim their profession while their neighbours furtively tried to attract your attention by showing you a packet of photographs, explicit if old-fashioned, and 'imported straight from Paris'. Here and there some lucky

Chinese – lucky because he was working – had been decked out in a grotesque uniform to advertise a new nightclub, and if you took the leaflet he offered it would surely promise you 'special arrangements'.

There were many beggars, often pitifully deformed, the legless sitting on small home-made platforms with tiny wheels, the blind led by small boys; and among them the occasional White Russian, dignified even in poverty, waiting patiently for someone to give him the price of a bottle of cheap booze.

You had to tread carefully on the pavements of the Bund to avoid, not so much the beggars, as the coolies carrying huge bales hanging like scales on bamboo poles arched across aching backs, each man with his eyes fixed on the ground ahead where his next footstep would fall, and giving short, sharp cries of warning as he tried to pass without altering his gait. Occasionally you would see a man crouching, his load on the ground yet with his pole still across his shoulders, resting like a worn-out beast of burden gathering strength for the long journey ahead. If it was summer and he wore only short blue coolie pants, you could catch sight of the angry scars which years of carrying had imprinted across his back.

With its kaleidoscope of movement the Bund was unique in those days, for it was the waterfront as well as Shanghai's main street, the noisiest tramcars in the world competing with a phalanx of motor cars, wheelbarrows, pedicabs, rickshaws. The street separated the handsome buildings from the bank of the Whangpoo, the jetties pointing into the water like fingers, the river alive with every type of ship from cruisers anchored in midstream to small steamers, often owned by the great companies, on the other side of the street. The companies' storerooms were beneath their offices; merely by sending coolies across the road, they loaded their ships with the produce of the fertile Yangtze basin which supplied half of China's food.

It seemed as though every vehicle in the rich hinterland had been pressed into service to carry the produce of China to the yawning holds of the ships tied up at the Bund. Along roads they came, on ancient carts drawn by mules or buffalo, or equally ancient wheezing trucks, hooting their way along the street, each with its load of cotton bales or hides piled precariously on the back, loosely lashed with frayed rope. By river and canal they arrived, boats always laden to their transoms. Boats of every shape and size seemed at times to cover the water entirely:

sampans bobbing fussily round the tramp steamers; lighters unloading a cargo of sausage casings from Manchuria; brown junks – their sterns high in the water, their sails patched, their prows decorated with glaring, painted eyes – some carrying precious wood oil, extracted from the tung tree, to be used in the manufacture of paint, others unloading silk or tea, or cargoes ranging from peanuts to sesame oil.

Once the holds had been battened down the vessels sailed towards the Yangtze, ten miles or so down the Whangpoo, and thence to the open sea, sixty miles away.

Overlooking the vessels in the Whangpoo were the big hotels, none more magnificent than the Cathay, a ten-storey ferro-concrete building which occupied almost an acre on and behind the Bund. Its finest suites boasted marble baths with silver taps. The water was specially piped from the Bubbling Well springs which had given their name to the long road leading to the outskirts of the city. Modern restaurants and a ballroom offered magnificent views over the river. The Horse and Hounds bar was the most fashionable in the city.

Every visitor of note registered at the Cathay, and if he was really famous the record of his stay was enshrined in a suite named after him; the most prestigious was the Noël Coward Suite where the 'Master' had written *Private Lives* in four days.

From this suite you could see the British Consulate, and next to it the Soochow Creek, remembered by every departing Shanghailander for its odour, as much a part of the city as the posh Cathay: an aroma compounded of refuse, human and otherwise, of drains pouring into muddy waters, of spices and the smell of the cooking pots on hundreds of river craft packed so tightly that a nimble man could reach the other bank on foot, jumping across the bobbing homes in which families were conceived, born, lived and died. From near-by skyscrapers you could see 'Creek children', as they were called, playing on the boats, their younger siblings tied round their waists with string to prevent them falling into the water.

Everywhere the city spilled from the normal into the unexpected. Just behind Nanking Road a narrow street led to the Gothic-style Anglican Cathedral, built by a grateful British merchant who had made a fortune. His memorial stood, with the Deanery, in a replica of the calm peace of an English cathedral close, somehow protected from the noise in the adjoining streets, where the jostling, hurrying, spitting Chinese made for the back-street tenements. Here they lived, twelve to a room, and the refugees on the pavements below huddled together every night, covered with old newspapers against the cold.

Half a mile away lay the old Chinese walled city, the site of the original township of Shanghai, which is said to date back to 1010. Though much of it had been rebuilt over the centuries, it retained a sense of intense national pride, so that the white man, if not excluded, was hardly noticed in the labyrinth of narrow, uneven, potholed streets flanked by ancient houses. Here, and here alone in Shanghai, he was a pale stranger in another world peopled by grave-looking Chinese in long black silk gowns, or artisans working in open shops with ivory, jade, brass or gold, the apprentices carving the first rude designs, the craftsmen giving each piece of metal or stone the final touch of the master.

Every narrow street was made more garish by its public display of laundry on poles, jutting out like flags from the windows of the tall, flimsy buildings. And then suddenly, turning a corner, you would stand entranced before a magnificent latticed front picked out in gold leaf, somehow incongruous amidst the puddles and the stench of sewers, lending an air of ravaged mystery as though – who knows? – strange secrets were locked behind its ornate doors.

A little further on, where Nanking Road ran into the Bubbling Well Road, stood the old race-course, used as a sports ground since the end of the war when Chiang Kai-shek decided that it was unwise to pander to the Chinese passion for gambling. One of the ornate stands, once filled with racegoers dressed to the nines, had become an American mortuary, used for the bodies of American airmen traced and recovered after the war from lonely village graves in which they had been buried after being shot down. The old grandstand was their last resting place in China before they were flown to their home towns for reburial.

Most of the city sprawled in disarray behind the Bund, bisected by wide avenues: the rue Lafayette and the avenue Joffre in Frenchtown; Bubbling Well Road leading to the western suburbs; Avenue Road, Connaught Road, even a Great Western Road, named in years gone by with nostalgic thoughts of home and Britain, with Nanking Road the greatest of them all. More than an artery leading from the Bund to the race-course and on to the villas of the rich in Hungjao, Nanking Road was a cross between Broadway and Oxford Street; yet it never lost its Chinese

identity. Every foreigner knew Nanking Road and its famous
department store, Wing On, though no Chinese ever dreamed of
using its foreign name, but always called it Dao Ma Lu, or Big
Horse Road. All day long sleek American cars diced with pedicabs
or – worse still – the clumsy Chinese wheelbarrows. These were
not wheelbarrows in our sense, but monstrous vehicles, each one
with a central wheel four feet in diameter, flanked by platforms on
either side; they were usually pushed by the man, with his wife
pulling on a rope in front.

From dawn to dusk Nanking Road was one huge traffic jam;
from dusk to dawn, when the neon lights were winking, it was
Shanghai's most patronised promenade, filled with impassive
waif-like (but tough) Chinese or sad-eyed White Russians waiting
for foreign 'escorts', or dancing at Roxy's which had a sign, 'This
nightclub will close at 6 a.m. unless requested to remain open
longer by our patrons.'

In every nightclub – the Metropole, Ciro's, the Lido, the
Caliente and a hundred others – a bevy of Asia's most beautiful
girls waited patiently for the evening clientele: well-heeled
tourists, rollicking sailors on shore leave, Shanghailanders taking
visitors to see 'the sights', quiet, earnest Chinese businessmen out
for a night on the town, all drawn there by the cast of thousands,
each slender, willowy girl more alluring than the next.

In most nightclubs a form of protocol was strictly observed. If
you saw a girl you liked, you beckoned to the manager, who then
whispered to her. She did not respond immediately – that would
have been vulgar – but took a good look at you to decide whether
you were worthy of her attention; only if she did not find you
repulsive or drunk (or poor) would she come to your table. You
danced a couple of times and bought her champagne (probably
cold tea). You asked after her parents (she was always, it seemed,
the sole supporter of a large, impoverished family). You sym-
pathised and told her how miserable you were to be alone in such
a strange yet glamorous city. Mutual sympathy was usually
followed by mutual understanding.

A visitor might have been troubled by this unacceptable
feature of a thriving city which allowed beautiful young girls –
not only Chinese, but Japanese, Filipinos, Koreans and White
Russians – to parade their wares so openly. It was a sight that
troubled many Shanghailanders too. But any problem involving
the Chinese was so enormous, so tangled, that no one could tackle
it. If you could not stop starvation, was it worthwhile trying to

stop prostitution? Or rather driving it underground?

In Shanghai of the late 1940s, the girls were no longer chattels of parents who sold them into prostitution; the era of the bound foot was largely over. But since the earliest days the Europeans had been unable to control the number of Chinese who had come to Shanghai; the city was wide open to exploitation – by Chinese, often of Chinese. In 1866 one out of every twelve Chinese houses in or around Shanghai was used as a brothel, almost all of them for Chinese workers who flocked into the city. Chinese girls, brought up in a cruel masculine country to believe that their main function in life was to please a man, drifted into the life without a second thought.

Nowhere was this attitude more evident than in the Foochow Road, whose unpretentious restaurants not only provided some of the best Chinese cooking in Shanghai, but also the best sing-song girls – willowy, gentle creatures between twelve and their early twenties who sang love songs and played their two-string lyres while you dined.

Through the years of growing they learned, in seven clearly-defined stages, the art of becoming courtesans. Their lives were devoted to making men happy – or at least to giving them a temporary illusion of happiness. There was nothing sordid about the sing-song houses. A man who ogled a girl or made improper suggestions would be asked to leave. Until they 'graduated' the girls belonged to the lady who owned the restaurant, and all approaches had to be made through her; private arrangements were handled with decorum.

Many of the girls had been sold into sing-song houses by starving village parents, to learn the arts and graces that could eventually lead a girl to the ultimate reward – becoming the concubine of a rich Chinese, who would not only keep her in luxury, but – as a matter of honour – provide her with ample pocket money so that she could send a monthly sum to her father as thanks for his help in guiding her to success.

For others there were 'the clubs', perhaps the greatest feature in the life of Shanghai's foreign community, for they provided links for shared interests and ideologies in a cosy atmosphere where no outside influences could intrude. Members were elected only after scrutiny by the committee. Once a member, you never paid cash but signed chits and settled your account at the end of each month. There were clubs for every nationality; there were clubs that prohibited women members, clubs that prohibited men.

There was a golf club at Hungjao, a rowing club on the Soochow Creek. There was a riding club, a shooting club, a gardening club, a 'Green Room' club behind the stage of the British-built Lyceum Theatre, with a convivial bar where members of the Shanghai Amateur Dramatic Society could keep in touch between productions, of which they gave four a year.

Without doubt the most prestigious was the all-male Shanghai Club, an impressive building, No. 1 the Bund, with columns on either side of the stone steps leading to its massive double entrance doors. The Shanghai Club was famous all over the East, and everyone had heard of its Long Bar, extending for more than a hundred feet and reputed to be the longest bar in the world. However stuffy and 'British' the club, however difficult it was to become a member, no visit to Shanghai was complete without an invitation by a member for a pre-lunch pink gin.

The bar itself was made of old and not very polished wood; it ran down the side of the room at right angles to the Bund. The bay window facing the street by tradition was reserved for the swashbuckling Yangtze pilots. These men enjoyed a monopoly on the river traffic; only they could be employed to guide a vessel through the shoals and sandbars of the Yangtze estuary. A rigid protocol ruled the position of others drinking at the Long Bar. The taipans – directors and managers of firms like Jardines, Butterfield & Swire, Patons and Baldwins, or of the banks – congregated by custom at the window end of the bar near the pilots. Newcomers played liar dice in the dark recesses at the far end. Over the months or years a member would, in some mysterious way, find himself moving up the bar as his importance in the business community increased.

Behind the bar was the billiards room, its tables covered with carefully brushed green baize. These were unlike any other tables in the world, for each was supported by short stubby legs resting on wooden platforms. New members were often puzzled until they found someone to explain: 'These used to be the finest tables east of Suez until those bloody Japanese dwarfs took over the club during the war and cut down the legs because they couldn't reach the tables to play.'

The Shanghai was above all a 'British' club – and proud of it. No menu was complete without roast beef, or saddle of mutton, or steak and kidney pie. The bedrooms on the top floor were serviced by the best boys in Shanghai, who ironed the morning paper before bringing it to you with your early tea, and who pressed your clothes daily before you descended to the breakfast room for kedgeree, or bacon and eggs, toast and Oxford marmalade (with porridge every day in winter).

For those who found the Shanghai Club too stuffy (or who could not find a sponsor to propose them for membership), there was the Dome, or the RAF Association Club, a few steps along the Bund. This was a good deal more boisterous; it had been founded by survivors of the RFC, and now drew its members from the younger people, who met for drinks or lunch on the top floor of the Hongkong and Shanghai Bank. The room was magnificent, its ceiling a huge painted cupola, and it had a splendid view over the river.

After the day's work there was the two-storey British Country Club with its ten tennis courts, squash courts, a pool (and a curry tiffin every Saturday), though the title was something of a misnomer, for the green fields on which it had been built were now packed with skyscrapers. There was also the French Club, near the avenue Joffre, generally regarded as the most chic of all, for it had the biggest ballroom, the best food, and made great efforts on special occasions. In 1948, a thousand members and guests had celebrated *le quatorze Juillet* there; the flowers on each table had been dyed blue, white and red, and a huge tricolour hung, fluttering, behind the orchestra. The American Columbia Club had gone one better, importing a cabaret and *two* bands to celebrate the Fourth of July; and the British St George's Society celebrated the thirty-seventh anniversary of its formation in May 1948, at the Country Club, with a dinner of asparagus soup; prawns; snipe; fillet of beef with mushrooms, new potatoes and green peas; *bombe glacée*; cheese and butter (American); followed by fresh fruit and coffee.

More than thirty nationalities jostled each other in the streets of Shanghai trying to earn either a fortune, a living, or at worst a bowl of rice a day. The most numerous of course were the nearly six million Chinese, their numbers swollen by the civil war. Yet the Chinese shared with every other nationality in the city one proud distinction: none had been forced to live there. Shanghai had always been a city of free choice. No colonial administrators had imported cheap indentured labour to work in the factories erected by the white men. To the Chinese, as much as to the Europeans, Shanghai was a magnet, for they knew that, even if they starved, the International Settlement, with its own police force, its Western code of justice, its independent courts, offered them a last despairing sanctuary in a country where half the people died before they reached the age of thirty. Life for the average peasant in China consisted of hunger, brutality, indignity, torture, humiliation, inflicted by corrupt authorities or venal landlords, men whom Chiang Kai-shek, once uplifted by visions of a purer and better China, was never able to control.

Before the end of 'extrality', when Shanghai was an open city where no visas were required, it had attracted more than its share of criminals who could hide safely there and continue to prey on the unfortunate. But for the most part the millions of Chinese were innocents blindly hoping for a better life. In 1948 many sons and daughters of earlier migrants had miraculously survived, so that even when the end of 'extrality' changed Shanghai's status, it had still not diminished its attraction in the eyes of the Chinese. More and more poured in after the war, an inevitable consequence among peasants whose lives and land had been uprooted by fighting and who still believed that the factories and mills would soon be working overtime again.

If the Western taipan, living in his huge villa with servants at his beck and call, seemed remote from the sufferings of the Chinese around him, nobody could pretend that the rich Chinese were not equally indifferent, and far more adept at callously exploiting the poor. Whatever their faults there were many more men and women of conscience among the settlers than among the wealthy Chinese in Shanghai. Efforts to help were pitifully inadequate, but at least some people tried. They opened schools, missions, hospitals, soup kitchens, which would never otherwise have existed. But often plans initiated by Europeans foundered simply because in China it was impossible for a man to see a project through to the end, to watch every development. If a European financed the construction of a tenement block for the poor, more often than not the Chinese builder would water down the cement, the salaried Chinese landlord would demand a kickback from prospective tenants, and the Chinese policeman would demand a fee for 'protection'. The European never got to the bottom of it.

Many Chinese-owned factories consisted of nothing more than groups of derelict houses or shabby apartment blocks operated as units, working on a round-the-clock Box and Cox system. In a city where more than a million houses had been destroyed during the war years leading up to 1945, entire families were grateful to

26

work for miserable wages and a daily ration of rice, cabbage and fish – and sleeping quarters, which they were allowed to use as soon as the other workers started their shift.

Most of the Chinese starved, but a few coined fortunes – especially the compradores to the great European companies, those independent linkmen between East and West. A compradore was not employed by a firm, but worked *with* it, as an agent who was responsible for seeing that goods were shipped or unloaded, dispatched to distant cities. The opportunities for enrichment were dazzling. The compradore engaged almost all the Chinese labour, from coolies to warehouse managers, from truck drivers to clerks; the steady jobs went to his family or friends for a consideration. The Europeans had a fixed 'coolie rate' for moving cargo – so much a ton paid to the compradore; he could hire coolies for a fraction of the money allotted to him and pocket the difference. No one asked any questions. After all, the European firm did not pay the compradore a salary. How he earned his living was his affair.

This age-old Chinese system of labour recruitment did much to increase the suffering even of the labour force; a worker considered himself *lucky* to know a compradore, however rapacious he might be, for otherwise he couldn't get work. The result was that though in theory wages rose, in practice a man working ten hours a day earned only enough to feed his family for two days a week.

When the British Chamber of Commerce investigated living conditions in Shanghai in 1948, they found that in one Chinese family the father worked nine hours a day for a tobacco firm, his wife eleven hours a day in a silk-reeling firm, their sixteen-year-old daughter twelve hours a day in a cotton-spinning mill, their nine-year-old daughter ten hours a day as an apprentice, for food but no pay. The family ate dried wheat cakes for breakfast on their way to work. They took cold rice for their midday meal, heating it in boiling water provided in most factories. They shared one room without running water with another family – fourteen people in all. Only after they had been given the strictest guarantees of anonymity would the family meet the Chamber of Commerce delegation, for they considered themselves the luckiest workers in Shanghai. 'We have a hot meal every night,' said the father proudly.

No one asked many questions in Shanghai. People minded their

27

own business, specially after the war when ex-Nazis mixed with German Jews, Gaullists with Vichy French, Reds with White Russians, even Indians with Pakistanis. All these worked alongside the hundreds of British artisans who kept Shanghai running – for all the meter-readers of the gas and electric companies, the bus and tram inspectors, the foremen in the waterworks, were British. Britons had built up the essential services and most of the big apartment blocks, hotels and hospitals, while American missions owned the Shanghai University and the St John's University.

Aloof from the rest of the city, even when begging in the streets, were the White Russians, perhaps Shanghai's most colourful community. Only a few were the dukes and countesses they pretended to be, but they had a way with them, whether they were the lucky ones managing restaurants, or the less lucky 'hostesses' in nightclubs like the Casanova and Del Monte. Rich or poor, they had style, they had panache, they helped in a curious way to lend a cosmopolitan air to the city which neither the British nor the Americans could ever have done.

The very first refugees had arrived in style – in three steamers carrying the remnants of the Far Eastern White Army, under the command of Lieutenant-General Glebov. He brought with him not only his entourage but the band of the officers' mess which played as he landed, thus marking the end of the voyage from Vladivostok from which they had been evacuated after the Bolshevik victory.

Necessity had driven them to Shanghai but that did not at first stop many from regarding the city's other Europeans with some disdain, especially those engaged in 'trade'. Glebov, it is said, politely declined an invitation to become a member of the Shanghai Club because he 'did not enjoy hob-nobbing with all those shopkeepers'. Russians with money usually settled in the French Concession because the restaurants were better there; they lived by selling their valuables one by one.

By 1948 the Russian community had dwindled to half of the original 25,000, for in 1945 the Soviet Union offered expatriates citizenship and repatriation. Youngsters who had never seen Russia, but whose imagination had been spurred by Russia's military victories, accepted; even many older people, tugged by memories, found their longing for their homeland stronger than their hatred of the government.

The original Russian refugees had fought a war and lost, but the 17,000 Jews who arrived in 1938–9 belonged to a different category. Mostly Germans and Austrians, they had been booted out of their own countries by a mad dictator, and while many Russians had arrived with money, every Jew was penniless. Yet they were potentially richer than the Russians who for the most part knew no other trade than soldiering. Many Jews brought with them skills which quickly became priceless assets in Shanghai. As doctors, dentists, teachers, engineers, writers, they became integrated into the life of the city more quickly than other refugees; they brought with them a determination to succeed, an ability to work hard, so that in many ways they echoed the ideals of the first settlers reaching Shanghai.

The Jews had lost everything but their optimism – and Shanghai was a city born of optimism. Even now its people refused to believe the worst could happen – whatever 'the worst' might be. *Maskee!* they cried – using Shanghai's very own special word which linked the babel of tongues, and was used by every one of its polygot people.

Maskee! It was the very symbol of the optimism which had for a century fired Shanghai's search for greatness. Derived from the language of the Portuguese, whose merchant adventurers had been among the first to sail the Eastern waters, it meant 'never mind' or 'don't worry'. So did *nichevo*, its nearest equivalent; yet the words were subtly different, for the Russian word was usually accompanied by a shrug of pessimistic acceptance.

But *Maskee!* Ah, that was something else! When the prickly heat was driving you mad in summer and a sympathetic friend said '*Maskee!*' it didn't mean, 'Never mind, there's nothing you can do about it'; it meant, 'Never mind, it's bound to get better.' The coolie whose rice bowl was empty cried, '*Maskee!*' not because he was starving, but because he hoped he would be luckier on the morrow.

And now, as the Communist armies pressed remorselessly southwards to the Yangtze, and the war news was bad – '*Maskee!*' And no one needed to add its implied hope, 'The news will be better soon.'

2

The People

Autumn – Winter 1948

Inevitably Shanghai threw up its quota of larger-than-life characters. Often at the daily tea dance at the Park Hotel, you could see a short, fat little man thoroughly enjoying each waltz and foxtrot though never with any of the professional dancers. Wang Hsiao-lai, chairman of the Chinese Chamber of Commerce, would never have risked dancing with a strange girl in a public place. Besides, why should he? Hard-working he certainly was, happily married he may have been, but he was rich enough to have forty-eight concubines, and he took them each in turn to dance at the Park Hotel or to dine at the St Petersburg, a spectacular Russian restaurant run by Mikhail Chernov, a middle-aged ex-officer in the White Russian Army who was (or so he said) the son of a grand duke.

Certainly Chernov was everything one expected of a Russian nobleman – he had excellent manners, he was a magnificent shot, a superb rider, he had an eye for the ladies. He was also the finest *maître d'hôtel* in Shanghai – when he chose to be. He had spent his smuggled jewellery on the lease of an old building in the avenue Haig, and transformed it into the St Petersburg restaurant, where you could eat shashlik on flaming swords, or blinis with caviare, your digestion soothed by the music of the balalaika, played against a background of a sumptuous Russian décor.

In immaculate tails, sporting a decoration on a blue silk ribbon round his neck, Chernov greeted customers at the door, kissing the hands of the most favoured female clients, until precisely midnight, at which moment he sat down at the best table in his restaurant with ten or a dozen guests. An invitation to dine at

Chernov's table was a signal honour.

Not far away, on the Nanking Road, an American ran his own restaurant – and he too was a character. Jimmy had been a sailor, who jumped ship in Shanghai after winning a modest fortune at poker. With the money he opened 'Jimmy's', offering American food only – hamburgers, ham and eggs, corned-beef hash, ice cream – served on plain wooden tables furnished with large blue enamel salt and pepper pots and bottles of ketchup. A late-night call at Jimmy's on the way home was the Shanghai equivalent of a visit to Les Halles in Paris.

Jimmy served 'American' portions – far too much to eat, but for a reason. His customers were provided with paper bags – surely Asia's first doggy bags, though the uneaten food was not for Shanghai's starving mongrels, but for the beggars outside, who learned to wait patiently for the revellers to leave. If you refused to take your bag, you were not welcome again in Jimmy's restaurant.

If the chairman of the Chamber of Commerce could have concubines, why should not a priest be allowed his worldly pleasures? Certainly the Abbot of the Buddhist temple in the Bubbling Well Road regarded it as perfectly normal to be married to an enormously wealthy wife, and also to have seven concubines. Khi Veh-du, with his shaven head, was famous. Six feet four inches tall, with a magnificent physique, he practised shadow-boxing and keep-fit exercises at dawn each day, before donning his magnificent robes in the temple.

There were many temples in Shanghai, Taoist and Confucian as well as Buddhist, where worshippers prayed to their ancestors and gave thanks for any good luck that had come their way. Several thousand Chinese Catholics said mass in their own cathedral with its twin spires; there was even a thriving Nonconformist chapel in the Bubbling Well Road. But no place of worship was like Abbot Khi's temple. Richly endowed, it contained forty or fifty huge Buddhas, some clothed in gold leaf, others in bright colours. Throughout the day hundreds of worshippers came in to light their joss sticks and place them in brass holders. All through the day, the priests conducted services, while the shifting congregation – standing, kneeling, squatting – chanted or joined in the incantations.

Not only was the temple rich in its own right, the Abbot and his wife saw to it that the temple was maintained as it should be. Mrs

Khi was a remarkable woman who drove round Shanghai in a new Buick with a White Russian chauffeur who, in cold weather, ostentatiously draped a sable fur over the front of the car if Mrs Khi stopped to do a little shopping. She and her husband had their own White Russian bodyguards who travelled everywhere with them – carrying an intriguing 'badge' of office. At first sight it looked like an ordinary leather briefcase; in fact the case was lined with bullet-proof steel so that it could be used as a shield should either of the Khis be attacked. The Abbot's seven concubines also had their bodyguards and each had a car and a house of her own, an arrangement cheerfully accepted by Mrs Khi.

One of the Abbot's closest friends was a remarkable Englishman, perhaps the best Chinese scholar in Shanghai. Norman Watts was a Southampton man who had come to Shanghai as a young man in 1929 to join a shipping firm. At that time a few British merchants were beginning to realise that a knowledge of the Chinese language could be useful; Watts, who was tall and extremely handsome, had been marked out as a man of outstanding ability. His firm sent him to universities in China for nearly six years; during the last three he lived at Soochow University as a Chinese, the only Westerner enrolled there.

Watts numbered as many Chinese as English among his friends, and in 1945, towards the end of the Japanese occupation, it was Chinese friends who hid him after he had escaped from an internment camp. He joined the Communist guerrillas to escape detection, and for the next four months, dressed in coolie clothes, his face hidden beneath a wide-brimmed straw hat, he fought with a guerrilla unit, mopping up isolated pockets of Japanese. Only when it was safe did he return to Shanghai.

Watts lived on the far bank of the Whangpoo River, in an area known as Pootung. As there was no bridge over the river he had to take a launch each time he visited the Bund or Shanghai proper. His company's wharves lay five miles or so down river, and his own house was behind the extensive wharf area which stretched for nearly half a mile. He had tried living in Shanghai, but preferred the country. From his veranda, facing inland, he could see the rough path leading to the village of Yangching. He kept a couple of ponies on which he explored the countryside. Sometimes he would ride to small villages, stopping for a slice of melon or a cup of green tea, talking to Chinese who had never seen a white man other than himself, and doubtless thought that they all spoke impeccable Chinese.

There were three other Britons on the wharf, with whom he 'got on well enough', but Watts realised that they thought him 'a little quirky'. It didn't worry him. He had a piano, a library of several hundred Chinese works, a tennis court, a pool, a good cook, plenty of spare rooms and a host of friends in Shanghai who enjoyed a weekend in the country.

When Watts felt like a change he would sometimes visit friends in Broadway Mansions, a sixteen-storey building of dull red brick overlooking the Bund, the British Consulate-General and the Soochow Creek. This was the headquarters of the Foreign Correspondents Club of China. The US Military Advisory Group occupied the lower nine floors of the building, and the apartments on the next six were used by the foreign press, with one floor serving as a club with a bar and an excellent restaurant.

The penthouse had been divided into two or three apartments, and in one of these lived an acquaintance of Watts, George Vine, the British assistant editor of the *North China Daily News*. Vine was a wiry, energetic man in his twenties, with an engaging smile and a shock of blond hair, who had served as an officer in Burma and later in Germany, and had vowed to return to Asia when the fighting ended. He fell in love with Shanghai the moment he arrived there in 1946 with the German girl he had recently married. Since then nothing had dimmed his enthusiasm.

Most mornings Vine walked from Broadway Mansions along the Bund to the *News* office, next to the Bank of China and the Cathay Hotel at the corner of Nanking Road. He had to work long hours, as in addition to his job on the *News* he was a correspondent for the American International News Service, and for two London papers, the *News Chronicle* and the *Observer*. Because of the time difference – midnight was early morning in London – George Vine often worked a sixteen-hour day.

For all the Westerners living in Shanghai, there was a sense of excitement, an exhilaration in this mercurial, unexpected city, and everyone in Shanghai had his or her own anecdotes.

When George Vine's wife Ellen decided to order a new dress, she went to Yates Road, a narrow street off the Bubbling Well Road known affectionately to the Americans as 'Pants Alley' and to the English as 'The street of a thousand nighties'. In Yates Road a woman could buy everything she wanted to wear for next to nothing – undies, new dresses dextrously copied from the latest fashion magazines, the models often displayed in small shops like the one with the sign 'Ladies Have Fits Upstairs', or Dong Chen & Co. the 'Bespoke Tailor and Ladies Cleaner'.

Ellen knew exactly what she wanted made by her tailor Han Son Loh (always known as Mr Loh): it was a dress that buttoned all the way down the front. The Chinese assistant understood, but was doubtful about one particular aspect of his customer's requirement. In a questioning voice which rapidly ascended the tonal scale, he asked anxiously, 'Missee want button, button, button, button, button, button, button, button?' or – his voice dropped to normal – 'Button, waittee little bit – button, waittee little bit – button, waittee little bit?'

One of the Vines' best friends, Nic Fogner, the young Norwegian Vice-Consul, had a meals problem, for he had 'inherited' a remarkable number one boy called Ah Tin who insisted each evening on producing the following day's menu for his master's approval. This was fine in theory, thought Nic; it had a certain old-world charm about it which he liked. Unfortunately Ah Tin couldn't read or write; consequently the proposed menu was in fact not written, but consisted of beautiful illustrations, often delicately coloured. 'Ah Tin drew a pretty prawn,' Fogner remembers. 'The drawings were so beautiful that I never had the heart to change the menu.'

Vine remembered an American lady who also faced a culinary problem: Mrs Passcote, the delightful young bride of a Shell executive, had arrived from California with a horror of dirt and disease. Taking one look at the antiquated wood stove in her new home she went straight to the PX and ordered an entire range of sparkling American kitchen fitments. After dinner one night she proudly invited her guests to inspect the transformed kitchen, and sure enough it shone like a new pin. As Mrs Passcote led her guests back to the balcony, Vine stopped to ask cookie how he managed to keep the kitchen so spotless. 'Missee velly angry if kitchen not clean,' explained a beaming cookie, 'so I do all cooking in my bedroom.'

Newcomers often had their first taste of Shanghai's way of doing things even before they landed. When David Middleditch, a new recruit to the firm of Jardine Matheson, arrived by ship from Hongkong in the autumn of 1948, he was met at the company wharf – opposite the offices on the Bund with 300 or more employees – by a Jardine man who tossed to him over the ship's side a parcel the size of several cigarette cartons. It was money – millions of Chinese dollars, worth virtually nothing – described as 'a little spare cash to ease your way through the customs'. Middleditch felt that 'The size of the parcel, the reason for the parcel, summed up Shanghai for me even before I landed – inflation and corruption.'

Now aged twenty-seven, Middleditch had fought with an armoured car regiment throughout the war until in 1945 he had a leg blown off near Ravenna in Italy. After leaving hospital he spent a year at Cambridge before joining Jardines. With remarkable determination he soon started playing tennis and squash again. He played a fine game of polo. He could dance till dawn.

Middleditch found it hard to believe the evidence of his eyes. Despite the poverty, shop windows in Shanghai bulged with goods, many people in the streets were well dressed. In his first week a colleague invited him home at a moment's notice to a banquet such as only the Chinese knew how to prepare without any warning. Wines and spirits, cigarettes, petrol, were plentiful. There was none of the rationing which Middleditch had left behind in England. When he was taken for the first time to the Shanghai Club, 'I just couldn't take in the sight of all those bottles behind the bar.' In England he had had to cajole a drink from a surly barman; here one could choose from fifty brands of Scotch.

Middleditch liked the Shanghai Club, but he made no attempt to join it, for 'I had been tipped off in Hongkong what the form was.' The taipans didn't relish their assistants joining. As one of them put it, 'It would have been damned embarrassing to prop up the bar at lunch with somebody after you'd played hell with him in the morning.' So if a newcomer unwittingly asked his boss if he could join, he was told vaguely, 'If you like, but it's rather expensive, and also we older chaps find that you youngsters tend to get bored in our Club.' (That was the reply Arthur Colley, a young American ex-pilot, received from his boss when he landed a job in Shanghai after VJ-Day. But Colley had an answer. 'Oh, I think I'll fit in, sir,' he replied cheerfully. 'After all I kinda know the place. I was made an honorary member when I helped to liberate Shanghai from the Japs.')

Though no one was prepared to admit it, a gulf did exist in the foreign population between the newcomers and the old China hands – an inability of each to understand the different world the other had inhabited during the war. Those who had lived most of their lives in Shanghai, and had been interned by the Japanese, had nonetheless escaped the bombs and mass destruction which had devastated Europe; so that when they emerged from internment and saw the European newspapers, the photographs of a demolished Cologne or Coventry had to them all the unreality of a film. Yet to newcomers arriving from Europe, it was Shanghai that was invested with unreality, and they could hardly believe the air of bustle, the wealth, the splendid shops stocked with goods, the elegant restaurants.

Almost all the newcomers were young men or women posted to branches of the big trading houses or aid programmes, and it was difficult for them to take the civil war seriously, for surely no one would be ass enough to waste time and money sending a youngster to Shanghai if there were any real danger of the business being closed down. It didn't make sense. Meanwhile there was a new and exciting city to be explored after all the miseries of war.

One newcomer summed up his impression of the summer of 1948 in two words, 'riotous abundance', and asked George Vine how it was possible, in a city living under the shadow of Communism and in the grip of inflation, to go on living a life which he, coming there from Europe for the first time, could only goggle at? One reason for this 'riotous abundance' lay of course in the large grants which China had been receiving from UNRRA and other aid programmes since 1945, most of which ended up in Shanghai. There was also massive direct aid from America – cotton, rice, oil, and particularly wheat, which with a certain irony was often shipped to the north and bartered for coal from British-owned mines in Communist-held territory. It was power from that source which kept the cotton mills in Shanghai busy weaving American-imported cotton, the mill-workers being paid with Chinese paper money printed in America, with which they could buy rice imported from overseas in American ships and paid for by the American taxpayer.

It was one way of hiding the fearful inflation which no one seemed prepared to try to cure. In 1944 20 Chinese 'dollars' (the gold yüan) had equalled 1 American dollar. By March 1946 the ratio was 2020 to 1. By February 1947 it had been officially pegged at 12,000 to 1. By the late spring of 1948 the black-market rate fluctuated above the million mark – and it was sliding not every week, but every day. Inflation was not only a human tragedy, it was a political tragedy which played into the hands of Communist sympathisers, for it was the workers who suffered –

the very people on whom the economy depended, factory-workers, soldiers, policemen, civil servants. What hope had any government of retaining their loyalty, if they starved while corrupt officials made fortunes?

For foreigners paid by their head offices, in their own currency which they could change to their advantage when they wished, inflation was a perplexing nonsense, as Gladys Hawkings tried to explain in one of the letters she wrote every Friday to each of her five daughters settled in different parts of the world. The Hawkings – Billy, aged fifty-eight, and Gladys, a year younger – were an institution in Shanghai, and they lived in a house called The Limit, set in ten acres at Hungjao, nearly ten miles from the Bund.

Billy Hawkings, who came from Bristol, was the Shanghai director of Wheelock, Marden & Co. Ltd, a well-known shipping firm, and over the years he had become one of Shanghai's best-known citizens. He was chairman of the British Residents Association, the Rotary and St George's clubs; he sat on the council of the Chamber of Commerce and the British Hospital committee. Gladys was the daughter of missionaries and had lived all her life in China. Warm-hearted, she had a face touched with lines of humour, and tanned by hours spent working in the gardens of The Limit, her pride and joy. The house was set in grounds studded with fragrant camphor trees, flame trees and bushes. In the grounds were a cricket pitch, a bowling green and tennis courts – and feeding trays to attract neighbouring tame pigeons which, in the fashion of the Chinese, often had bamboo whistles fitted under their wings so that they made a gentle, plaintive, piping music.

The Hawkingses' number one boy and the cook now got $8 million a month each, the amah and the coolie $6 million, and the driver $10 million; $38 million for the five of them. In English money this fluctuated between £10 and £15. Butter was $750,000 a pound or about 25p; eggs $10,000 each, or less than ½p; American apples $1 million a pound; chicken $200,000 a pound; beefsteak $130,000; fillet of beet $240,000. Coffee cost the Hawkingses $1½ million pound, or about 50p; imported powdered milk $1 million a pound; ham $400,000; cheese $650,000; flour $45,000; fresh milk $400,000 a pint. A packet of American cigarettes cost $100,000. As Gladys said in her letter, 'I hope I have got my arithmetic right.'The rates vary from day to day.'

More and more, people were turning to barter, trying to avoid possessing any money. The Hawkingses had decided to pay their servants in rice. Others had similar ideas – though sometimes with unexpected results, as the Hawkingses discovered when they dined with Alec McShane and his wife, a White Russian. McShane owned a small import–export firm, and a year previously had only been able to obtain some urgently needed supplies from a Chinese merchant by 'paying' with some cases of tinned sardines worth £4000 which had just arrived in his godown.

The sardines had had a long history. The original consignment was split up, various cases going the rounds of Shanghai as they were exchanged for the most improbable items of merchandise, until finally a few cases arrived back at McShane's godown in payment for something he had sold. It was then that McShane decided to prise open one case and take a few tins home to his wife. They were bad. Repeated handling, bumping, dropping, as they travelled round and round Shanghai, had dented several tins and ruined the sardines.

When McShane told the dinner guests that, after all, there would be no sardines on toast as a savoury, one remarked cynically, 'Serves you right, Alec! Opening those cases was like tearing a banknote in two. They weren't sardines any more – they'd become money.'

Two other guests at that dinner party were good friends of the Hawkings; they too had missionary parents. Robert T. Bryan Jr and his wife Gertrude, both Americans, had particular cause to view the onrush of Communist forces with apprehension.

Bob Bryan was a lawyer who had been born in 1892 in Shanghai's Chinese walled city where his father was a Baptist missionary. As a youngster he had been the only American to attend Shanghai's Ming Jang Academy, and he spoke better Chinese than English until his father sent him to America to study law at the University of North Carolina. In 1928 he was, much against his will, appointed municipal advocate, or public prosecutor, to the Shanghai Municipal Council in the then International Settlement. Four times in fourteen years he tried to resign, but each time he was told, 'There's no American in town who knows Chinese like you do. You're indispensable and we simply won't let you go.'

In those fourteen years Bob Bryan and his staff were responsible for sentencing 10,000 underground Communists to prison terms in Shanghai's mammoth Ward Road Jail, a huge penal institution supervised by the Municipal Council (and to which Bryan faithfully went on a monthly tour of inspection as part of his duties). 'I even prosecuted one case,' he told Hawkings, 'in which one of the wives of Mao Tse-tung was involved, so I don't think I'll have many friends if the Communists take the city.'

Bryan's wife Gertrude was a schoolteacher who had arrived in Shanghai in 1924 after a friend had written to her, 'You must try and get a job here. There are ten men to every woman and you can't miss.' A cheerful extrovert, Gertrude was an instant success with the 500 pupils of the American School in the avenue Pétain. She also married Bob Bryan whose first wife had died, leaving him with three young children. She was an equal success as wife and mother. They lived in a three-storey house with a red-tiled roof at Columbia Circle.

The Bryans had been interned after Pearl Harbor, and when they were freed, Bob had set up in partnership as a lawyer. With the abolition of the old International Settlement, he found that 'The roof had suddenly collapsed and the old International Settlement was in chaos'. He had more work than he could handle, in 'a businessman's nightmare in which corporations which had done business in China for fifty years were suddenly required to register as foreigners through a hailstorm of forms, documents and affidavits'.

He and Gertrude discussed over and over again whether they should leave, and their friends urged them to go before it was too late, but as Gertrude remembers, 'Somehow Bob and I never really got around to making a decision. Reason told us we ought to go, and we did compromise by sending the children to America, but I guess that we loved Shanghai so much – after all, it was our home – that we couldn't bear to make the final decision.'

Bob had no illusions, as he wrote later: 'I knew that Shanghai had reached the soft, fat and frustrated state that opens the door to Communism, and the Communists were already knocking at the door,' and he realised that 'my role as municipal advocate would surely cause me trouble in the coming months'. Yet he not only loved Shanghai, it was the only place where he could recoup his fortunes. He had lost everything but his house during the Japanese occupation, and now American businessmen were beseeching him for help – at any fee he cared to name. 'My risk was calculated, but thus committed I had a grandstand seat to wait for the spectacle of Communists taking over a great city.'

3

The Reason Why
Autumn–Winter 1948

George Vine had been asked by a London newspaper to write a major feature article summing up the problems facing Shanghai, and the recent history leading up to the ever-increasing Communist threat. Briefly he sketched in the latest military situation, from which it was clear that a dynamic, disciplined Communist army was inflicting defeat after defeat on Nationalist forces led by Chiang Kai-shek, which were beset with corruption, intrigue and defectors. Some of the defectors were training Red Army troops in the use of modern American weapons which they brought. with them. By now the Communists were rampaging over most of Manchuria (where they had in 1945 collected a huge stock of Japanese arms), isolating the few remaining Nationalist strongholds which Chiang's troops found difficult to supply or relieve because of the great distances involved.

It was hard sometimes for the people in Shanghai to appreciate the vast numbers of people in this campaign, in a country where estimates of population varied from 400 to 600 million – numbers so large that the difference in estimates was greater than the entire population of the United States. Yet all over China people were killing each other, or were locked up in long sieges of the great walled cities north of the Yangtze. These cities remained under siege until, as so often happened, their garrisons defected with their arms, enabling the Red Army to transform itself slowly from a force of foot-sloggers – each man with a bandolier holding enough rice for ten days – into a modern army, using the weapons which the Americans had originally supplied to Chiang Kai-shek.

John Leighton Stuart, US Ambassador to Nanking, reported,

'Even high-ranking officers said that whereas there seemed to be some point in endless fighting when the enemy was Japan, there is not much stomach for fighting when it is against China. This lack of morale appears to be reflected among the troops who do not understand what the war is all about and who, in some instances, have been susceptible to Communist appeals to lay down their arms.'

Many had certainly 'been susceptible', and as a result the size of the armies had changed dramatically. In a secret session of the Nationalist Yuan, or parliament, in the summer of 1948, deputies were told that when Japan surrendered, the Nationalist army totalled 3.7 million men. Apart from rifles and machine-guns, they had 6,000 artillery pieces. The Communists had 320,000 regular troops, of whom only 166,000 were armed. By June 1948 the Nationalist army had been reduced to 2.1 million, with 21,000 artillery pieces, while the Communist army now totalled 1.5 million with nearly a million rifles and 22,800 guns. Hundreds of thousands of those rifles – to say nothing of other guns – had been 'made in America'. As Dean Acheson pointed out,[*] they had fallen into the hands of the Chinese Communists 'through the military ineptitude of the Nationalists' leaders, their defections and surrenders, and the absence among their forces of the will to fight'. In all, the US was providing China with grants and credits totalling $2 billion and also selling her Pacific war surplus *matériel* which had originally cost $1 billion – including 300 aircraft and dozens of naval vessels – for $232 million, payable in instalments. Now all the Americans could do was watch wryly as American equipment was used against their allies, and wonder how far the explosion rocking China would spread across Asia.

Throughout the Asiatic continent nearly a billion people, tired of the starvation, brutality, corruption that made up their daily lives, were ready to throw off their chains; people hitherto impotent and apart, but spurred on now by proof that the power of the West was not enough to halt the new tide of the East. Mao was no magician; he could lie and cheat and make false promises as much as Chiang, but he knew what everyone wanted, and he guaranteed everyone at least one square meal a day. Chiang Kai-shek might have his powerful American allies with their arsenals of democracy, but he also had to live with the past which had

---

[*] Writing in 1949 in *United States Relations with China*, published by the US State Department in the same year.

been discredited. Mao Tse-tung had the people – and the future, which no one could discredit in advance.

As grave as the military defeats was the wickedness of Nationalist government officials, who in 1945 had been hailed in Shanghai as victors over Japan but who were now interested only in making their fortunes. They sold patronages, printed worthless money, diverted food and aid from relief programmes into their own black market. Corruption was not confined to Shanghai alone. The American Consul-General in Mukden commented on the food situation in the north: 'Puerile efforts have been made towards price control and to combat hoarding but in general the results of these efforts have been largely to enforce requisitioning of grain at bayonet-point for controlled prices and enable the re-sale of requisitioned grain at black market prices for the benefits of the pockets of rapacious military and civil officials.'

In Shanghai the millions of refugees were victims of negligence by the authorities. No serious attempt was made to feed or house families without work. Their only 'homes' consisted of flimsy straw and bamboo lean-to shacks, erected nightly under the lee of the imposing buildings where the taipans worked during the day. Hundreds died daily of cold or starvation, and each morning a fleet of municipal trucks set out to clear the main streets of corpses.*

Sometimes if George Vine was on the 'early turn' he saw the bodies being collected. The driver and his mate jumped out of their cab, gave the figure in the doorway a kick, and if it didn't react, the corpse was thrown on the pile of bodies on the open truck. One morning Vine saw a truck piled so high that when it turned a corner too sharply three or four bodies fell off into the street. The driver never noticed. Only the previous week Vine had seen a body outside the Palace Hotel near the *News* office. Vine had contacted the manager, a White Russian, whom he happened to know.

'But do you realise there's a man right outside your entrance – he's either dead or dying?' asked Vine. 'It's not a very good advertisement for your hotel, is it?'

'No, no, it's nothing to do with us,' replied the agitated manager. 'He'll be collected in due course.'

---

* Official statistics show that even in 1938 when unemployment was rampant – but not as bad as ten years later – 101,047 'exposed corpses', as they were called, were found in Shanghai.

'I'm going to send for an ambulance,' Vine insisted.

'You'll have to pay,' the manager warned him – and he was right. The man was collected. He was dead. And in due course Vine received a bill.

'Nevertheless,' Vine wrote, 'millions of people in Shanghai are living better today than they have ever done before. Before World War Two the Chinese youth smoking a cigarette or the Chinese girl wearing nylons were exceptions. Today you can see them everywhere.'

Vine went on to comment on the

astonishing serenity of people living on top of a volcano. Two of the most severe afflictions that a country can suffer – civil war and inflation – are with us. I can partly understand indifference to civil war because China has been a hotbed of wars in one form or another for centuries, but how things manage to tick over when the dollar is worth one-5000th part of its value in 1939 defeats me. The whole economic situation is unreal.

How was it possible for this indifference to continue among a people with one of the most ancient cultures on earth? Norman Watts, who discussed it time and again with his Chinese friends, came to the conclusion that the Chinese themselves didn't know. 'It was hard for people in Europe to realise that the Chinese were subjected to one of the most ruthless censorships of all time. Every Chinese newspaper carried only stories of Nationalist victories. The average Chinese had not the faintest idea of the magnitude of defeats that were tearing Chiang Kai-shek's armies apart.' Among all Watts's Chinese friends, only one seemed to be really aware of the danger – and that was the remarkable Mrs Khi. The Abbot's wife told him on one occasion, 'We are lost. The Communists will conquer all China, and our world will be forgotten.' Mrs Khi, however, was a lone voice in Shanghai. Perhaps the Chinese who did have doubts preferred, as the world's greatest fatalists, to hide them even from themselves.

Shanghai was more a mirror of China than New York is of America. It was hard for its people to follow the shifting ideologies that divided the two sides which had been locked in intermittent civil war since 1927; yet their leaders, Chiang and Mao, had at first been fired by much the same lofty ideals. They had both begun as romantic revolutionaries, dazzled by the opportunity to rid their country of oppressive warlords, to ease the burden of tyranny which almost (but, miraculously, never quite) broke the backs of toiling peasants.

To the Shanghailander, busy with making money or dancing the night away, it was all so much ancient history; and not even their history because Shanghai had only recently become part of China. When Dr Sun Yat-sen led the revolution against the Manchus in 1911, they were unconcerned at his attempts to 'westernise' China. They only became concerned when the good doctor turned to Russia, for though he was no Communist, Sun Yat-sen had been deeply impressed by the success of the Bolshevik revolution. So had his son-in-law, Chiang Kai-shek, a brilliant soldier who jumped a few rungs on the ladder to success by marrying 'the boss's daughter'.

The new member of the family despised communism as much as his eminent father-in-law, but he did admire what the Communists in Russia had achieved, and it is ironic to reflect that the collaboration between Russia and China started when Chiang Kai-shek visited Moscow in 1923 to solicit help for the hard-pressed Sun Yat-sen. Chiang saw both Stalin and Trotsky (Lenin was ill), and within two years a thousand Russian military and political advisers were helping China to overthrow the warlords. It is even more ironic to remember that when Chiang opened the Whampoa Military Academy in 1924 – the first professional military school in China – the Russians were the first to congratulate him on his plans 'to supply the army with junior officers of political understanding', while Sun Yat-sen frankly felt that 'it was the lessons of the revolutions of Soviet Russia that have led us today to inaugurate this academy'. The policy of Whampoa was to train young officers along Leninist lines to become political commissars who would ensure that the army always remained under the direct control of the government. On Russian advice the Nationalists grudgingly allowed left-wing elements to join the Academy so that, in a bizarre twist, Chiang Kai-shek, as director, was actually supervising the training of the Communists who would one day become his enemies.

Before long Chiang could sense the danger of a leftist trend. He might have admired Russian organisation, but never its doctrine, and he was not in command at Whampoa to obey the Russians. When he discovered that Communist cells were being organised in Whampoa by the Russians, and that officers were even being discreetly incited by Russian advisers to strike, he struck first. Without warning he disarmed all left-wing 'rebels' at a moment when the leading Soviet advisers, including Field-Marshal Galin, were on a visit to Moscow. The coup was so successful that Stepanoff, the senior Russian military adviser, commented bitterly, 'The Russians are beginning to realise that they are not using Chiang, but are being used by him.'

Next, Chiang removed all Soviet advisers from executive posts. The result was a head-on clash between Russia and China. Chiang could not eliminate the thousands of non-executive Russian advisers, and they were now ordered by Moscow to foment unrest, form Communist cells in the army and generally stir up trouble. Thus, out of Chiang's brave stand against Russian interference was born the force which would one day become known as the People's Liberation Army and which would hound him from the Chinese mainland.

No one can doubt that in the beginning Chiang Kai-shek had only one thought – for China. Yet the first flaws in his character began to show soon after he succeeded Sun Yat-sen, who died in 1925, four years after the Chinese Communist Party convened its first meeting in Shanghai. Chiang's march to Chungking, his heroic stand against Japan in the early years, made it easy to label him as a patriot. But Chiang's patriotism was marred by early signs of paranoia.

This first manifested itself when in 1927 he felt strong enough to move his army into Shanghai to liquidate the Communists who were increasing their hold on the Chinese in the city. Chiang could not of course touch anyone in the International Settlement, but outside its boundaries, in outer Shanghai, not a single suspect's life was spared. Several hundred thousand Chinese – thousands of them innocent – were slaughtered in Shanghai and in a similar purge in Canton. The purge was so horrific, so brutal, that had it been ordered by a Communist or Fascist government it would have been reviled all over the world.

It was this bloodthirsty essay that more than anything else sparked off a hatred of Chiang by Communist leaders; it lasted until they were able to cheer his death. And it was the personal animosity between Mao and Chiang, born out of this purge, that made it virtually impossible to halt the civil war, to try to fashion China even temporarily into a loose federation of north and south under different rulers. To Mao, Chiang was as bestial as Hitler had seemed to Churchill, and he would never settle for

anything but 'total surrender'. Many of the old-time foreigners
still living in Shanghai hardly realised that now, in 1948, twenty-
one years after the massacre, the two leaders were still the same
men, with Mao Tse-tung hating the man who had 'torn the heart
out of Shanghai'.

Soon after the rape of Shanghai, another factor entered the
bloody picture. In 1931 Japan occupied Manchuria. The Communists, who had retreated to the mountains on their famous
Long March, declared war on the Japanese – an ineffectual
military threat, since their nearest troops were thousands of miles
distant, but a brilliant stroke of propaganda, for their declaration,
and their demand for a 'united front' to fight the Japanese,
eventually forced Chiang to form an unholy alliance with his
enemy.

By the time the Japanese attacked Pearl Harbor they controlled
not only Manchuria, but also 800 miles of the Yangtze coast north of
Shanghai. They had settled in huge numbers in the Shanghai
suburb of Hongkew on the north side of the Soochow Creek, and it
was an easy matter for them to walk into a defenceless
Shanghai. From the various national organisations such as the
British Residents Association, they obtained lists of every
foreigner in Shanghai, and interned them all – except their allies,
the Germans. Men like Norman Watts were ordered to report at
the Bund on a given day and sent to one of the several camps
which the Japanese hastily improvised. Japanese businessmen –
each one with an exact task – took over the rich prize of
Shanghai's industry. Japanese bankers took over the British and
American banks; administrators took over every business excep-
ting the big German companies like Carlowitz & Company.
Every foreign-owned house or apartment block was requisitioned. Troops moved into big houses like The Limit, while the
Japanese shipping manager deputed to run Watts's wharf lived in
his house.

To the Americans, China had to be helped with every dollar
that could be spared; not only did Chiang Kai-shek tie down size-
able Japanese land forces, but he was the instrument that would
help to stop the spread of communism in Asia. The China lobby
in Washington backed Chiang to a man. Arms poured into China.
So did advice, which the Americans felt would help to bolster
Chiang's morale. It did nothing of the kind. Chiang found the
advice unpalatable, Madame Chiang found it even more so. American generals and politicians begged, cajoled, bullied, threatened

Chiang, all to no avail. Even when his troops were weighed down with American arms, trained by American instructors, Chiang refused to intensify his attacks against Japan. Surrounded by cliques, nagged interminably by his domineering wife, Chiang had become so obsessed with his fears of communism that he allowed the US to arm his troops, even train them, but would not commit them to major battles. The West was powerful enough to beat Japan with its own forces, he reasoned, and after that he, Chiang, would have the finest army in Asia, fully trained, fully equipped, ready for the one task for which it had been formed: to annihilate the Communists.

At the end of the war Chiang was authorised to dis-arm the Japanese armies. But the Nationalists were concentrated in central and southern China, while the vast stocks of war booty lay to the north, much of it in Manchuria, near Communist guerrilla units. Lin Piao, one of the most brilliant Communist leaders, marched at the head of a rag-tag 'army' of men who had no more than a hundred rifles among them. Long before Chiang arrived on the scene, Lin had taken the surrender of half a million panicking Japanese, all terrified by rumours seeping out of the ruins of Hiroshima and Nagasaki. They handed over 138,000 machine-guns and 2,700 pieces of artillery, together with hundreds of thousands of rifles, and so the nucleus of the People's Liberation Army was born. Thousands of former Manchurian soldiers were freed and within weeks Lin Piao had organised eleven divisions. By the time Chiang arrived on the scene the Communists had distributed free land to the peasants who had been under the Japanese since 1931. This helped to reinforce Lin's argument that the Communists were the real conquerors of Japan.

For this fiasco the American government must be held partly to blame. There was no way that Chiang could have rushed sufficient troops to the area in time, but American military chiefs in China realised the danger of leaving the Manchurian door wide open. General Wedemeyer was among the first to warn the Pentagon that if it did not act quickly the Communists would seize power in Manchuria. Wedemeyer asked the US Joint Chiefs of Staff for permission to dispatch seven American divisions to Manchuria and northern China to make sure that the Japanese surrendered to the properly designated forces. Washington turned Wedemeyer's proposal down flat – and by so doing helped significantly to create a rival army to the one which the

Americans were equipping and training. (Wedemeyer did at least manage to airlift troops to Shanghai, Peking and Nanking.)

After the American refusal to send troops north, Chiang made a fatal strategic error. His ego bolstered by the fact that he was still one of the 'Big Four' and the legal ruler of a victorious country, he felt it was imperative to maintain at all costs a strong military presence in Manchuria. Only vanity or the whisperings of an ambitious wife could have made him risk such a foolhardy venture, for though he maintained garrisons in big cities like Mukden, Chinchow and – further south – the vital city of Hsuchow, which dominated the Yangtze delta, they had to be supplied by air at enormous cost in men and money. For what? To maintain islands that were isolated in the Communist-dominated countryside, and were thus of no military value whatsoever.

Chiang had started out with 'every favouring grace on his side' as one writer put it. But he was fighting a revolution that he could never understand – a revolution that had supplanted his own. It was this, combined with the corruption of his colleagues, that had brought him defeat after defeat. Chiang never really understood what the people wanted, while the Communists did. They knew the changes that had to be made to win support, and they made short-term promises which they had no intention of keeping. It did not matter. A free plot of land, a guaranteed bowl of rice each evening – this the Communists could and did give to the people. Chiang never made such gestures, so that by 1948 the billions of dollars of American aid counted for nothing any more.

Even General Marshall, who had become US Secretary of State in 1947, felt constrained to declare that the Chiang regime 'has lost the confidence of the people, reflected in the refusal of soldiers to fight and the refusal of people to co-operate in economic reforms'. The image that had once captured the heartbeat of all China – and had mesmerised men like Roosevelt – had vanished. Never again could Chiang capture the glory and triumph that had been his when he set out to improve the quality of China's history – the history that Lawrence Durrell once described as 'the endless repetition of the wrong way of living'.

None of these political events made much impact on the foreigners in Shanghai, and even now, in 1948, people rarely discussed 'the war'. In a sense the foreigners in Shanghai were like unwilling spectators of an event in which they had no real interest and whose outcome they could in no way influence. Anyone who tried playing Cassandra went unheeded. Even John Cabot, the US Consul-General, remembers how 'it was fascinating to watch this enormous problem – like an avalanche. The question was: Could I do anything about it? I couldn't.'

Added to this sense of unreality, this sense of uninvolvement, was – the weather. The Indian summer of 1948 was among the most beautiful the people of Shanghai could remember, warm but with cool breezes, so that the sunny, flowering days seemed to run endlessly into each other.

It was not deliberate self-delusion that made people ignore what was happening, for in fact nothing was happening – on the surface. So the people of Shanghai behaved in much the same way as the people of Britain behaved during the 'phoney war', lapping up the sun every day, and refusing to worry until the guns started firing.

Even in Shanghai's four English-language papers, the war seemed to have been relegated to second place. Since June much of their attention had been focused on Western Europe – from the New Look in Paris to the Berlin airlift. They seized gratefully on any scrap of news that had nothing to do with China, so that all who lived through that last 'normal' Shanghai summer, eagerly striving to ignore the prospects of violence to come, seem to have remembered it with affection and a sigh of nostalgia for 'the good old days'. Perhaps the beautiful weather helped to create a kind of hiatus; certainly the diaries and papers, the notes and memories, are concerned with trivial incidents.

Nothing, of course, could disguise the soaring inflation, though in August Chiang Kai-shek had made an ill-fated attempt to stop the slide in currency. Unfortunately Chiang, whose credibility had all but gone, appointed one of his sons, General Chiang Ching-kuo, as economic dictator of Shanghai to introduce a new 'gold' dollar whose value at first was pegged at four to the American dollar; the old currency could be exchanged at the rate of 3 million old dollars to one new one. With the monetary reform came – for the moment – a freezing of wages, prices, foreign exchange, and young Chiang started a 'tiger hunt' against black marketeers and currency speculators. He arrested the son of Tu Yush-sheng, one of the most notorious mobsters in Shanghai. He had one small-time speculator shot – to warn off the bigger fish. He blackmailed the less important members of the underworld, threatening to arrest them for collaboration with the Japanese unless they contributed $5 million American to his 'war chest' – in which case their crimes would conveniently be forgotten. They paid up, but then papa Chiang stepped in with a warning to his son to be 'less severe' with those racketeers who supported him. The warning came too late. By the autumn Chiang Kai-shek had lost the support of the two groups which had not only helped to put him in power but kept him there – the bankers and the big-city racketeers.

At the same time the government found it impossible to decrease expenditure; nor could it increase revenue. Within two months the ceilings on wages and prices were removed; the government had to print hundreds of millions of worthless banknotes. At the end of October Chiang Ching-kuo resigned, apologising to the people of Shanghai in an open letter in which he said:

> After the past seventy days of my work, I feel that I have failed to accomplish the duties which I should have accomplished. Not only did I not consummate my plan and mission, but in certain respects I have rather deepened the sufferings of the people which they experienced in the course of the execution of my task. . . . Today, aside from petitioning the government for punishment so as to clarify my responsibility, I wish to take this opportunity of offering my deepest apology to the citizens of Shanghai. But in so doing . . . I sincerely wish the citizens of Shanghai to use their own strength to prevent unscrupulous merchants, bureaucrats, politicians and racketeers from controlling Shanghai.

Prices soared as never before, in the mad rush to spend every cent as soon as it was earned. While beggars starved, the rich unloaded wheelbarrows of money – because shopkeepers were still prepared to deal in hundreds of millions since big sums could be changed into silver. Yet if you gave a beggar a million dollars few shopkeepers would sell him goods for such a trifling sum.

Price fluctuations caused problems no economist could hope to solve. When Walter Roncaglione, an American working for China National Airways Corporation, decided to lay in stocks of sugar for the airline's commissary, he found a dealer with a hundred sacks in his warehouse and offered to buy the lot if the man would make him a special price. To his surprise the Chinese dealer said that if Walter wanted the *entire* stock, the price would be three times as much per bag. To the mystified American, he explained patiently, 'If you buy all my sugar I must replace it and this will cost me three times as much as the amount I paid for my present stocks. So if I sell you the lot, you'll put me out of business. But if I sell a little at a time, I can raise my prices every day and stay in business.'

All inhibitions vanished. Walking towards the Bund one day, Darrell Berrigan, an American writer who knew China well, saw a large American car driven by a liveried chauffeur draw up outside the Royal Jewellery Store in the avenue Joffre near the French Club. Two things about it intrigued him. The passenger – a good-looking middle-aged Chinese lady – was sitting in front with the chauffeur, a rare sight in snobbish Shanghai. A brief glance into the back of the car made the reason clear: it was filled above the window-line with the loose-woven wicker baskets normally used by the Chinese to transport earth on building sites. The baskets were filled with 'bricks of notes'.

The Royal was a first-class jeweller's. Berrigan recalls how 'She walked inside and as I stopped for a moment to look, the chauffeur started to unload the entire contents of the automobile.' The Chinese lady was one of dozens of rich people who were indulging in the biggest spending spree Shanghai had ever known, buying up everything that could be carried easily, from the biggest diamonds to the greenest jade.

'Aunt Beattie' Brayne, who had lived all her life in Shanghai and was the sister of Gussie White, the city's best-known money broker, was married to an UNRRA official, so was able to use the commissariat. Once a week she bought a packet of prunes and raisins there and used them to pay her greengrocer for a week's supply of fresh vegetables. Another time Beattie went to collect some shoes and, as she prepared to pay, sensed that the old shoemaker was anxious to ask her a question. Finally, with a rush it came out: 'Instead of money, missie, could you pay me with something I used to eat every day and is now hard to get?'

Beattie Brayne put her money back in her capacious shopping basket and cheerfully obliged, returning later in the day to pay for three pairs of hand-made shoes with a pot of jam.

Autumn was nearly over, and as the first winter log fires crackled in the open hearths of Hungjao villas, Shanghai was shocked into an awareness of impending disaster. Almost without warning the illusion of peace was shattered by rumours of major battles about to erupt in the north, including Manchuria, where Mao controlled most of the countryside while Chiang's garrisons were holding out in isolated cities.

Now the moment had come when Mao Tse-tung felt that he could finally change from a military policy of mobile defence to attacking in force, and he was poised for what would become one of the most decisive battles in China's military history: the battle for the key city of Hsuchow, in the Yangtze delta north of Nanking. This was the last in a series of battles to mop up Chiang's isolated strongpoints and thus liberate all north China and Manchuria.

Before the battle for Hsuchow could be joined, however, other cities had to be attacked, including Changchun, Mukden and Chinchow in Manchuria which Mao had been besieging for months. Changchun lies on roughly the same latitude as Vladivostok; Mukden is further south; and Chinchow lies between Mukden and Peking, which was also held by the Nationalists together with Tientsin. The Red Army was content to ignore these last two cities, for Mao had already occupied Tsinan, hundreds of miles to the south, thus isolating Peking.

For eighteen months Mao had laid siege to Hsuchow. This important strategic point on the main railway between eastern and central China in the hands of the Red Army would open up the way to the Yangtze itself; to Shanghai, less than 300 miles away; to Nanking, the Nationalist capital. Meanwhile Mao had bottled up large concentrations of the enemy in the three other cities. In Chinchow – the main supply base for Chiang's troops in Manchuria – 70,000 Nationalist troops were virtually prisoners inside the city walls. In Mukden, 120 miles to the north-east, 150,000 men were isolated. In Changchun, 50,000 defenders had been under siege for more than a year.

But this was not all. Chiang had insisted on keeping some sort of 'government' offices in Changchun to prove that the area belonged to him. There was nothing for them to administer, but the 'government' staff together with the troops in these cities now totalled nearly 700,000 people. It cost the Nationalist government half of its entire military budget for 1948 to supply Changchun by air for only two months.*

---

* Figures revealed in a secret session of the Nationalist parliament in September 1948.

For all the cooped-up garrisons, living on cats, rats and dogs, life had been reduced to the ultimate choice: fight or starve. And since the Nationalist generals had little stomach for fighting, a third ugly option presented itself – defection.

As the first attacks were launched, Chiang panicked. Bypassing his own general staff, he took personal charge – but not all the time, only when the mood took him. Without warning he would stride into the map room at GHQ and issue direct briefings, often without telling the Minister of Defence what he was doing. Sometimes his orders would take twenty-four hours to reach units in battle areas and consequently were unsuitable for rapidly changing circumstances – but a personal order from the Generalissimo had to be obeyed on pain of severe punishment. In one case the commander of an army group was on the point of crushing a trapped Communist army when he received three different sets of instructions. As the Nationalist general stood by, impotent and angry, the Communists escaped.

Then Chiang flew to Peking – and confused matters even more, for here he was trying to run a war from an island surrounded by Communists. After appointing two cronies of no ability to top military positions, Chiang issued an Order of the Day urging the vital strongholds to 'fight to the last man'. But the High Command was now in a state of hopeless confusion. Nobody in the besieged cities knew which of the conflicting orders to obey.

In an effort to stop the increasing number of defections, Chiang promulgated a ruthless decree while in Peking. Wives and families of all high-ranking army officers north of the Yangtze were ordered to live in Shanghai or Nanking, obviously as hostages against their husbands' good conduct. Admiral Kewi, commander of the Navy, was quite blunt. He ordered all senior naval families to go to Taiwan 'for security reasons'. But in a speech to the Navy, he added, 'If you want to go, I won't ask you to stay. Nor will the government prevent you from leaving. The only thing I must tell you is that you must think of your families, who will now be living a comfortable life in Taiwan.'

The threat was implicit, yet it had little effect. In early October Mao launched his first major attack, striking at Changchun, whose garrison was already starving. Chiang ordered the commanding officer in Mukden to break out and relieve his comrades in Changchun. The Mukden garrison made only a token effort. After the relief columns failed to arrive, one of the armies in

Changchun, realising it had been betrayed, opened fire on another Nationalist army to try to force it to defect. The Seventh Nationalist Army, a key defence force trained by Americans, handed over all its weapons when the Communists marched into the city on 20 October, distributing rice to the starving inhabitants who greeted them as liberators.

Within a few days the Red Army launched an attack on Chinchow. Once again Chiang ordered the commander in Mukden to march to the relief of Chinchow. Once again only a token effort was made. The Red Army bombarded Chinchow ferociously for four days before it fell, with the loss of 8 infantry divisions, 36 generals, 197 field-grade officers, all taken prisoner (most of them with relief).

Now only Mukden, whose garrison had held out for two years, remained to be cleared before Manchuria was entirely in Red Army hands. Under a shield of devastating artillery fire, the Red Army troops charged in human waves, yelling, 'Chinese should not fight Chinese!' Some men did fight – until they learned that General Wei had made an 'agreement' to hand over the city providing the Communists allowed him to 'escape'. He did get away, only to be arrested later in Nanking.

The Nationalist losses were staggering. In all, a third of the weapons captured by the Red Army in Manchuria were of American manufacture.

Now only Hsuchow remained.* The Communists launched their attack with two field armies totalling just over half a million men. They were backed by an extraordinary 'army' of nearly two million civilians – not only political commissars and technicians, not only logistic experts and intelligence units, but a motley assembly of part-time soldiers, some trained as hit-and-run guerrilla units, others acting as anything from cooks and baggage-carriers to stretcher-bearers. Many had been wooed and won by the Communists during the months of siege with promises of land.

From the start the Nationalist defenders had been beset with bickering among the commanders in Hsuchow, and while they quarrelled, hundreds of thousands of peasants-turned-guerrillas harassed the Nationalist troops night after night. Moving on foot

---

* Because Hsuchow is situated on the Huai River, and on the east–west railway which starts at Haichow on the coast, this struggle has always been referred to by Chinese historians as the Huai–Hai campaign.

with intimate knowledge of the countryside, surrounded by sympathisers, they made life impossible for the government troops, without at first attempting any major attack. The Nationalist air force, which could have become a decisive factor in Chiang's favour, was kept on the ground by its hesitant commanders, while guerrillas probed for weak sections in the defences and began to shatter Nationalist morale.

By the end of November the Nationalists had lost 178,000 dead or wounded, prisoners or defectors. Now, with the enemy tottering, the crack Communist troops which had been kept in reserve, moved in. Though the Red Army fought magnificently, a share of the credit for victory must surely be awarded to the incompetent Nationalist generals. Defence plans were an impossible jumble of disorder. Relief columns never arrived. Attempts to break out were cancelled at the last moment – without other units involved being informed. The air force never flew. One division defected to the Reds at the start. The rest of the armies, encircled in their camps outside as well as inside the city, were fighting each other – sometimes with knives and guns – for a share of the meagre rations that were occasionally parachuted down. The surrounding fields were stripped of crops by troops which time and again were attacked by the civilians as robbers. Resentful troops refused to fight. Three other divisions followed the first and defected from the starving defenders. General Tu Yu-ming, one of Chiang's most incompetent generals, found the three armies he commanded completely encircled. He tried to escape by disguising himself as a 'prisoner' of his own bodyguard, but failed even in this pitiful subterfuge and became a real prisoner. All was chaos.

In a country where pestilence, famine and filth hardly excite the imagination, the first hard-bitten Communist troops to reach the city were profoundly shocked. Accounts in the Communist magazine *Red Flags Flying* tell of huge, Belsen-like open graves into which hundreds of carcasses had been tossed without ceremony; of a local hospital where every patient was dead – but the bodies left in the wards; of early patrols probing the narrow streets of the old city having to don gas masks because they could not stand the stench of putrefying flesh; yet the inhabitants, who were found to be wearing jackets made from the skins of cats and dogs they had eaten, hardly noticed it. There were numerous cases of cannibalism, especially of unwanted girl-children by ravenous parents. 'When our men arrived with rice,' said one report, 'men fought like animals for their share, gouging and knifing each other, trampling the women underfoot.' For a time the Red Army actually had to suspend the distribution of rice to starving civilians, for more were being killed in the riots than would have died from hunger. Some of this may be Communist propaganda, but the general description is too fantastic to be pure invention.

After sixty-six days of ferocious fighting, the battle of Hsuchow was over.* In the campaign Nationalist losses totalled 400,000 men of whom, according to the US Military Attaché in Nanking, 200,000 were successfully integrated into the Red Army (together with 140,000 American rifles).

* Historians differ on the actual date when Hsuchow fell. Most believe it fell in early January 1949. The US State Department's *United States Relations with China* says in its chronological lists of events that the Communists occupied Hsuchow on 1 December 1948, a month after the occupation of Mukden. The city was probably occupied piecemeal and at different times.

56

4

'No Immediate Threat'
October 1948–January 1949

In Shanghai only the barest details of these great defeats were known, for Chiang still imposed a rigid censorship in the battle areas. Yet rumours were rife, and there was no way of hiding the magnitude of the disasters from foreign diplomats. Nanking and Shanghai were obviously the next targets. Sudden chilling warning signs appeared. There might be no shortage of drinks or luxuries, since these were imported and paid for with foreign currencies, but at the end of September bread suddenly disappeared from the Shanghai shops. Bakers didn't bake any more – even for black-market money – and no one could explain why. Most Americans were able to obtain supplies from the PX and other institutions, but the British were not so fortunate and when it became apparent that the bread shortage would continue, the British Residents Association started a rationing plan. Every Briton was issued with a card, and a system of fair rationing was organised with the Bakerlite Company. At the same time the BEP – British Emergency Planners – was formed to arrange further food distribution if needed and to work with the Royal Navy on evacuation plans. As Alec McShane, the Scots businessman, said, pointing out of the window of the Dome Club to the grey outlines of two British warships in the deep channel: 'There's *one* guarantee of safety, the good old *London* and the *Amethyst*. No bloody Chinese are going to fire on them.'

Warnings of potential danger varied starkly, and so did suggestions for safeguarding the foreign community. The Americans urged women and children to get out while there was still time. The British urged people to remain at their jobs. The

British had large investments in Shanghai and it seemed to make sense to stay and look after them in a country where civil war had always been a part of life. On the other hand, much of America's investment of $3 billion in arms and aid had been taken by the Communists or had gone up in smoke, so why should the Americans stay? Besides, the Americans had openly supported Chiang Kai-shek; if the Communists did arrive they could only expect short shrift.

The US Consul-General in Shanghai, John Cabot, had been appointed in January 1948, somewhat to his own surprise. Tall, distinguished-looking and athletic – he played tennis, squash and loved swimming – Cabot had gravitated naturally to a diplomatic career after Harvard and two postgraduate years at Oxford. Having been told late in 1947 that he was being posted as Ambassador to Nicaragua, he had instead abruptly been transferred as 'C-G' to a country of which he had no special knowledge. However, he had some experience of Communism gained during a spell as chargé d'affaires in Yugoslavia, and his wife Elizabeth, whom he had married when serving in Mexico, was convinced, as she put it, that 'Jack was sent to Shanghai because he had been through the Communist mill in Yugoslavia and the State Department wanted to know more about the Communists in China'.

Certainly American policy in China needed some clarification. Against all the evidence of Chiang Kai-shek's corruption, the China lobby in Washington was as powerful as ever. Cabot had soon discovered that a rational approach was not made easier when dealing with men like the founder of *Time* magazine, Henry Luce, who was the son of a missionary in China and was a key man in the lobby. His 'idea of telling a story', according to Cabot, 'was telling it the way it should have been, not the way it was'.

Cabot also found it hard to fight the influence of Madame Chiang Kai-shek, 'an extremely intelligent, attractive woman, though the fact that she was unscrupulous in gaining her ends was not so evident. Nor was it evident in Washington that members of her family had their hands in the public till.' Cabot also quickly realised that Chiang Kai-shek himself might want to take some of the advice suggested by American experts but was powerless to do so for, as Cabot said,* 'he could have been out had he tried to

* In conversations with the author.

implement some of the measures. China has always been largely ruled by different factions, and it was hard to know which one was the power behind Chiang.'

Almost immediately Cabot had decided that his first priority must be to organise large-scale evacuation plans, and by the time the Huai–Hai battle ended he had managed to persuade almost all American women and children to leave Shanghai; but it had been a tough job because many Americans believed that if the Communists did assume power, conditions and business might actually improve. 'First of all I had to shout to all the women and children to get them to leave,' Cabot remembers, 'then I spent months trying to stop them returning.' Cabot knew that legally he could not force any wife to leave Shanghai, 'but I made damn sure none of them found that out'.

The same happy-go-lucky attitude was echoed back in Washington, particularly when Cabot insisted to the State Department that every one of its employees in China should plan for immediate evacuation when necessary. Washington, he felt, was more concerned over the actions of Russia in the Cold War, culminating in the Berlin blockade. 'Russia was threatening to take over the world, and no doubt to the State Department China was a long way off.' He had already sent a signal to Washington suggesting that a definite list of evacuation priorities should be drawn up 'just in case', and had received a frosty reply with words to the effect, 'The Department does not comprehend. . .'.*

The British took the opposite view, summed up by the new Consul-General who took up his post in Shanghai in November 1948. Robert Urquhart was fifty-one and had a sense of the dignity of his position, feeling (quite rightly) that since Shanghai was the heart of China the C-G was (in his way) as important as the Ambassador in the backwater of Nanking. Perhaps Urquhart's forthright character is best illustrated by one of his first decisions on reaching Shanghai. He was the first British C-G to ask the Royal Navy to provide him with a private launch to be moored in front of the Consulate-General. The Navy meekly obeyed.

Urquhart outlined his views when addressing the annual meeting of the British Residents Association at the Country Club

---

* When Cabot returned to Washington in 1949 after the Communist take-over, he ran into an old friend who greeted him with a grin, 'Oh – by the way, Jack, the Department *does* comprehend now.

in Bubbling Well Road: 'We are under no immediate threat,' he insisted. 'Most of the fears which have been conjured up are founded on rumour and pure imagination. It takes all sorts to make a world, but give me always the man or woman who looks twice at a rumour – and who thinks twice before abandoning his settled ways.'

The prospect of a Communist take-over damaging the British community was hardly discussed at that meeting, because, as Urquhart put it, 'We British know too well that we belong to a country which has long since learned never to attempt to put the clock back politically.' The C-G pointed out that all the British had to do was be patient and maintain their equipment so that it could be ready for a 'resumption of full trading activities'.

Any possibility that these trading activities might not be forthcoming was ridiculed by the Consul-General on two counts: first, the wisdom of the Chinese and, secondly, the stalwart character of the British community. He told his audience:

> Of course stabilising conditions will return and nothing in the world can stop China from becoming a prosperous commercial and industrial power. Now, as the situation unfolds we may have our ups and downs. We shall worry off and on whether or not we have cause for it. But we will stand by Shanghai if we possibly can. It will take the extreme of human folly, of military disaster, to dislodge us; as a community, we have seen Shanghai in the days of prosperity, under foreign occupation and now under the approaching threat of civil war; Shanghai is home to us as a community, not merely a trading post, and we are not going to up and leave our community home at the first signs of an approaching storm.

He added:

> Does anyone suggest that if there is a change of government here, the new one will be so unreasonable that they will make civilised life and normal trading impossible? I have great confidence that the government of China will not fall into the hands of any but responsible men, who will have the interests of their country at heart – and we foreigners ask for nothing more.

Urquhart did warn the British that there could be a period of anxiety. If that time arrived, a scheme had been prepared under which British subjects would gather at fixed rendezvous points, each one carrying one suitcase, two blankets and food for twenty-four hours. But this was simply a fall-back position; indeed, as Cabot was finalising his evacuation plans, Urquhart was promising his listeners, 'I will not lightly expose you to the miseries of evacuation. I will in fact expect this community to stay put and face reasonable risks.'

To discourage further any would-be quitters, Urquhart added a stiff penny-pinching warning that 'if anyone leaves his or her house on my advice - if it is looted - it is the wish of HM Government that I absolve myself - and them - in advance from any financial responsibility'.

After all, everything was relative and there is nothing that a distant community enjoys hearing more than words that reinforce hopes and help to banish doubts. 'Of course the Commies will want to do business with us,' one taipan told Vine at the Club. 'They can't bloody well live without us.'

Meanwhile, there was Christmas to prepare for. Plans had to be finalised for entertaining 700 naval ratings from the *Amethyst* and the *London,* organising Christmas carols at the Cathedral, visiting hospitals and institutions. There were also Christmas cards to be sent - including a novel one which must have bewildered some of the recipients in far-off England or America, for it consisted of a genuine $5000 bill with 'Happy Christmas' scrawled across it. Chinese dollars, of course.

Though the temperature fell below freezing point that winter, members of the Foreign Correspondents Club held a Christmas party in Broadway Mansions, helped out by supplies from the American PX. The Hawkings, settled in The Limit with the last traces of the hated Japanese eradicated, had thirteen guests staying for the holidays. Gladys made two Christmas cakes together with four pounds of mincemeat; after all, as she wrote to her daughters, 'This is the first Christmas since 1940 that we've had the family festival here at home, free from wars and their anxiety.'

Ward Price, the distinguished foreign correspondent of the *Daily Mail,* summed up that Christmas: 'There is no sign of uneasiness among the British residents here. British businessmen mean to carry on unless physically forced to leave. They are confident that a Communist government would find the co-operation of the British import merchants indispensable to keep up the standard of living among the Chinese population.'

If Gladys Hawkings could write of a Christmas 'free from wars' and Ward Price could find no signs of uneasiness, why should the Chinese be more afraid of impending disaster? Though thousands died that grim winter, thousand more poured into Shanghai every day. Despite warnings, Shanghai was still a magnet for refugees, a city in which there might at least be a glimmer of hope. Norman Watts remembers asking a frail old man hawking peanuts from a small paper bag why he should have come to this friendless city. 'If I sell just a few peanuts,' explained the man, 'I might be able to buy a cup of rice. But in my village I *know* I could not sell one peanut – and I know I would starve, for Chiang's soldiers have taken everything.'

Many refugees still had a foolish faith in the ultimate power of the Westerner to solve all problems. One man told Watts, 'Why! It's unthinkable that the Europeans will let the Communists win.'

Most European firms tried to help in some small way. Chinese working for foreign firms were given their Christmas presents, usually food or clothing. National organisations like the British Residents Association arranged special distribution of food – yet this was a drop in the ocean. Even Norman Watts, a lover of everything Chinese, who had arranged special festivities for the workers on the wharf, had to admit, 'Though conditions in Shanghai were terrible, they had to be seen in relation to the enormous, recurring problems of China. When you think of the millions of people who die in the regular natural disasters that engulf China – floods, famines, drought – and the refugees who wander across the length and breadth of the country without any government to rescue them, with no aid funds, you realise how cheap life is in China. And however angry or sad or frustrated you feel, you realise that you cannot look at their problem through Western eyes because you will never get an answer.'

All that people like Watts, the Hawkings and other foreign families could do was to brighten the lives of the few people with whom they came in contact.

In the early part of 1949 the staff of the British Consulate-General in Shanghai was increased by one; Commander John Proud, after a distinguished war record with the Royal Australian Navy, arrived to become Land Consul. It was a curious appointment. In the heady days of the International Settlement, the Land Consul had been a very important fellow, handling all the property problems; but since 1945, when Shanghai became a Chinese city, the position had been vacant. The presence of a new Land Consul in Shanghai at this juncture seemed redundant, for his duties were apparently restricted to performing the occasional marriage service. Yet the Consul-General had received instructions from Whitehall that the new Land Consul would be sending regular coded messages to London, the contents of which would not be divulged to the Consul-General.

For Proud was in 'Intelligence'. Just turned forty, a man with a wry, sardonic humour, he was dark-haired, with a thin figure which seemed to slide into a chair rather than sit; he had an equally mobile face, full of expression and movement when he talked. He had been trained with, among others, Kim Philby, in London,* and his mission in Shanghai was tricky: he was to recruit agents and try to make contact with the Communists. The British Government realised by now that the Chiang Kai-shek regime would probably collapse within months or even weeks. Yet all attempts to talk with the Communists had failed. This worried the British far more than a similar lack of contact worried the Americans, for it was imperative that British investment should be safeguarded, preferably by carrying on when the Communists took over. But this needed preparation, and one stumbling block separated these fanciful Foreign Office dreams from reality: every tentative approach by the British had been firmly rebuffed, not with impoliteness but with silence, by Communist leaders who (officially anyway) pursued the equally fanciful notion that Britain did not exist.

Proud, who had served in Chungking in 1941, was soon in touch with several Chinese. Even though the Communists had not yet reached the Yangtze, their fifth-column agents were circulating in Shanghai in their hundreds. After several weeks, mainly through the efforts of a Chinese agent nicknamed 'Charlie Chan',† the first meetings were arranged between Proud and high-ranking Communists. It was Britain's first real contact, and Proud now had a base from which he could plan, for he quickly discovered that if or when the Communists did become masters

---

* They were both trained to lose skilled 'tails' in the wild chases at Harrods, in and out of various departments, up and down escalators, as Proud and Philby tried to shake off the instructors following them.

† His real name is withheld as he may still be in China.

of all China, it would not be enough for Britain to decide loftily to recognise the new regime. The Communists' pride in their achievements and their bitterness at being ignored were monumental. They would *allow* Britain to recognise their government only on *their* terms. Proud would have to spend the next few months finding out in secret what those terms would be.

At about the same time, another Australian arrived in Shanghai. He too wanted to contact the Communists, but for different reasons, and had already made arrangements to join the Red Army as a war correspondent. Graham Jenkins worked for Reuters news agency, and in Hongkong some weeks previously had received a confidential letter from Sir Christopher Chancellor, the head of the agency in London, asking if Jenkins thought he could get into Communist China and report from there.

Jenkins made contact with Mao Tse-tung's unofficial 'representative' in Hongkong, Chow Wou Wa, who had an office in Lockhart Road. Somewhat to his surprise, Jenkins had found it comparatively easy to make the preliminary arrangements. Within ten days Chow told him that the Communists were prepared to receive him. Chow gave Jenkins two separate letters of authority, and added, 'My advice is for you to go to Tientsin which is still in Nationalist hands. Register in the Grand Hotel and wait.'

'Wait in Tientsin?' Jenkins looked disappointed. 'But I might have to wait for ages till you take the city.'

'Tientsin will fall in the second or third week of January,' said Mr Chow smoothly. 'There will be very little fighting. When the moment comes, just sit in the lounge of the Grand and you will be contacted – and you'll be the only newspaper man from the West to tell the story.'

This was heady stuff for Jenkins, still in his early twenties, a youngster with a great sense of humour and adventure. But first he had to go to Shanghai and when he arrived there the Reuters China manager made it quite clear that he was not happy about the arrangement. 'I was on his territory with instructions from the big boss in London,' Jenkins remembers, 'but that wasn't the only reason. He felt that if Reuters were seen to be flirting with the Communists, Chiang might pounce on a lot of Chinese people working for Reuters and even break up our news-gathering organisation in Chiang territory.' The following morning the manager told Jenkins bluntly that he had cabled Chancellor advising him that the trip was not in the best interests of the organisation. Jenkins was sent to Nanking.

He had not told anyone about the two letters of authority, and he still harboured a vague notion that he might be able to get to Tientsin. He knew that if he landed some exclusive eyewitness stories all would be forgiven – or, if not, he would find it easy to get another job. It didn't work out that way. After ten days or so in Nanking's International Club, Jenkins realised he was being followed. He suspected that his room in the club had been searched.

A few days later he received a message from the British Ambassador, Sir Ralph Stevenson. He would like to see Mr Jenkins at the Embassy at 10.30 sharp. Jenkins recognised this as a summons. He found Stevenson 'very dapper and dressy. I remember he was wearing an elegant double-breasted waistcoat.' He offered Jenkins sherry and ladyfingers, 'the first time I'd met that sort of refreshment at that time of day'.

After a minute or two of small talk, Stevenson asked the Australian, 'Jenkins, are you trying to go and report the Communist side of the fighting for Reuters?'

Jenkins had to answer carefully. He couldn't be sure how much Stevenson knew of his plans, and of course if he did go to the Communist side it would be against the direct orders of his boss. He replied diplomatically, 'That's rather a matter for my employers, sir. If there are any problems, surely the FO could talk to Reuters in London about it.'

'I'm concerned only with your safety – no, not in Communist hands: I don't want any trouble here in Nanking,' said Stevenson.

'I don't understand.' Jenkins was genuinely puzzled.

'Have you seen these?' The Ambassador pushed some newspapers across his big mahogany desk. They were Communist underground newspapers, usually referred to as 'mosquito papers'. Stevenson also handed him a slip of paper. 'Here's a translation of one article in the papers,' he said. Jenkins read it aghast. It told the complete story of his supposedly secret negotiations with Mr Chow in Hongkong, of his plans to go to Tientsin; it even quoted at length from his two letters of authority.

'But how on earth—'

The Ambassador cut him short. 'Does it matter?' he replied sternly. 'Possibly the Communists felt they could gain some public credit from being approached by such a powerful

Western organisation as Reuters. But one thing is certain, the Nationalists will take a very dim view of your activities.' He was silent for a moment then asked, 'Have you got those letters, Jenkins?'

'Not on me,' Jenkins replied. 'They're in my room at the International Club.'

'You've got a Jeep, I believe?' Jenkins nodded. 'Then I suggest,' said the Ambassador, 'that you get in it now, go back to the Club, pick up those letters and bring them here. I'll put them in the Embassy safe. My concern is for your safety – if we do this, both you and the letters will be safe.'

Jenkins acted just in time. That afternoon two Nationalist officers called on him and demanded to see the letters. Jenkins denied any knowledge of them. The officers insisted on searching his room, without any result of course. As they left, one officer said quietly, 'We will be keeping an eye on your activities, Mr Jenkins.'

Jenkins never did get behind the Communist lines. On the other hand, the meeting with the Ambassador led to a different kind of exclusive story, because Stevenson invited Jenkins to dinner at the Embassy, where he met – and immediately liked – the young Assistant Naval Attaché, who had just been posted to Nanking. His name was Lieutenant-Commander John Kerans.

5

The Traitor

January–March 1949

With the Chinese New Year in January a great surge of hope swept not only through Shanghai, but through all parts of China still in Nationalist hands. There was a chance that Chiang Kai-shek might retire. Everyone knew of Chiang's pathological hatred of Communism, and surely with him out of the way the road to peace would be wide open.

Chiang gave the news in a nation-wide New Year broadcast in which he hinted that the Nationalist government would be willing to enter into peace negotiations with the Communists; even more exciting, he added, 'If peace can be secured, I am not at all concerned about my own position. In this I will only follow the consensus of the people. During this national crisis I cannot but blame myself for my inadequate leadership. I am sorry that I have not lived up to the high expectation of the people.'

Surely this could only mean one thing: Chiang was going. To most diplomats the speech at first made a highly favourable impression. They found it a message of dignity and promise. But then the doubts started to creep in. Leighton Stuart, the US Ambassador, commented that 'On further thought the fatal flaws reveal themselves . . . it has the gracious tone of a powerful ruler dealing with troublesome rebels. . . . Communist reaction can easily be surmised. Their attitude will doubtless be uncompromising. Flushed with success and with victory in sight they want to complete the task of eradicating once and for all the evil influence of the Kuomintang.'

This belief was shared by many Westerners. They had lost faith in Chiang's good intentions. On 8 January when the Nationalists asked the United States to try to initiate peace talks with the Communists, through a four-power mediation team which would also include Britain, France and the Soviet Union, the State Department refused to help on the grounds that such a move would serve 'no useful purpose'. The other three countries also refused.

Within the week Tientsin fell – captured, in the words of the US Consul-General in the city, 'by Communist armies equipped almost entirely with American arms and other military equipment handed over practically without fighting by Nationalist armies'.

For Chiang Kai-shek the loss of Tientsin was the final signal to go. Within the week he resigned, leaving Nanking for retirement in the pretty seaside town of Fenghwa where he had been born. All China – weary Communist soldiers as well as dispirited Nationalists, penniless peasants as well as rich foreigners in Shanghai – breathed a collective sigh of relief as Chiang declared, 'With the hope that the hostilities may be brought to an end and the people's sufferings relieved, I have decided to retire. As from 21 January, Vice-President Li Tsung-jen will exercise the duties and powers of the President.'

No one could have made a more categorical handover of power, but was it the end? 'I just didn't believe it,' Graham Jenkins told a colleague. 'Quite apart from the fact that Chiang is a wily old bird; his wife has such a colossal ego and power complex that she'd never give up the good life just to sit at home knitting sweaters by the seaside.'

Jenkins predicted that the fighting would go on and since his failure to reach the Communists in Tientsin still rankled, he was determined that if or when the Red Army crossed the Yangtze, he and Reuters would be better informed than any other agency. He travelled up and down the south bank in his Jeep, stopping at each town, even in some villages, making friends with local leaders, schoolmasters or newspapermen – and making notes of their telephone numbers. If the Yangtze were crossed, then all movement on the south bank would surely be restricted, but Jenkins reckoned that he would be able to keep track of all the details by telephoning his new part-time assistants.

Vice-President Li might have harboured doubts similar to Jenkins's had he had time. But almost immediately he faced the need for action. Within days of his appointment Peking fell after a token attack in which – following prior agreement with the Nationalist general in the city – the Red Army sprinkled a few 75 mm shells on the city before it capitulated. The Communists had hardly installed themselves in Peking before Li sent an unofficial mission from Shanghai to arrange for a peace conference. The first Nationalist delegates faced stony opposition, and demands so intransigent that there was little room for discussion. Yet Li had to carry on negotiations, even if it were only to gain time, for now, following the fall of Peking, the Communists were marching towards the north bank of the Yangtze.

At first the Nationalist delegation tried to bluster and intimidate the Communists. After all, the Nationalists did have around 600,000 men on the south bank of the Yangtze and another 100,000 earmarked for the defence of Shanghai itself. But when the Nationalist delegates bragged about their strength, General Chu Teh, Commander-in-Chief of the Red Army, took them into the map room at his new GHQ in Peking. Picking up a long wooden pointer, he touched the wall map of the Yangtze at various places. Each was marked with a small blue flag showing the position of a Nationalist unit. Every single Nationalist military unit from regimental to divisional strength had been pin-pointed.

In fact the Communists were now definitely stronger than the Nationalists. On 1 February the US Department of the Army had reported:

The Nationalists entered 1948 with an estimated strength of 2,723,000 troops. Recruitment and replacement of combat losses kept this figure constant through mid-September. By 1 February 1949, however, heavy losses had reduced Nationalist strength to 1,500,000 of which approximately 500,000 are service troops. This represents a reduction of 45 per cent of the Nationalist government's total troop strength, in a 4½-month period.

Communist strength, estimated at 1,150,000 a year ago, has mounted to 1,622,000 virtually all combat effectives. This increase of approximately 40 per cent represents the creation of new units, particularly in Manchuria and East Central China. Whereas the Nationalists began 1948 with almost a three-to-one numerical superiority, the Communist forces now outnumber the total Nationalist strength and have achieved better than a one-and-a-half-to-one superiority in combat effectiveness.

Talks reached deadlock and the hopes of peace that had gripped Shanghai in January were replaced by 'peace-at-any-price' fever. It was not confined only to the rich foreigners; rather it was a highly infectious 'disease' among the Chinese who felt that their loyalty to the Nationalist cause had reached breaking point.

Mariano Ezpeleta, the Filipino Consul-General, a handsome man of forty-three who, because he was from the East, had a special relationship with the Chinese, remembers trying to explain to Hawkings that the defectors in the Nationalist army were not traitors; it was the other way round. He could see around him, he said, in everyday life, that the Nationalists were betraying the citizens. Ezpeleta was no Communist, but he had no illusions about Chiang. 'The Kuomintang which began so auspiciously as a revolutionary party of all classes but especially of the intellectuals, the peasants and the shopkeepers, has degenerated into the party of the industrialists, financiers, the big land-owners and militarists.' In a country where 80 per cent of the people lived by agriculture it was inevitable that a party catering only to the privileged class must lose the trust of the people. To a responsible Chinese any loyalty to one side in a civil war was subordinate to loyalty to his country. The tragedy was that both sides preached the three cardinal principles of Sun Yat-sen, but each blamed the other for violating those principles. It was not a question of supporting one set of principles against another but of how the same principles were interpreted.

In Shanghai throughout the spring of 1949, this inward conflict among liberal-minded men who dreaded the prospect of a Communist regime found an outlet in a new wave of anti-Americanism. In the previous year 15,000 university students had demonstrated against America's benevolent attitude towards Japan, picketing the US Consulate-General in Hangchow Road and the US Navy building on the Bund. Now there was an increasing tendency to blame America for the mess in which the Nationalists found themselves. An editorial in one newspaper blamed President Truman for publicly requesting Chiang to take Communist leaders into a coalition government. This proposal from China's powerful ally had, they thought, undermined Chiang's prestige and strengthened Mao's.

Others delved deeper into recent history, blaming the débâcle on agreements made by Roosevelt with Stalin at Yalta in 1945, which had recently been publicised in books by James F.

Byrnes and Harry Hopkins, both intimates of Roosevelt who had been at Yalta with him. As a price for entering the war against Japan when it was almost won, Stalin had demanded an immense extension of Russian territory at the expense of China, and Roosevelt had agreed – but secretly, without telling China, his ally in war. As the *Herald Tribune* scathingly pointed out on 19 January 1949, 'If China refused, then under the agreement Roosevelt would "on advice from Marshal Stalin" take measures to establish concurrence.' It was, said the *Herald Tribune*, 'profoundly offensive to China'.

Almost all businessmen in Shanghai blamed Roosevelt for being, in the words of George Vine, 'bamboozled by missionary and left-wing propaganda'. Above everything else they blamed Roosevelt for giving away Shanghai. Vine wrote, 'Roosevelt's brotherly love, complain the aggrieved businessmen out here, extended even to signing away something that was not even American but which belonged to people of a dozen other nationalities – namely the Municipality of Shanghai, which by any law could only be held to belong to the ratepayers who had built the city. Now it hangs like a plucked bird waiting for the Reds. Roosevelt hoped to gain China's goodwill and later, military and naval agreement. In the event America has gained nothing and lost most of what she already had.'

Bob Bryan felt much the same. Though he agreed that 'extrality' was undemocratic and the change had had to come, it should have been accompanied by safeguards to protect the International Settlement from destruction. 'But in 1943,' he wrote at this time, 'the United States recklessly led the way in tearing up old treaties, abandoning the foreign investors in China and abruptly ending a century of free trade between East and West.'

Roosevelt was of course violently anti-imperialist. As he once bitterly remarked during the war, 'The British would take land anywhere in the world, even if it were a rock or a sandbar.' One wonders what the hard-pressed Shanghailanders would have thought of him had they known that, in addition to being the prime instigator in ending Shanghai 'extrality', the American President had time after time tried desperately to persuade Churchill to give up Hongkong. In 1941 he urged Churchill to sell the colony to Chiang Kai-shek, offering to pay on behalf of the Chinese. In 1943 he again urged Churchill to give up the island colony 'as a gesture of goodwill', and when Churchill again refused, Roosevelt suggested privately to Stalin at Yalta that it should be turned into an international free port.*

Li knew that if the Communists maintained their intransigent attitude, he would have to fight, but he felt sure that the Yangtze would prove to be the natural military barrier all believed it to be. This would give the Nationalist armies time to regroup in the south, for though they had suffered humiliating defeats, the military situation was by no means hopeless – provided Li, a one-time general, could as leader with complete responsibility make energetic troop dispositions and use the all-important Nationalist Air Force which had hardly been used in battles north of the river.

Chiang had piously hoped that by his departure 'hostilities may be brought to an end'. Had Acting President Li been allowed the power that was his by right he might have won an uneasy peace by achieving a military stalemate. But unknown to Li, Chiang – the so-called patriot – was secretly plotting against his own deputy, making sure that 'his' Armies, Navy and Air Force would not be wasted on fighting, but would be kept intact for the retreat he was already planning to Taiwan; he was already transforming the island into an impregnable bastion. Already dozens of government arsenals all over China had been dismantled and transferred to Taiwan. New armies were being trained there; it was now the source of men, munitions, money.

The first danger signals of Chiang's extraordinary behaviour reached the Americans in February when Leighton Stuart reported to the State Department that 'The Generalissimo is interfering in military affairs, thus hampering rather than helping the Yangtze defence. Li Tsung-jen may eventually be sufficiently thwarted by these factors to feel forced to retire south, prematurely abandoning peace efforts.' Three days later, the Ambassador noted, 'Li is in a fundamentally weak position, because he does not control the larger portion of the army.'

China in fact – to say nothing of the US, its arsenal – was being betrayed by Chiang in a manner so cunning and devious, on a scale so massive, that in a work of fiction it would be ridiculed as impossible. A whole series of catastrophic moves was secretly

---

* Though Roosevelt failed to persuade Churchill, only the swift action of a former Colonial Secretary, Franklin Gimson, kept Hongkong in British hands in 1945. He raced from Stanley prison, where he had been incarcerated for three years, ran up the Union Jack before the Americans or Chinese could forestall him, and in the words of one colonial officer 'resumed the administration as though he had just been interrupted'.

engineered by the 'retired' Chiang Kai-shek behind the Acting President's back. He bribed high-ranking military officers not to fight, promising them final refuge from the relentless pursuit of the Communists on the island of Taiwan. There Chiang planned to become the puppet ruler of an ineffectual country, conveniently surrounded by water and dependent for its existence on American charity. Now he set about abandoning the people who had trusted him and died for him for eight years or more.

It seems incredible that Chiang could have acted as he did, and even more so that he could have persuaded others to abet him; that in so-called retirement he could gather around him so many powerful men and mould them to his will. There are two possible explanations. Chiang (to say nothing of Madame) had a magnetic personality; many were hypnotised into obeying him even though they knew what he was doing was wrong, in much the same way as the German generals were mesmerised by Hitler. The second reason was more down-to-earth: Chiang was offering them security in the face of defeat. As Ezpeleta put it, the Nationalist leaders 'saw in every Red uniform the spectre of the hangman's noose'. They were not the first Chinese to act on that pearl of Taoist military wisdom, 'Of all the thirty-six alternatives, running away is the best.'

As the secret plan unfolded, members of the cliques that had supported Chiang through the years made their way to the calm beauty of Chiang's old house near the sea at Fenghwa. Success depended on many deceits: American arms and other equipment had to be stored in Taiwan; the country's gold had to be spirited out of China; the bulk of the army had to be so positioned that it could not be drawn into battle and thus face possible decimation – instead troops had to be ready to beat a hasty retreat. The Navy and the Air Force had to be neutralised, so that when the time came for Chiang to bolt he would still be seen to be surrounded with the trappings of power. Finally these plans depended on the government forces being totally defeated on the mainland of China – with Chiang Kai-shek out of office and consequently in no position to be blamed – for only with total defeat on the mainland could he hope to pose as the 'saviour of real China'.

The uncharitable might say that Chiang was an out-and-out traitor, and it is difficult to dispute this; yet he was not of the stuff of which traitors are made. He was a supreme realist. He knew defeat was inevitable and believed it was imperative to keep the old China intact in some form. But whichever way you look at it, he had stabbed Li in the back.

Li at first knew nothing of what was happening, though doubtless he had his suspicions. He had never nursed great ambitions, but as an army general had performed well. He was a patriot, and saw no reason to abandon the Yangtze as a natural line of defence if the peace talks failed. This in turn meant that Nanking and Shanghai should be defended, for that, he estimated, would allow the Nationalists to hold south-western China for perhaps another twelve months – in which time anything could happen, including a change of political climate in the West and a resumption of American supplies which were now trickling to a halt. In short Li was playing for time.

As for the actual crossing of the Yangtze, Li reckoned that he could repulse it. The Nationalists had a navy, an air force; also they still had some crack American-armed regiments. What was to stop their combined forces from blowing this horde of cockleshell invaders right out of the water? Even a few sorties of fighter planes raking an enemy that had no planes of its own could stain the yellow waters of the river with the Communists' favourite colour! There seemed no reason to worry.

So, as the peace talks at Peking dragged on, Li decided to prepare. His Intelligence warned him that the Communists were using the time to assemble an assortment of river craft for the crossing, and putting the final touches to the gun emplacements that would cover those crossings.

Li decided that his first task must be to transfer to the impending battle area some of the mountains of *matériel* which had been stockpiled 'for safety' in Taiwan. There would be plenty of time to transfer it by sea to Shanghai while the peace conference dawdled on. But his request was met with a blank refusal, though it was couched in evasive and apologetic terms, by the Ministry of Defence representatives in Taiwan. There was no shipping available, they were having labour problems, and so on. An exasperated Li decided to enlist Chiang's personal help. But Chiang Kai-shek was 'too ill to interfere with affairs of state'. In fact Chiang had himself sent secret orders to Taiwan that on no account should any military equipment be sent to the mainland.

One slender hope remained. A last shipment of American arms was on its way to Taiwan. Li tried personally to persuade the American Ambassador to divert the shipment to the mainland. The plea was in vain.

Worse was to follow. Li decided that one crack Army Group,

numbering 200,000 men, armed mostly with sophisticated American weapons and under the command of General Tang En-po, should be transferred from the Shanghai area up river to join other troops already stationed nearer Nanking. There they could defend sections where the river narrowed and where the Communists would obviously attempt mass crossings.

He asked General Tang to come and see him. Somewhat to his surprise Tang was not with his army. He had left on a 'secret' mission; nobody seemed to know much about it. In fact Tang was sunning himself in Fenghwa with Chiang Kai-shek, who now gave him the firm order that on no account must he move his troops up river. When General Tang did finally meet Li he explained that his troops were 'not in a fit state' to move. He said nothing, at that time, about Chiang's secret orders.

Li now sent for the local officers in charge of the Navy and Air Force. Some Nationalist naval units were actually stationed at Nanking and Commodore Lin Tsun, a one-time aide to Chiang, made vague promises, but could not be pinned down to a definite plan of action. The Air Force chief in Nanking simply refused to fly his planes without firm orders from Taiwan. In fact the Air Force was still under the strict control of Chiang Kai-shek who had ordered it to remain grounded.

Li was not a strong man; he was not the kind to seize power by a *coup*. He had been an ardent admirer of Chiang Kai-shek, and now, more than anything else, he was anxious to show the rest of the world that Chiang's resignation had not caused any rifts in the Nationalist ranks. Perhaps Li thought of twisting the Americans' arm for more supplies. Certainly he felt that it was important for the world to see that all was well in his government.

It was a forlorn hope. As John Cabot reported from Shanghai: 'Despite the steady increase of Li's prestige and popularity, his actual power should not be overestimated. There is little indication that he has been able to instil any new fighting spirit into the Nationalist armies. . . . The Generalissimo, though outwardly co-operating, is maintaining in effect independent political and military authority.'

Poor Li was also being duped in other quarters. The Communists, content to allow the peace talks to drag on while they prepared their flotillas on the Yangtze, were fully aware of Li's problems with Chiang, and they decided to exacerbate them with pre-planned defections which would make the crossing easier.

It was as well for Li's peace of mind that he had no inkling of these other sinister moves taking place behind his back. During the peace talks, Communist fifth-column agents had been operating almost at will along the southern bank of the Yangtze, especially in Shanghai and Nanking. They had been moving freely in Nationalist territory for more than a year, reporting on the growing discontent, not only in the army but among civilians, particularly in big cities where refugees and inflation were fomenting the kind of chaos on which communism thrives.

General Chen Yi, one of the most brilliant Red Army commanders, had dispatched a group of highly-placed Intelligence operators to work in two particular areas of disaffection: first, among the naval units at Nanking and, secondly, in the army garrison at Kiangyin, on the south bank, a highly strategic fortress because it commanded one of the narrows of the Yangtze. The operation was led by Colonel Teng Tsu-fo, who had been trained in Moscow. His task was simple – to bribe the weak naval Commodore Lin at Nanking to remain 'neutral' (that, according to General Chen Yi, would be enough), and to bribe the commander of the Nationalist garrison, a General Chang, to take more drastic action: at the moment when the Communists made their crossing the Nationalist general would turn on his own troops defending other parts of the river. We do not know the details of how Colonel Teng achieved his objectives, though Western Intelligence did discover that when he left Peking for Nanking he had five trunks filled with silver dollars. It seems that large sums of money were deposited with third parties trusted by both sides; for though the Communists always kept their word when bribing people, they never paid out actual cash except on results. Certainly, long before the peace talks finally broke down, Colonel Teng had recrossed the Yangtze; and he travelled without luggage.

These defections were planned in advance. Others were spontaneous. During the peace talks five Nationalist regiments crossed the river and joined Communist-inspired guerrillas. Worst of all was the defection of Chiang's most powerful naval vessel, the cruiser *Chungking*, given to the Nationalists by Britain on VJ-Day. On routine duty in the waters around Shanghai in February, she just vanished. Three days later Peking Radio triumphantly announced her arrival in a Communist-held port, and the vessel's commander, Teng Chao-siang, said that he and his crew had defected 'for the good of the Chinese people'.

Though Nationalist planes bombed and sank the *Chungking* a week later, the Nationalist Navy never recovered its morale.

While Communist spies were operating south of the Yangtze, the Peking talks were drawing pathetically to an end: as John Cabot noted in his diary on 17 April, 'Peace talks seem confused and confusing.' From the start the Communists refused absolutely to budge from Mao Tse-tung's eight-point peace formula, which demanded, in brief, the punishment of war criminals; abolition of the constitution; abolition of the Nationalist legal system; a democratic reorganisation of the Nationalist troops; confiscation of 'bureaucratic capital'; reform of the land system; the abolition of 'treasonous treaties'; a new Consultative Conference, from which 'reactionary elements' would be barred, to establish a democratic coalition government which would take over all authority from the 'Kuomintang reactionary government'.

Though the formula was in effect a demand for unconditional surrender, it did not, in fact, seem unduly hard to the masses of war-weary Chinese. It was, however, a very different matter for the Nationalist delegates who were faced with an ultimatum to accept the eight points by 12 April or take the consequences. The ultimatum was postponed, but by 15 April the dispirited Nationalist delegates had obtained virtually no concessions from the Communists, who then issued a second ultimatum: the Nationalists would be given two days to accept Mao's terms. If they were not accepted, the Communists would break off negotiations, and would begin the crossing of the Yangtze at midnight on 20 April.

There was nothing the delegates could do but return home.

One other major problem faced Li as he prepared for the inevitable battle: he would need cash. There had always been large reserves of gold and silver in the vaults of the Bank of China; alas, they now vanished as a result of Chiang's most daring *coup* of all – nothing less than a plan to rob the Bank of China of its stocks of bullion, of all the gold reserves in the country.

Plans were laid with the utmost care. A freighter was tied up almost opposite the Cathay Hotel at the corner of the Bund and Nanking Road. Its crew, dressed in ragamuffin style befitting a coastal tramp, hardly merited a passing glance; in fact it consisted of hand-picked members of Chiang's naval forces, suitably disguised. The officers in the chart room had already studied every detail of the swiftest route to Taiwan.

Several senior executives of the Bank of China had been admitted to the secret, for they would have to open the vaults. There was no question of coercion, for after all the orders came from on high, but the bank officials were promised passage on the freighter; this was not only an effective bribe, since it assured these people's safety, but an effective way of keeping the affair secret in Shanghai. The robbery could not be kept secret for long, of course, but Chiang needed a few days' grace before it leaked out – certainly time to get his vessel into open waters. However, one Englishman, by the purest chance, actually saw the robbery himself.

As Nationalist troops in the early hours of the morning cordoned off entire blocks surrounding the bank – including the Cathay, part of Nanking Road, and the Bund almost to Foochow Road – George Vine was putting the cover on his typewriter and preparing to leave his fifth-floor office at the *News*. Suddenly he heard a sound almost never heard in the heart of Shanghai after dark – the peculiar chant of coolies carrying heavy loads and the soft *pad, pad, pad* of their feet.

Vine had stayed late to send a cable to his London newspaper. 'I went to look,' he remembered later, 'and I could hardly believe what I saw. Below was a file of coolies padding out of the bank. I could even make out their hats or the sweat-rags on their foreheads, and their uniforms of indigo tunic and short baggy trousers.'

Each coolie carried two pans or parcels, each attached by a rope to one end of the bending, dancing bamboo pole arched across his bony shoulders. Across the Bund the freighter was drenched in light from powerful arc-lamps on its masts. George watched the coolies pad across the Bund, lope up the gangplank, hand over their cargo and return for more. He realised immediately what was happening, and after cabling the news to London remembers thinking, 'There was something pleasantly ironic about the fact that all the gold in China was being carried away in the traditional manner – by coolies.'

This was the culminating point of Chiang Kai-shek's treachery. He had managed to keep control of the army units needed for the defence of Shanghai and Nanking. He had neutralised the Navy, and the American-trained Air Force which was surely powerful enough to have shot the Communists out of the water. But all that was as nothing compared to this latest master-stroke. China was broke.

6

The Armada – and the *Amethyst*

April 1949

Mao Tse-tung was now poised in force on the north banks of the Yangtze, yet one problem remained to be solved before he could attack the enemy. Throughout the years he had fought them on land. Now he had to mount his first waterborne assault against the Nationalist forces which included naval units he could never hope to match. He needed an armada of boats of all kinds – and the men to sail them.

Always a man of broad vision, Mao Tse-tung in his planning had scorned the first tentative advice of his commanders to make just two or three powerful thrusts opposite Nanking, Chinkiang and Kiangyin which lay ·between the capital and Shanghai. Instead he decided to attack simultaneously along a 400-mile front using four field armies – more than a million battle-trained troops. Two armies would attack on the 200-mile front between Nanking and Shanghai, where the Yangtze flowed from west to east until it reached the sea. It was along the south bank in this area that the Nationalists had built their strongest defences. The Yangtze, however, does not run from west to east along its entire course. From the city of Kiukiang, hundreds of miles to the south of Nanking, the river pursues a north-easterly course, turning right, so to speak, when it reaches Nanking: thus these two stretches of the river form an obtuse angle.

Mao had decided that he would, in the months of preparation, bluff the Nationalists into expecting a major offensive across the river between Nanking and Shanghai, but in fact he concentrated huge armies around Angking south of Nanking, where he planned to cross the river and land on what was in that area the east

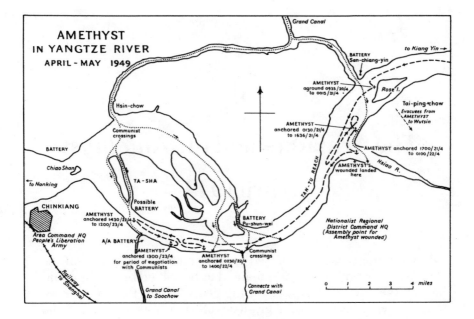

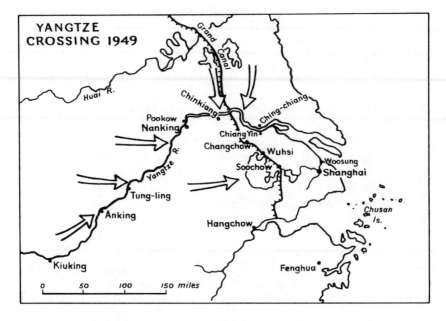

bank. He could then race eastwards, well south of the Nationalists on the south bank between Nanking and Shanghai, and cut them off. At the same time he could march in a north-easterly direction to positions south of Shanghai where his forces would link up with troops which had crossed the Yangtze near the capital.

Strategically it was brilliant, but even if Mao could find enough boats, the Yangtze was rarely less than a mile wide, and where were the sailors versed in the vexing local currents and shifting shoals that had always made the river so dangerous to cross? To allow a soldier to manoeuvre a frail sampan through currents of which he was ignorant was unthinkable – or was it? General Chen Yi had once boasted that given good instructors he could train a peasant to be a soldier in six weeks. Now he suggested that, given the help of skilled local river-dwellers, he could turn a soldier into a sailor in two weeks.

First the local peasants who lived along the north bank of the Yangtze had to be recruited. It was not difficult. Until a few weeks previously the peasants and fishermen had been caught up in the Chiang regime, in which landowners had kept them under the lash. Because of transport difficulties, the peasants south of Nanking might be starving while those on the north bank of the Yangtze were producing, in a good harvest, more than they needed. It was always the long-suffering peasants who paid, while the wealthy manipulators of agricultural produce increased their fortunes.

Yet this northern bank was peopled by sturdy men and women who asked only to be allowed to carry on living as they had done for centuries. The Communists, most of whom had come from the far north, discovered a life of luxury and richness they had never seen before. There was fish for all – caught by the teams of cormorants perched on the gunwales of the fishermen's boats, who darted for their prey but were never allowed to swallow it because of the rings fastened round their necks. Old forts dotted the river banks, giving better shelter than makeshift tents. Every possible inch of the marshy land, laced with inlets and dikes, was cultivated by women, their black hair coiled and shining with oil. Behind the swamp bamboo groves provided perfect camouflage for guns. Fir, cinnamon and camphor trees shielded many of the inland villages; others were surrounded by groves of mulberry trees carefully protected to feed the silkworms. To the men from the north, it seemed to be a magical country, with ducks and squealing pigs in every village, with lush crops of wheat and beans grown in one season and rice and tea in the hot summer.

The first thing the Communists did was to expel the landlords and give every peasant an acre and a half of land. Local political commissars made certain that it was distributed fairly. This was the first time any of the villagers in the area had achieved even a simple form of security in their farm holdings; but even more important, in a way – since man always dreams of escaping his bonds – it was the first time any of them had been influenced by that most magical of words, 'progress'. The commissars instituted the first 'schools'. At this stage they did not bother with the children so much as with the adults. Using a method that had been successful elsewhere, the Communists chose men who knew, perhaps, 500 basic Chinese characters, and made them teach their fellows 5 characters a night. Their pupils would then pass on their knowledge to their children.

From every swirling creek, from every hidden inlet along hundreds of miles of this north bank of the river, a motley flotilla of river boats slowly emerged. Many had been holed by the retreating Nationalists the previous autumn. Almost all had been hidden in the reeds and swamps and the scrub where water and land met. The vessels ranged from junks that could hold a hundred men, or sampans that might take a dozen, to narrow fishing boats in which there was barely room for three or four to crouch. Every one was pressed into service and repaired. At the same time local peasants started constructing bamboo rafts big enough to transport tanks, while long snakes of landing craft which could hold small vehicles made their way slowly from Tsinan, hundreds of miles to the north. These vehicles had originally been captured from the Japanese, and were now transported on China's famous Grand Canal which ran all the way to the north shore of the Yangtze.

Along the river bank there was the intense activity and training that precede a great offensive. One Communist general, Liu Chen, remembered later how 'every road leading to the Yangtze was alive with a continuous movement of guns, armoured cars, cavalry "like a gust of wind", while behind them thousands of peasants arrived with masts, ropes, sails, anchors, which they had hidden from the Nationalists. Some pushed wheelbarrows, some carried stretchers, others used their buffalo to pull carts towards the river and its forest of masts.' Liu had made his headquarters in the small village of San Chiang Ying, on the banks of a typical Yangtze creek known locally as the Sim Ni Mu Ho. Behind the creek lay dozens of boats, all hidden in reeds or fingers of water shaded by trees. But they had been immobilised by peasant farmers and fishermen who had dammed the waterways to provide irrigation channels, so that General Liu found many of the craft landlocked. There were thirty-seven of them, mostly in good condition: he had to get them to the river somehow.

There was only one way: 5000 troops stripped to the waist, armed only with spades and hoes, worked for 13 days and nights, in shifts, to break down the dams and then dig a connecting channel 50 yards long. Women carried the earth away in wicker baskets, while men shored up the banks with huge squares of criss-crossed bamboo plastered with stones or earth. When the canal was finished the boats were towed to hiding places under trees near the river.

East of Nanking, a retired railway engineer called Fein Rui-lai invented a remarkable contraption. Using laths of thin wood, he constructed a kind of miniature water wheel powered by a hand crank. When this was fastened to a boat, even those unversed in the art of handling a sampan could turn the handle and increase speed noticeably. Soon every village was making water wheels, and hundreds were ready by the middle of April - not only to increase the boats' speed, but to ensure that they could be propelled even if there was no wind.

While this was going on, every soldier who could not swim was given a daily lesson. As a precaution, specially selected men were trained in rudimentary 'navigation'; for though the boats would, in theory, be taken across the river by their owners, there was always the chance that a boatman would be killed. Gun emplacements were hidden in trees behind the river. Shells – more than a hundred to each gun – were brought south along the roads or the Grand Canal, the convoys always facing the danger of air strikes by Chiang, though these rarely materialised.

Across the river, the armies of Chiang Kai-shek waited, 300,000 men at key defence points on the south bank. They had thrown up artillery emplacements, concrete block houses, machine-gun posts, and dug trenches. Another 300,000 troops were stationed further south. A dozen Nationalist gunboats could patrol the river. The Air Force had half a dozen landing fields which could put fighters over any battlefield within ten minutes. So, though the Communists had by now a numerical advantage, the Nationalists, fighting from entrenched positions, with an air force and naval units, should in theory have been able to repulse any crossing easily.

By 18 April, with barely forty-eight hours to go, all was ready for the Communist gunners to tear off their camouflage and prepare to lay a massive barrage across the river to protect the crossings. Every unit held its 'ceremony of dedication', with triumphal arches in the village square and red pennants fastened to every tree, building, even to the rocks, with a huge portrait of Mao behind every arch under large red flags. Junior officers distributed small red flags to the 'shock regiments' which would lead the crossings. The flags were to be planted on the south bank. There were martial bands, pep talks, even free cigarettes, for this was to be the greatest river crossing in the history of Chinese warfare.

As chance would have it, a ship of the Royal Navy was caught in the ensuing conflict, an event which was to hold the attention of the British press, and to affect relations between Britain and Mao's government, for some time to come.

While the Communists were making their last-minute preparations in hundreds of camps along the Yangtze, Billy Hawkings had got up before first light on the 19th to drive from The Limit down to the Bund, then beyond to a bend in the Whangpoo opposite Pootung, with six sixteen-year-old youngsters, all neatly dressed in the uniform of boy-seamen of the Royal Navy. They had been staying the night at The Limit, having received special dispensation to remain ashore, and now Hawkings was taking them back to rejoin their ship, which was to sail that morning. When they reached the wharf opposite the berth where their frigate lay, her code F116 painted neatly on the side, Hawkings looked at his watch. 'Just in time,' he remembers saying. The boys chorused their thanks. Hawkings turned the car round and made for his ofice as the youngsters climbed aboard the sampan waiting to take them across the Whangpoo to board their ship. She was called *Amethyst*.

The 1495-ton *Amethyst*, with her complement of 183 officers and men, had been docked at the wharf run by Norman Watts at Pootung. She was due to sail up the Yangtze to Nanking carrying supplies for the Embassy, and to replace HMS *Consort* as guard ship in the capital of Nationalist China. All had been arranged in advance; the Nationalist naval authorities had been notified and had given permission for the voyage to take place. So the

Amethyst duly set off that morning, anchoring for the night at Kiangyin, roughly a hundred miles from Shanghai, as all shipping movements after dark were forbidden.

At eight o'clock on the morning of the 20th, while some of the crew were having breakfast, a couple of shells landed twenty yards from the ship, sending up giant plumes of water; other shells whistled overhead. To most men, rushing on deck to see what was happening, there was a feeling of excitement rather than apprehension, for everyone assumed that the Communists were shelling the Nationalists on the south bank of the river. 'What the hell!' one cried, 'it isn't our war!' He seemed to be right. Fifteen minutes later, the firing stopped abruptly and the *Amethyst* proceeded on course.

Half an hour later, she started to negotiate a bend in the river where she had to steam within 400 yards or so of the north bank because of a small island surrounded by shoals: its sandbanks posed a danger even in mid-river, so that the ship was nearer the Communist-held north bank than she would have preferred. In fact, opposite Rose Island, as it was called, was the inlet Sim Ni Mu Ho which spilled into the Yangtze at the village of San Chiang Ying, the headquarters of General Liu. The ship's captain, Lieutenant-Commander Bernard Skinner, had half expected trouble, for British Intelligence had given him fairly detailed placings of the main Communist batteries on the north shore.

Someone in the wheelhouse cried: 'They've started firing again!' Almost at the same moment there was 'a bloody terrific crash' and the man at the wheel was jerked from his post and thrown to the ground, leaving the wheel spinning. The shell had scored a direct hit on the wheelhouse, and the frigate turned with the current and headed straight for the mud of Rose Island; the wheelhouse area was strewn with dead and wounded. Two more shells hit the *Amethyst*. Both scored direct hits on the bridge and 'men were falling around like skittles'. Another shell blew up the machinery operating some of the guns, killing the man in control.

The ship's navigator and one of the river pilots were among the score of men who were badly hurt; some had their clothes ripped off by the blast. Skinner, the captain, was mortally wounded and Lieutenant Geoffrey Weston had to assume command even though he too was hurt. He took over control of the ship just at the moment when it was heading straight for Rose Island. All Weston could do was to telegraph the engine room, 'Full astern'; but the signalling mechanism had been hit and he was unable to contact the engine room before the *Amethyst* slid into the oozing mud without so much as a tremor, her bows stuck in three feet of sludge. The time was 9.35 a.m. Still the shelling continued at what was now a sitting target. Five minutes later *Amethyst* sent out an SOS in plain language, 'Under heavy fire. Am aground. Large number of casualties.' It was just in time. A shell hit the low-power room, and the radio was immobilised for the time being. But at least the message was picked up by *Consort* in Nanking and relayed to Sir Ralph Stevenson, the British Ambassador.

The crew of *Amethyst* were issued with Bren guns and rifles before receiving the order to abandon ship. As *Consort* in Nanking had acknowledged the SOS, Weston hoped that she might come to their rescue. So two men were deputed to fix a wire hawser to the stern so *Amethyst* would be ready to be towed. Every boat except the ship's whaler had been smashed, but Weston ordered most of the ship's company ashore, leaving a 'steaming party' on board, even though he was convinced the Communists intended to sink *Amethyst*. Skinner, who occasionally regained consciousness, suggested they fly a white flag of truce. It made no difference, for now the Communists started to rake the crippled vessel with machine-gun fire as some of the wounded and those of the crew who could not swim were taken aboard the whaler. Those who could swim jumped overboard and made for the island, which was only 400 yards from the Nationalist-held south bank of the Yangtze.

The survivors could see the Nationalist troops on guard in their trenches, and it was only now that the Nationalists realised this was a British ship. They sent several sampans across the narrow channel between the mainland and the island and carried the wounded to some small huts behind the lines, where two Chinese women brought hot water and attended the wounded sailors.

When the news reached Shanghai that same morning, the first question people asked was – why? Britain was not at war with the Communists. By the time the firing had ceased *Amethyst* had been hit fifty-three times by shell fire. Twenty-three men were dead or dying and thirty-one more were wounded.

The old brigade at the Shanghai Club, nurtured from their first days in the East on a diet of gunboat diplomacy, demanded immediate retaliation. When George Vine went into the Long Bar before lunch the first words he heard were, 'Christ! First the Japs – now the Chinese!' To everyone in Shanghai the attack made one thing abundantly clear: the British residents could expect no help from that symbol of Britain's might, the Royal Navy, which was being humbled in a manner that spelt once and for all the end of British gunboat diplomacy.

In the *News* office after lunch, details of the one-sided engagement began to pour in on the tape machines and over the telephone. But George Vine was more intrigued by the reasons for the obviously unprovoked attack than by the results. He had thought the voyage of *Amethyst* was ill-conceived in view of the Communists' clear declaration that they would cross the Yangtze in force at midnight on 20/21 April 'and launch a full-scale offensive'. *Amethyst* had only a few hours to make the trip before the battle started. Vine's first reaction, echoed by many others, was, Why on earth hadn't the British sent *Amethyst* to Nanking a week earlier? As one Club member remarked, 'They can't have suddenly discovered at the last moment that the Embassy in Nanking was out of Scotch!'

Graham Jenkins of Reuters was convinced that the Communists had been furious because *Amethyst*'s wash had smashed up newly-built rafts. Certainly she had had to go near the north bank as she rounded Rose Island, and it was there that Liu's men had been striving to unlock thirty-seven precious boats. If the wash had wrecked those boats, it was possible that Liu had flown into a rage and ordered his guns to open fire; otherwise, why had the Communists ignored a deadline which they themselves had proclaimed?

However, most people took the view that the Communists had assumed that any warship moving along the Yangtze must be Nationalist. 'Well, if it was a mistake,' said several people, 'we'll soon know because they'll let her go. She'll be back in Shanghai in a few hours.'

There was another possibility of which only a few – among them John Proud – was aware. British Intelligence had received repeated information that Nationalist naval units on the Yangtze river had already agreed to defect; the Communists may well have believed that Chiang's navy had done a classic double-cross, and instead of remaining, as agreed, at Kiangyin, was proceeding up river. Since the Nationalist defections were known to British Intelligence, it seemed incredible that the Royal Navy would send *Amethyst* up the Yangtze. Or had they ignored advice from Intelligence?

George Vine was not simply engaged in producing the fullest

possible story for the *News*; he was being bombarded by cables from London, asking for coverage of the story itself and for the local reaction, for evidence of possible retaliation or at least official protests. It was still morning in London. Vine managed to file his cables, but at the back of his mind was a niggling fear which he tried in vain to suppress. The sustained nature of the attack indicated clearly that this was no accident, but deliberate. What was the British Government going to do about it? By midnight, absolutely nothing had been done, except for a 're-quest' to Mao Tse-tung from the British Ambassador in Nanking for a cease-fire. A request! Vine had a premonition that nothing at all would be done to avenge the dead.

Earlier in the day *Consort* had sailed from Nanking. She reached Rose Island that afternoon, guns firing almost non-stop at the Chinese batteries which were pinning down the *Amethyst,* then turned and headed up river. But *Consort* could not know that General Liu had assembled in the creek near his headquarters one of the biggest concentrations of guns on the north bank. As she returned up river, Liu opened up with every gun, mainly rapid-fire anti-tank guns which had been concealed near the river bank, together with any other artillery he could find. He hit the *Consort* in two vital places – the bridge and wheelhouse. Her captain was wounded, the coxswain killed, and two gun turrets silenced. Her steering was disabled, making it practically impossible to manoeuvre in narrow waters. In all eight men were killed and thirty wounded, as the *Consort* received scores of direct hits. Even so, she blinked out a lamp signal to *Amethyst,* 'Is it possible to tow you off?'

Weston, who was bleeding badly from his injuries, knew that if *Consort* did try, both ships would be blown out of the water, so he warned her that it was not possible unless the shore batteries were first silenced. *Consort* replied that she couldn't do that. After flashing a few messages of encouragement, she turned and steamed away.

This was the moment when Weston decided to try to refloat the *Amethyst* after dark. He had a shell splinter in the lung, which made it difficult for him to speak, but he ordered everything that was 'loose and heavy' to be thrown overboard to lighten the bows in the mud. At midnight *Amethyst* slowly began to move a few inches as the slime and mud loosened their grip. Before long she was able to sail slowly a mile and a half further up river.

The British naval authorities in Shanghai, once they learned that *Amethyst* had moved, decided that the only way to save the wounded and the ship was for her to try to reach Nanking. For that she would need protection, so the 10,000-ton cruiser *London* and the frigate *Black Swan* sailed up as far as Kiangyin, and at 9.30 on the morning of the 21st – the day of the Communist crossing – *London* made a signal to *Amethyst* that she would sail alongside at 11.30 and instructed her to be prepared to move. But *London* never reached *Amethyst*. An easy target for General Liu's shore batteries firing at short range, the cruiser was pounded mercilessly by guns hidden in the paddy-fields. She was holed in several places, and soon fifteen of her men had been killed and twenty wounded. She too had to turn back.

When *Amethyst* learned that *London* was on her way, she moved into midstream. The crew could plainly hear the sound of firing, and it never entered anyone's head that *London* was getting the worst of the encounter until they received a signal 'Am sorry we cannot help you today. We shall keep on trying.' It was the moment when, as one of the crew remembered, 'Everybody's spirits reached an all-time low.'

By now some of the wounded had been taken to hospitals, in some cases by train to Shanghai; but for those aboard there was nothing to do but wait – and hope. The frigate was virtually helpless. Seventeen bodies lay waiting to be buried. Many of the wounded left on board, including the captain, would die without urgent medical attention. The *Amethyst* had no doctor and no boats.

And the Communists were expected to cross at any moment.

In Nanking the first thought at the British Embassy was that a doctor and medical supplies must be rushed to *Amethyst* at all costs. At 10 a.m. on the 21st Lieutenant-Commander John Kerans, the Assistant Naval Attaché, and his opposite number in the Army, Colonel Raymond Dewar-Durie, decided to try to reach the ship. After all, the south bank still seemed to be in Nationalist hands.

The only Jeep in the Embassy was too unreliable for the rough journey ahead, so Kerans phoned Graham Jenkins at the International Club and asked to borrow his.

A Jeep in Nanking was more precious than a Rolls in London. 'But I use it every day,' Jenkins protested. 'I *need* it.'

'It's urgent, really urgent,' Kerans insisted.

'For how long?'

'Might be quite a while,' admitted Kerans. When Jenkins asked why, Kerans explained.

Jenkins agreed, though according to him he made one condition. He would have to send his driver with the Jeep. 'He knows its funny ways,' he explained. 'He's the only one who can keep it in running order.'

This was not strictly true; the Jeep was in excellent condition. But Jenkins gave his driver, who spoke good English, a wad of dollars, outlined what had happened to the British ship, and told him, 'Listen carefully to everything that's said – and watch everything that happens. *Everything*, you understand. Then you telephone me every evening.'

For weeks no one could understand how Reuters managed to get regular exclusive stories about the *Amethyst*.

Not only was the Yangtze a natural barrier, but the terrain on the south bank was very different from the flat fields north of the river. Here it was studded with rocky promontories, long stretches of roadless country. Yet Kerans had to hurry, for he knew that soon the ground along which they were travelling might be swarming with Communist troops. Whatever happened, he had to reach *Amethyst* before the Communists. It took the two men and their driver more than three hours to cover the seventy-two miles from Nanking to Chinkiang, which was choked with refugees. This was the area headquarters of the Nationalist Navy which they had hoped would be able to provide a craft to take them to the *Amethyst*. It was out of the question. The only boats available were a few slow, unwieldy sampans. So they decided to try to go overland, across fifteen to twenty miles of very rough country. As they set off, around noon, Nationalist troops were sending the first batch of wounded from the *Amethyst* to Shanghai.

Meanwhile Kerans and 'D-D', as Dewar-Durie was always called, were driving cross-country, along rutted cart tracks. They averaged about five miles an hour, until they reached a tiny Nationalist-held village called Tachiang. There they left the Jeep, and set off on foot, with a dozen coolies carrying the medicines which were loaded on to two ancient Chinese wheelbarrows, each with its huge single wheel. It took three coolies to manage each barrow – two pushing and one pulling with a rope harness over his shoulder.

When they finally reached the spot where *Amethyst* should have been, there was no sign of her. They did not know that during the night, the *Amethyst* had slowly moved a short distance up river and dropped anchor there. Kerans and his party trekked back to the nearest village, gleaned what information they could, and set off on a new course. It was nearly midnight when they stumbled on the first British naval rating half a mile from *Amethyst*.

Much had happened to *Amethyst* while Kerans was travelling towards it. The RAF in Hongkong, 750 air miles from *Amethyst*, had decided to fly in medical supplies. Also in the aircraft was a naval doctor and twenty-five-year-old Dr Michael Fearnley, who was nearly at the end of his national service in the RAF. Their Sunderland flying boat landed on the Yangtze within seventy-five yards of *Amethyst*. Fearnley, with his haversack and pockets stuffed with medical supplies, waited impatiently. As the Sunderland slid on to the water, the Communists opened fire. However, a man from *Amethyst* had, at revolver point, forced some terrified coolies to row him out to the aircraft.

As the plane landed and the door was opened, the Chinese coolies panicked. Fearnley, seeing they were on the point of rowing away, grabbed his haversack and jumped into the sampan. The coolies paddled madly away from the Sunderland under the Communists' fire. Seeing that in a few moments his aircraft would be blown to bits, the Sunderland's pilot took off, taking with him the naval doctor and most of the drugs still on board.

In the sampan Fearnley managed to reach *Amethyst*. Taking one look at the shambles, he remembers thinking, 'This is hopeless.' But that night, after treatment, some of the more seriously wounded were evacuated to the shore and thence to hospital, after a Chinese Nationalist doctor reached the ship and arranged to commandeer some sampans.

Despite the shell splinters in his lung, Weston refused to be taken to hospital. 'I can't,' he said. 'If I go there would be only one executive officer on board. That isn't enough to operate the ship.' Nothing would persuade him to go.

That night a signal came from Hongkong ordering *Amethyst*, which could still move, ten miles up river before the moon rose at 1 a.m. This would take her out of range of the Communist battery. The ship moved easily in the dark, only to be fired on by nervous Nationalists. It took some time to persuade the Nationalists that this was not the enemy.

Meanwhile, the rating whom Kerans met in the dark was looking after the less dangerously wounded who had been left behind in local houses. Kerans telephoned the British Embassy in Nanking.

'The only executive officers left aboard the *Amethyst*', he explained, 'are Weston who is badly wounded and one other officer. I think I ought to try to get on board and take the ship up to Nanking.' The Ambassador agreed and Kerans set off to join the ship, using a landing craft 'borrowed' from the Nationalists. 'D-D' saw him off at the water's edge and then started the return journey to Nanking.

Kerans's first job was to see Weston, who by now could hardly move. Worse still, he was finding it increasingly difficult to speak. Kerans asked Fearnley, 'Is this officer fit to carry on?'

'No,' replied Fearnley. 'He ought to go ashore to hospital.'

Weston protested, but Kerans insisted. 'I'm sorry,' he said, 'but I'll have to *order* you to go.' Weston, bitterly disappointed, left on the landing craft that had brought Kerans to the ship.

A few minutes after he had gone *Amethyst*'s radio stuttered out a message of a different kind. The Communist attack had started. Troops had not only crossed at Kiangyin, but under cover of darkness they had crossed the Yangtze near Nanking. Now the *Amethyst* with eighty-one men left on board was trapped.

7

The Crossing

April 1949

There is some confusion about the actual moment when the Red Army launched its crossing of the Yangtze, doubtless because it was impossible to synchronise river movements, in which winds and tides played such an important part over a front stretching for at least 400 miles. Because of the river's course, some units would be attacking due south while others would be striking north-east. The historian L. M. Chassin in his book *The Communist Conquest of China* (1965) says, 'The Communist push was launched on 20 April', without giving a time, while F. F. Liu in his *Military History of Modern China* (1956) says the Red Army crossed the river at several points 'at midnight on 20 April'. The Communist General Bao Hsien-chi, who crossed south of Nanking, described in detail how he started the attack late on the 20th; while the *New York Times* of 21 April 1949 reported that 'a top-ranking General of the US Defence Ministry said Communist firing had started to gather momentum at 5 p.m., seven hours before the formal expiration of the deadline for the surrender ultimatum'. On the other hand Mariano Ezpeleta, the Filipino Consul-General, one of the best-informed diplomats in Shanghai, states categorically that 'At midnight on 21 April the Reds struck in five places south and east of Nanking'. Peking Radio itself broadcast eyewitness accounts of the crossing 'on the night of the 21st'. According to plan, the crossing should have started at midnight on 20/21 April; but two factors are indisputable: Kerans only *left* Nanking to try to reach *Amethyst* on the morning of the 21st, and was able to move freely along the south bank near the vital defence fort of Kiangyin during the night of 21/22 April; and though directly in the path of the battle, the crew of

Amethyst only saw their first Chinese attacking craft on the 23rd, 'two motley fleets . . . civilian craft of all sorts; junks predominated, but there were also some motor craft and dozens of sampans.'

When the moment came to strike, Mao Tse-tung had concentrated two Army Groups under General Chen Yi, conqueror of Hsuchow, between Nanking and Shanghai; and two more Army Groups were poised south of Nanking under General Lin Piao, hero of Mukden and Peking. Their combined forces now numbered more than a million; and they had almost two million – some put the figure higher – civilian auxiliaries, recruited willingly from the surrounding countryside.

Though the attack was by river and not on land, it was in many respects almost a carbon copy of the classic German *Blitzkrieg* used against the Low Countries in 1940, in which fanatical shocktroops, utterly dedicated to their cause, attacked unrelentingly and with astonishing mobility a dazed and doubtful enemy. In place of German dive-bombers, the Chinese employed tremendous firepower, mostly from 75 mm and 105 mm guns.

The New China News Agency report broadcast by Peking Radio summed up what happened more or less accurately:

On the night of 21 April [24 hours late?] there was some anxiety because of a westerly wind but it veered at dusk and boatmen said Chairman Mao had 'borrowed the east wind' for the crossing. Officers synchronised their watches and troops armed with American-made automatic weapons took up positions covering the opposite bank. Forward units near the river were in communication with headquarters by field telephone. Suddenly heavy guns opened up from behind infantry lines and a signal flare was the sign for the boats to set sail across the river. Shock-troops jumped into the shallow water thirty-five metres off the south bank and waded ashore. More signal flares showed that Nationalist troops had either been driven off or mown down by automatic fire.

In most cases, the attack did open with a ferocious barrage, sometimes lasting for four hours, and aimed at softening up the enemy defences. General Liu – who had literally jumped the gun by opening fire on *Amethyst* – recalled how 'shortly before midnight we poured four thousand shells on the enemy around the Kiangyin sector, determined to destroy their defence works'.

South of Nanking, near Angking, General Bao remembered: 'We started at 5.05 p.m., and through binoculars I could see the enemy forts crumbling. By 6 p.m. the time to attack had arrived. The band played "The March of the Guerrillas". The artillery cover intensified and the artillerymen were so hot they had to take off their tunics.' He added graphically, 'Even Heaven was alarmed' as the first boats set off. At that moment he had a more down-to-earth thought: 'Oh, for some outboard motors!'

On the north bank opposite Rose Island (but with his troops spread out eastwards towards a point opposite Kiangyin) General Liu had much the same experience. 'I stood there proudly as my helmeted shock-troops, each man knowing just what to do, passed through a hero's arch while the civilians tried to stop up their ears to shut out the roar of our guns. There were pillars of black smoke from fires on the opposite bank as our first boats prepared to leave at nine o'clock.'

The boats poured out in some sort of ragged formation from all the creeks that laced the bank; hundreds of boats of all kinds, each with its complement of armed troops. The landing craft followed, and against virtually no opposition, certainly not in the Kiangyin sector, most boats made the crossing in a matter of minutes. On the north bank General Liu was waiting for a signal. When two green flares lit up the sky, proof that the first wave of his shock-troops had landed, 'I jumped on the next boat, standing in the bow. The wind smelt of gunpowder.' General Liu was not afraid – and there was no reason why he should be, for though Kiangyin boasted a heavily defended fortress on the promontory at a narrow part of the river, the defending guns had been silenced by bribes long before the Communists started to cross the river.

General Tai, the Nationalist commander of the fort, had taken good care to earn the Communist bribe that was being held for him by a neutral banker. At the first sign of any instinctive reaction by his colleagues, he turned the guns under his command on loyal artillerymen and silenced them. He also shelled two small Nationalist gunboats anchored at Kiangyin when they suggested moving into the river to attack the Communists' boats. Of the Air Force there was no sign. In the end one full Nationalist division and an artillery regiment defected, many of the men turning their guns on 'loyal' colleagues who were retreating. So Kiangyin had the doubtful honour of being the first city on the south bank to fall to the Communists.

When Liu crossed with the victors and landed, he was, he said, horrified to find thousands of Chinese refugees in rags, with no shoes, straggling from the scene. 'Enemy documents were scattered everywhere. So was ammunition, supplies, clothes, blankets, cooking utensils.' But Liu was really intrigued to find among the debris, 'pictures of women, items of ladies' under-clothes, women's shoes, even rouge' – proof that the Nation-alist officers, even in the front line, were still provided with that most welcome of all camp comforts. Comforts of a nature denied to members of Mao's austere regime.

While General Liu was inspecting the fortress of Kiangyin, hundreds of barges and boats were pouring towards the larger ancient walled city of Chinkiang, which nestled in a semicircle of hills behind the river. Once a British treaty port, it had long since run to seed – except as a sector headquarters of the Nationalist Navy. Half a dozen gunboats were stationed there to help to protect Nanking fifty miles or so up river. The Nationalists had built pillboxes, erected gun emplacements and barbed-wire fences, and dug foxholes. They poured in enough men and equipment to enable the city to hold out for a long time while the Navy blasted any approaching vessels out of the water; this should have been an easy task, since at Chinkiang the Yangtze was considerably wider than in other parts of the area.

Without a shot being fired on either side, the mixed fleet of Communist vessels drew abreast the Nationalist warships station-ed at the edge of the city. 'Nobody made a belligerent move, the men looked at each other and understood,' according to one eyewitness. The Communists were well aware that Commodore Lin Tsun, head of the squadron at Nanking, had been bribed and had, as part of his treachery, previously visited Chinkiang during the peace talks. There he had called all hands to a mass meeting and, warning them that the Communists were bound to win, had suggested that it would be wiser to defect. A vote was taken, the motion was carried.

When the attack on Chinkiang started – and when it was obvious that the Navy was not going to fight – the loyal head of the Nationalist Navy, Chief Admiral Kewi Yung-chun, who was in Shanghai, radioed Commodore Lin, begging him to order the naval units to flee to Shanghai, from where they could go to Taiwan. Lin refused. Then Admiral Kewi managed to get through on the telephone. This time he offered to promote Lin to the rank of Vice-Admiral, 'stationed safely in Taiwan'; he suggested a bribe, and finally offered Lin 'all the medals you care to choose'. Lin refused apologetically. He had already accepted a huge bribe, and he could not go back on his word – whether because of a twisted sense of honesty, or whether because he feared that the Communists would ferret him out if he double-crossed them, nobody knows. Within twenty-four hours the red flag was flying above the roofs of Chinkiang.

South of Nanking the armies of General Lin Piao also met virtually no opposition, largely because Communist strategy had given the Nationalists the impression that the main thrust would be launched between Nanking and Shanghai, and that only a secondary attack would be made below Nanking. Thus the Nationalists south of Nanking were almost unprepared for the ferocity of the attack. 'The men had a pleasant junket. The attack was unopposed, the crossing uneventful, the weather fine,' wrote one of the officers. Entire divisions moved easily in a north-easterly direction across undefended country, to cut off the retreating Nationalist troops and effect a link-up with General Chen Yi's army which was quickly advancing south of Chinkiang and Kiangyin, taking in thousands of square miles of paddy-fields in the Changchow and Wusih area, a rice 'granary' which fed most of Shanghai's six million people. Worse: by executing a turning movement the attackers from the south were able to cut vital railways and trap the Nationalists' eastern flank.

In Nanking the British and Americans had already made hasty preparations for evacuation. All but six men of the platoon of US Marines guarding the American Embassy property in Nanking were withdrawn to Shanghai, and the US Embassy sent a circular letter to the 262 Americans still in the capital warning them that Nanking was now 'a war area', and suggesting that they leave while transportation was available unless they had 'pressing reasons to stay'. Both Embassies warned that there could be no assurances that Nanking would be spared military assault, and that the Yangtze was blockaded.

In Shanghai, however, evacuation of Westerners was still a fairly simple matter. British warships might not be in the best condition after their drubbing from the Communist guns, but there were enough American vessels in the area to evacuate all American nationals and many foreigners. They included the flagship of Vice-Admiral Oscar Badger, Commander of the US Naval Forces in the Western Pacific; the auxiliary communications vessel *El Dorado*; the hospital ship the *Repose* (in which several *Amethyst* survivors were recovering); the troop transport *Chilton*, a floating barracks for Marines; the destroyer *Duncan*. An American President liner was due any day and plans were being discussed with the owners to use her for the evacuation of American refugees. Clearly there was plenty of room for anyone who wanted to leave – but he would have to go quickly.

In the event, there was no bloodshed at Nanking. Indeed, nothing illustrates the ease of the Communists' advance more clearly than the manner in which Nanking fell. Hardly any of the million inhabitants of Chiang's capital knew what had happened until they woke on the morning of 24 April, for the Communist troops entered the city at 2.30 a.m. marching behind a Jeep crowded with several Communist officials and three Nanking politicians. With the dawn, students chanting patriotic songs walked out to meet troops marching in from the north-west gate and down North Chung Shan Road, past the imposing executive Yuan Building until so recently the office of the Nationalist Prime Minister.

By early morning crowds of Chinese gathered along the line of march. Some were manifestly pleased, but without doubt the dominant emotion was one of curiosity. The troops were armed with a motley assortment of weapons – some Japanese-made rifles, but more often American-made sub-machine-guns. Many carried baskets of vegetables dangling from bending bamboo poles across their shoulders. It was in no way a staged 'triumphal' entry arranged with ceremonial pomp. Soldiers just marched to their new barracks as quickly as they could or, if not, those on immediate duty sat in neat rows all over the city singing in unison or listening to talks by their officers.

The first men from *Amethyst* had reached Shanghai by train late on the afternoon of 21 April and were transported in two busloads to the British Consulate. Mrs Urquhart, wife of the Consul-General, had telephoned round to ask British wives with spare rooms to take one or two home for a night, thinking that a complete change of surroundings would act as a kind of anti-shock therapy.

No one knew exactly what time the train would arrive, so the ladies gathered in the Consulate early and played bridge until the fifty-three men arrived from the station around five o'clock, 'dirty and ragged, unshaven, many bare-footed, all looking utterly dejected'.

What really dismayed the British in Shanghai was the timid, almost frightened reaction of their government. Of course, as the *New York Times* commented on 21 April, 'With the likelihood increasing that South China too will be overrun by the Communist armies, the British are not willing to involve themselves at the moment in a dispute with Communist leaders that might end in complete loss of British property and possible further endangering of British life.' It is interesting to note how time after time in newspapers and documents, the question of property came before people. It was a point echoed forcefully by one taipan, who said to Hawkings in the Club, 'My dear fellow, we've got millions tied up in China, to say nothing of the thousands of Britons who earn good money here. I don't think it's a good idea to start off on the wrong foot by quarrelling with the next government.'

That might have been true, but still there had been no protest note to Peking, even when the Communist newspaper headings screamed 'People's Liberation Army Beats British Navy' and 'British Navy Runs Away'. For decades the Royal Navy had enjoyed complete supremacy in the East. When a British naval squadron arrived off Canton in 1923, its mere presence had been enough to compel Sun Yat-sen to withdraw. In the Arrow War of 1856 the British Navy had attacked Tientsin for no other reason than a disregard of the British flag. Everyone agreed that this sort of adventure had no place in the twentieth century; yet British blood had been spilled on a peaceful, neutral mission, the Communist newspapers were jeering, and all that Urquhart, the Consul-General, could say was, 'We think we have the situation in control.' It was a massive blow to British naval prestige in the Far East, and it did more for Communist morale than a dozen victories against dispirited Nationalist troops.

Even when it became clear that *Amethyst* had been trapped, after the Communist crossing, the news was hardly given the prominence it deserved in local newspapers. Mariano Ezpeleta noted that 'three days after the incident and the burial of the dead, Shanghai papers were deliberately silent on the *Amethyst* affair. Neither the British nor the American newspapers made any reference to it.' Ezpeleta believed that this was due to requests from 'higher officials'.

The Communist newspapers had no such inhibitions. They made it clear that 'the British have no business helping the gangster Chiang Kai-shek by bombarding our troops on the

Yangtze. It is a patently unfriendly act. The British Government must pay – and apologise.'

The crossing of the Yangtze had been so brilliantly executed that there seemed to be no reason why Shanghai should not be attacked immediately, for no one believed the Communists could not take the city whenever they wished. True, there was the question of stores and equipment, but what about the American *matériel* they had taken from the defecting Nationalists? The delay was puzzling until certain considerations were taken into account. The Communists had advanced more than a thousand miles in a year; they now controlled all China north of the Yangtze, and some territory south of the river. They had to administer a population of at least 200 million, perhaps many more. The Communist forces were spread thinly over the areas they held; in itself this was an argument against an immediate advance. There was another important reason for not pressing home their advantage: Mao Tse-tung had already established a potent fifth column in the south, which included three regular divisions in the mountains behind Canton. They posed an ever-increasing threat to the Nationalists and meant that Mao would not sacrifice any military advantage by waiting.

None of this was known to the millions unwittingly involved in the war; Chiang Kai-shek's censored newspapers saw to that, with accounts of 'victories' and strategic withdrawals so reminiscent of the Second World War. The *Chung Yang Jih-pao*, a government-backed newspaper in Shanghai, explained patiently that a strategic withdrawal must not be confused with a military defeat. The fact that many cities on the Nanking–Shanghai line had been abandoned had only been done to concentrate government forces. The newspaper added, 'The Communists massed two-thirds of their entire military forces so as to encircle our main forces defending the Yangtze. As a counter-measure the Nationalist Army effected a strategic withdrawal of its main forces, so that the Communists failed to realise their plans. Since our main forces have not yet fought with the enemy, where is the defeat?'

Whether anyone believed this drivel it is hard to say, but perhaps they did. For suddenly the *Blitzkrieg* across the Yangtze was over and, for the moment anyway, an attack on the city seemed to have been abandoned. The people of Shanghai seized upon the respite gratefully in what came to be known as the month of the lull.

8

The Month of the Lull

April 1949

On 23 April martial law was proclaimed in Shanghai. Nationalist armoured vehicles clattered through the streets and guarded key bridges; after dark, troops brandishing bayonets halted cars and examined papers at almost every corner. All that day and night Shanghai was drenched by a canopy of rain, soaking the thousands of refugees trying to find a place to rest in a city already bulging with the homeless. Roads leading to Shanghai were jammed with families carrying everything they owned on rickshaws, pedicabs or wheelbarrows. The road between Hungjao airport and the city was impassable, and when George Vine went out to see what was happening at the airport, he (together with would-be passengers) had to go to Lunghwa airport and fly the five miles due west to Hungjao. It was the only way to reach it.

Trigger-happy Nationalist troops no longer waved foreigners on at city entrances – especially after curfew at 10 p.m. They insisted on opening parcels and handbags, and Walter Sullivan of the *New York Times* told how 'they made one carload of Americans uncomfortable by fingering the pin on a hand-grenade and loading a rifle magazine at the car window to show they meant business'. Nationalist troops were also searching for looters, most of them trying to steal food. Ellen Vine was looking out of the window of her flat down towards the Garden Bridge when a truck stalled. It carried not only a family but a few bags of rice. Before the driver could re-start his vehicle beggars swarmed over the truck, punctured every sack and carried off as much rice as they could in any container that was handy – hats, pockets, and of course their hands. She saw one man put the raw rice in his mouth and gobble it down.

Both the British and American Consuls-General warned their nationals that, in view of the *Amethyst* incident, evacuation posed new problems. Mr Urquhart told British subjects that the warships had left their moorings near the Bund and moved down river to the mouth of the Yangtze. There was now no hope of implementing original plans for an evacuation from the Bund directly on to the British ships. 'It cannot now be guaranteed and indeed in certain circumstances may be impossible,' he said. John Cabot warned those Americans still in Shanghai that they could not expect guaranteed protection if fighting broke out.

'I assume that all those who are not prepared to face the dangers of remaining in a war area have already left,' he told them. Recent incidents on the Yangtze showed clearly that American nationals remaining in Shanghai 'cannot count on safety through emergency evacuation if the situation in Shanghai should become so hazardous as to make it inadvisable to stay'.

There was, however, an almost mystifying lack of response by the foreigners to suggestions of evacuation. This was undoubtedly because most of them regarded Shanghai as home. They were worried, of course, but the men had livings to earn, factories to protect, loyalties to a distant head office, and most wives felt that their place was by their husband's side. Besides, this was only another 'local war' which, like all the others, would resolve itself given patience and good sense.

Even practical plans for evacuation fell on deaf ears. When the Dutch offered 2000 berths to foreigners on their comfortable liner the *Boissevain*, details were advertised in the English-speaking and Chinese press. About 150 registered to leave, but when the moment came to board the ship, 60 had changed their minds.

The decision to remain had nothing to do with bravado among any of the races in Shanghai; nor was it evidence of complacency. The foreign refugees were in a heartrending category of their own, for many had no place to go to until aid programmes began to help. And the bulk of the Chinese had nowhere to go, and would have fared even worse in the countryside; indeed many hoped that they might live better under Communism. The rich and marked Chinese did get away mostly to Hongkong – by bribing officials for exit permits.

Many people were encouraged to remain by the recent Communist take-overs of Peking, Nanking, Tientsin, for all had fallen without bloodshed. Why should the Communists destroy Shanghai, the greatest prize of all? And not one man in a thousand believed that the Nationalists would really *fight* for Shanghai; all the bustle and military preparations were part of a huge demonstration of how to save face. As one man put it, 'Surely if Londoners could stick out the blitz, we'd look bloody fools running away from a war in which both sides know we're neutral.'

There were, nevertheless, many anxious discussions. Gertrude Bryan, whose husband had been involved in the prosecution of 10,000 illegal Communists, remembers telling Bob, 'It's madness for you to stay! You must be a marked man.'

Bob just laughed. 'We've sent the kids back to America,' he replied, 'but I *can't* go. I've got enough work to last me for six months, at sky-high fees. If I left now, it'd be like throwing a pot of gold down the drain.'

It was true. Bob Bryan had never been so busy, advising American and British firms how to unravel the tangled skeins of red tape that had proliferated since the end of the International Settlement.

Billy Hawkings received much the same reply when he suggested that Gladys should be evacuated, that she owed it to her five daughters not to put herself at risk. 'And leave you?' asked Gladys. 'I'll go if you'll go!'

'I can't go,' said Hawkings. 'What about the British Residents Association? What a fine example I'd set if I bolted.'

Many of the White Russians were faced for the second time in their lives with the prospect of a Communist regime, but now a new haven suddenly opened for them, though it had none of the glamour of Shanghai, nor the opportunities. After a lot of hard work by John Cabot and the International Refugee Organisation, the government of the Philippines had agreed to offer sanctuary on the small island of Guiuan, at the tip of Samar Island, to up to 6000 stateless persons. There, after processing by Filipino officials in Shanghai, they would be looked after by the IRO in a sort of oriental Ellis Island until they could be admitted to other countries as immigrants.

Many of the Jewish refugees from Hitler faced problems similar to those of the White Russians, and even though some thousands had by now left for Israel, they still constituted the biggest single group of foreigners in Shanghai, waiting patiently for the day when a magnanimous United States would admit them. Nearly all could look back on a blank in their lives or more than a decade during which relatives and friends in Europe had vanished without trace.

Doubtful cases among the stateless people anxious to go to Samar who were being vetted by the Filipino consular authorities, were weeded out personally by the energetic Consul-General, Mariano Ezpeleta. He found that 'some of those who applied were downright adventurers and desperadoes wanted in several European capitals who had found sanctuary in Shanghai'. On the other hand, he thought the White Russians exhilarating, especially the so-called 'aristocrats' who insisted on claiming direct descent (legitimate or otherwise) from the Romanovs.

One morning Ezpeleta faced 'an irascible-looking, moustached individual in a seedy suit and stiff Victorian collar'. On examining the man's application form he saw that opposite the space for 'Profession or Occupation' the White Russian had written, 'Prince'. Ezpeleta explained that he wanted to know his profession, not his title. The Russian answered icily, 'I am a prince of the royal blood, and a prince does not need to have any profession.'

Ezpeleta enquired what he did for a living, at which the Prince answered haughtily, 'That is different. I work in a barber shop when I need money, but that is not my profession.'

Another morning the Countess Alexandra announced that she wanted to go to Samar. Ezpeleta found her 'a sweetly-scented matron in her fifties, complete with pince-nez and a mink coat'. She asked him to help her fill out the form, and wrote '38' against her age. He decided not to query it, but when he came to her profession she said with a conspiratorial smile, 'I don't have any.'

Ezpeleta insisted, 'I must know your profession, madam; but you needn't worry, I will keep it confidential.'

He wondered whether he had 'a smirk in my voice' because she said, 'Please do not misunderstand me, sir. I am a very moral woman.' In fact, it transpired that the Countess had left Russia thirty years previously with plenty of money and all her family jewels. After the money ran out, she sold a piece of jewellery whenever she needed funds. According to Ezpeleta, 'She had a beautiful villa, a car and driver and enough jewels left to live comfortably for another twenty years. Why then did she want to go – to Samar of all places?'

Countess Alexandra 'tilted up her royal nose' and replied disdainfully, 'What! Live with the Communists? That riff-raff! Never!'

One young White Russian called Tina, who sang with one of

the Filipino dance bands that were a feature of Shanghai life, applied to go to Samar. Tina was only seventeen and Ezpeleta had met her several times in the fashionable Russian cabaret where she sang, finding her 'blonde, bosomy and hip-swinging'. He admired her, for her father had died and 'life was hard and she was trying to make it rosy; she was kind and frank and gay'. There was some discussion, however, as to whether older people wanting to go to Samar should not be given preference.

Nothing daunted, Tina asked Ezpeleta if there was a way in which she could be given Philippine nationality. When the Consul-General told her that the only way was by marrying a Filipino, Tina returned several days later with a Filipino widower of sixty-five called Jimenez who played in the orchestra at the nightclub where Tina sang.

'Mr Jimenez is ill,' she explained, 'and I can help him financially. He is free, so we can get married today and I can then get a Philippine passport. He will not demand anything from me after we are married, and I will pay all the bills.'

Ezpeleta saw nothing wrong in the arrangement – except that, as he remembered, 'at the word "marriage" Jimenez jerked up, apparently ill at ease. Then all of a sudden he stood up, mumbled something about having to see somebody at the other end of the city, and without saying goodbye was gone like a flash. That was the last I saw of him.'

On the other hand, some women did get away by conveniently marrying virtual strangers. One elderly Chinese woman who kept a well-known bordello – known fondly as 'The Vice-Consulate' because of its rather special clientele – was able to move to a comfortable living in Europe, thanks to the good offices of an ambassador whose diplomatic relations with her ladies-in-waiting had always been conducted on a horizontal level.

Madam was known to the whole of the diplomatic corps. But she had always been the soul of discretion. Moreover she had been very generous, as many a potential ambassador suffering from a temporary shortage of cash gratefully remembered. But Madam knew that when the Communists arrived they would arrest her and probably execute her. In desperation she appealed to the ambassador. She had accumulated a great deal of illegal currency (paper money had never been accepted in her establishment) and at first the ambassador was dubious, for obviously it was not easy for him to arrange for a Chinese woman to leave China. Then he had an idea. He knew of one of his nationals who was down and out yet eager to return to his homeland. He introduced the two of them. They were married hastily and left for Europe on one of the last boats.

Most foreigners who fled in April were in theory allowed to take out their personal belongings with no questions asked, but the Chinese were not so tolerantly treated and several rich Chinese who tried to smuggle out valuables were discovered at Lunghwa airport. They faced uncompromising treatment. An official tore up the person's ticket, cancelled the passage, and sent the man or woman back to Shanghai. One rich Chinese did get away with a small fortune; she had long been known as a 'character' because of her collection of handbags, and these she insisted on taking with her when she fled to Hongkong. She and her handbags had often been featured in Chinese newspapers, so the customs let her through not knowing that each of the handles which pulled open the zip fasteners consisted of a small gold ingot.

Smuggling became a way of life among the wealthy Chinese, and led to some agonising moments in the customs shed at Lunghwa airport, and sometimes the British became involved. Mrs 'Billie' Woosley, whose husband worked for Babcock & Wilcox, the international construction firm, was unwittingly duped. Billie Woosley had decided to leave and on her last night she and her husband were invited for dinner by a Mr Chang, the number one Chinese of the B & W operation in Shanghai. As she remembers, 'It was a great honour, but after a fabulous meal came the nitty-gritty. Would I carry a few bits and pieces to a friend of Mr Chang's in Hongkong? Ah well! Was I not full of wine and very young and a sitting Peking duck?'

She agreed. Mr Chang said he would meet her at the airport – her husband had left that morning for Woosung – and sure enough he arrived at Lunghwa, handed her a small cardboard box, bowed his thanks and made for the exit.

'I made straight for the ladies' loo, locked myself in and opened the box,' Mrs Woosley remembers. 'It was filled with rubies, diamonds, jade.'

She closed the box, ran out into the airport lounge and looked in vain for Chang. She couldn't just dump the box; nor was there anyone she could give it to, so she put it in her handbag and walked, heart palpitating, to the customs. 'Almost immediately an angry-looking Chinese woman customs officer came up to me, pointed to my bag and told me to open it.' Mrs Woosley did. The

106

Chinese woman seized the box inside, took the lid off, and gazed at the glittering contents.

Billie Woosley stuttered something about 'a few family trinkets', while the Chinese woman examined the contents 'for hours it seemed', looking up at her from time to time and glaring. Mrs Woosley was quite sure she would soon be heading straight for jail. But suddenly the inspector closed the box, handed back her handbag and waved her through. 'I could hardly believe it,' Mrs Woosley wrote later, 'but not long afterwards I was told that the customs had all been bribed and the look of suspicion was put on only for show.'

Some people benefited unwittingly from the zeal or cupidity of others trying to smuggle their possessions out of Shanghai, among them a Mrs Kang, a poor elderly widow who planned to join her eldest son in Hongkong. She went by train to Canton with only one small cardboard suitcase containing everything she owned in the world. When the family said goodbye to her in Shanghai they presented her with the traditional Chinese peasant farewell gift – a leg of ham. She noticed that many of the other travellers carried similar insurances against hunger.

When the passengers reached the Hongkong border near the Lo-Wu bridge everyone had to disembark and luggage was taken to the customs sheds. Old Mrs Kang had nothing to fear. She was told to pass through the immigration where her suitcase, and her ham, of course, would be waiting for her. She did so, and a few minutes later was weeping for joy as she hugged her eldest son in free Hongkong. The fact that her son's one-room tailor shop was on the verge of bankruptcy – for lack of capital, he explained – didn't matter. They were together; and at least they could look forward to a good supper of ham on that first night.

As Mrs Kang started to prepare the meal, however, she suddenly realised that the ham wasn't hers. It was wrapped in a newspaper that came from the north; she remembers that hers had been fastened with a loop of old string. This one had no string. It didn't matter, of course, one ham was more or less like the next; and there was nothing she could do about it anyway, for she hadn't the faintest idea who had taken her ham by mistake in the customs mix-up.

But then she made a startling discovery. At the narrow end of the leg – where it came to a point – the bone, which almost stuck out, seemed to be covered with a strange substance.

'It's wax,' said her son, and started to peel it away with a knife.

As the first flakes of wax came off, a small piece of glass fell on the table – then another, and then another. They were diamonds.

Neither Mrs Kang nor her son had the faintest idea that for months many rich Chinese had been hiding valuables in scooped-out hambones, often carried by innocent boys or amahs who would be unlikely to invite suspicion. But the Kangs had been presented with a small fortune in diamonds – all by mistake.*

Another tailor founded a fortune in Hongkong by exporting a touch of genius that came to him during a party. He was the Han Son Loh of Yates Road, alias 'Pants Alley', who had made Ellen Vine's first dresses and who was always addressed as Mr Loh. Among his friends and clients was Mrs Brayne, who had bought three pairs of shoes for a pot of jam.† 'Aunt Beattie', as she was called, was a 'Jill-of-all-trades'. At one time she had done a stint as social columnist for George Vine on the *North China Daily News*; she had later started up a wine and spirits firm supplying the Shanghai Club. She met Mr Loh at a party where she wore a short evening jacket that had been sent to her straight from Paris. Mr Loh was entranced by it, felt it and then asked if he could copy it.

'Certainly, I'll lend it to you one day,' she said.

'No – now!' Mr Loh said urgently. 'There's very little time left in Shanghai.'

Aunt Beattie took the jacket off, Mr Loh signalled to one of his assistants, the coat was whisked to his shop in Yates Road just round the corner and was brought back, and draped over Aunt Beattie's shoulders, long before she left for home.

The next day Mr Loh rang up and told her, 'We can make a fortune in Hongkong with your jacket. Would you like to open a dress shop for me there – and run it until I can get over?'

Aunt Beattie never hesitated; she left within the week.‡

Aunt Beattie's brother, Gussie White, had something rather more difficult to smuggle out of Shanghai – himself. Mr White was a perfectly legal foreign-exchange broker, but though he was careful to operate within the law some of his more distinguished clients, particularly those in the diplomatic service, had no scruples about changing dollars or sterling or other currencies

---

* The money was used to establish her son on a sound footing, and today Kang owns a shop in the Ocean Terminal in Kowloon, and is recognised as one of Hongkong's finest tailors.
† See above, p. 51.
‡ She opened Mr Loh's shop in Hongkong, trading as Ying Tai, and handed it over to him when he left Shanghai. It was highly successful until Loh died in 1978.

through Mr White. For them it was strictly illegal – but in fact it was the only way many of the young foreign diplomats and businessmen could make both ends meet. Mr White was also extensively patronised by American servicemen on leave in Shanghai.

Mr White had nothing to fear, but with the possibility of a Communist takeover many junior members of the diplomatic service certainly had. They were convinced that all account books would be examined, and many a future ambassador trembled at the prospect. They urged Gussie White to get out of Shanghai. There was one snag, however. If Mr White was seen to be closing down his business, it might alert Nationalist officials who were trying to crack down on all suspicious currency transactions.

Finally two young members of the American Consulate and one British Consulate official arranged a meeting with a senior officer of the US Air Force, which still flew into Lunghwa. There they hatched a plot. As a result, Gussie White was spirited out of Shanghai disguised as the navigator of an American war plane.

To the world of Shanghai, Gussie White just vanished. One day he was at his office as usual, the next he wasn't. But at least his many friends were able to learn that he was safe and well. Other people vanished, never to be seen or heard of again, including Khi Veh-du, the remarkable Abbot of the Buddhist temple in Bubbling Well Road, who disappeared with his enormously wealthy wife, and his seven concubines. No one has ever been able to pin-point the date of their disappearance. One of the last people to see the Abbot was Norman Watts, who remembers, 'We had a magnificent formal dinner in the Khi house – a large Tudor-style building off Seymour Road.' They started with the customary four cold dishes placed in the centre of the table, followed by shark's fins which in Shanghai were always the first hot dish of a meal. Watts was not one to despise what Western visitors call 'rotten eggs'; he knew that they were in fact fresh, preserved for a few days only in a fluid which penetrated the porous shells transforming the white of the egg into a tasty dark brown jelly. He ate everything from chicken's tongues to lotus seeds boiled with oranges, washing down the different dishes with plenty of Shao-hsing wine.

After dinner an astonishing thing happened. The Abbot, who was a renowned calligrapher, took a sharp knife, rolled up one sleeve and deliberately made a cut in his arm. As Watts looked on dumbfounded, the Abbot took out of his desk an exquisite Chinese scroll of silk on paper, unrolled it, then dipped a brush into his own blood and wrote on it five characters: courage, endurance, purity, integrity, good fortune. He waited for the blood to dry, wrapped the scroll in silk, and handed it over to Watts 'in a rather formal manner'. No one in Shanghai has ever seen him since.

No details of these sudden journeys or mysterious disappearances ever appeared in the Shanghai newspapers. At the best of times secrets were well guarded in Shanghai and now, a few days after the introduction of martial law, the Shanghai military authorities imposed a rigid censorship on all Shanghai newspapers, English-language and vernacular, together with news bulletins from the agencies.

The move followed mounting criticism of government policy in newspapers which could normally have been trusted to turn a practical defeat into a theoretical victory. The *Chung Yang Jih-pao*, a government paper, actually admitted on 27 April that the Communists outnumbered Nationalist troops and added, 'The military reverses suffered by the government lately were partly the result of mistaken policies. The lesson of this defeat must be thoroughly reviewed and drastic measures for reform must be undertaken immediately in order to restore public confidence' and to rebuild our defence line in our fight with the Communists.' Another newspaper, the *Ho Ping Jih-pao*, which spoke for the Army, said flatly that there was need for more harmony among the military leaders, adding, 'In past battles some generals were jealous of their colleagues, so their assistance was lacking, allowing the enemy to defeat them individually.' The paper went on to warn, 'There must be no repetition of the mistakes committed at Peking when the time comes to defend Shanghai.'

Actually the censorship brought a little light relief into the lives of the Europeans, thanks to Randall Gould, the irascible American editor of the American-owned *Shanghai Evening Post*. From the start he fought the censors as a matter of principle – and made them the laughing-stock of the city.

On the first day, the censors ordered Gould to take out a three-column story on the front page. Gould did not feel the order was justified, but he had to do as he was told. However, he refused to replace it with a substitute story, but merely inserted a paragraph in the blank space saying 'Material which occupied this space was deleted by censor'.

The censors were furious – because the blank space on the front page of the *Post* conjured up awful possibilities to readers. No news is not good news when people are jittery. There was even a rumour that the blank space had originally contained a picture of Stalin who had promised to give aid to the Communists. Mariano Ezpeleta found that 'people began speculating whether the suppressed cut referred to the peaceful surrender of Shanghai or the final split between Chiang and Vice-President Li. The deleted material caused more uneasiness by its suppression than it would have done by its publication.' The censors retaliated by issuing an order next morning – under martial law – making it a punishable offence for a newspaper or magazine to leave blank spaces on its pages. Gould replied with an announcement on page one: 'The *Shanghai Post* had no intention yesterday either to contravene the censorship regulations nor to serve readers with anything less than a heaped dish of news. . . . But we have no complaint. The censors know best.'

From the moment this tongue-in-cheek apology was published it was war. While other papers published their censored stories without comment, Gould, every time a story was censored, inserted sentences like, 'Six lines deleted by censor', according to the size of the cut. If the cut was large, Gould inserted a boxed story, looking like an advertisement, and reading, 'All the News That's Fit to Print (passed by censor)' or 'Pardon! Our slip is showing (approved by censor)'. On one occasion, the box read, 'We are in favour of Good Government. We also Favour Eating (passed by censor)'. The *Post*'s circulation zoomed, and Gould took great care with his 'advertisements'.

Gould had no compunction in attacking politicians in ways that could not be censored. In the last weeks before the attack on Shanghai, the Mayor, General Chen Liang, organised a 'Health Week' and also issued a decree begging the people of Shanghai to grow more food in 'Victory Gardens'. (It was the kind of palpable nonsense that the Governor of Singapore had uttered during the weeks before the fall of that city.) During the fighting, said the Mayor, produce from the Victory Gardens would supply the city with fresh vegetables. He himself had just planted a Victory Garden of his own. Gould commented in the columns of the *Post*, 'Shanghai's Mayor urges us to plant Victory Gardens, but the problem is, who will reap what we sow?'

* * *

The foreign correspondents also faced censorship problems. When Chiang Kai-shek came into the news, most correspondents were concerned that any references to him would be deleted. Fred Hampson, bureau chief of Associated Press, got his story past the censor by referring to Chiang as 'The Peanut' – and the AP back home in America knew perfectly well that this was the name bestowed on Chiang by General Stillwell. Stanley Alberto of the International News Service mentioned Chiang by name and his copy was censored, so remembering how proud Madame Chiang was of her perfect nose, rewrote the cable referring to Chiang as 'Shapely Schnozzle's Suitor'.

Most correspondents took great care, but suddenly Broadway Mansions – headquarters of the Shanghai press corps – was shattered to learn firstly that two of its members had been arrested, and then a few hours later that they had been sentenced to death. The two men were George Vine and Graham Jenkins.

What had happened was this: Just before the Yangtze was crossed, Jenkins had come to Shanghai complete with the telephone numbers of 'friends' he had contacted along the south bank of the Yangtze. He immediately started a marathon session of telephoning, and from his informants built up an exciting and detailed picture of various places where the Communists had crossed in strength. It was a Reuters scoop. The *South China Daily News* subscribed to Reuters, and when George Vine read the story, he immediately visualised it in terms of a graphic map, and set about having one prepared in the office. He printed it that night on page one – complete with arrows, details of troop concentrations and so on, all based on Jenkins's story.

Then all hell broke loose. 'I'd only arrived in Shanghai from Nanking a couple of days before,' Jenkins remembers, 'and at nine o'clock that morning a man in a black tunic arrived in the Reuters office and took me to a secret headquarters.'

There he was faced with a Colonel Yeh who asked him how he had learned the details of his story. Jenkins refused to tell him – at which Colonel Yeh reminded him sharply, 'Don't you realise that if you don't tell me I can sentence you to death under martial law?'

'You do that,' said Jenkins.

'I will,' shouted Colonel Yeh. He sentenced him there and then.

Vine was picked up later that day. 'I was young and impetuous,' he remembers, 'and I didn't really appreciate how tricky the situation was – and that Shanghai was under strict martial law. Sometimes we all found it hard to remember that we were living in China – subject to Chinese laws – and not in the International Settlement.'

Three Chinese in civilian clothes asked to see him in his office and asked who had decided to publish the map in that morning's paper.

'I did,' admitted Vine. 'But it was based on information that was common property of any newspaper in the city.'

The leader of the Chinese, a short, dapper man with close-cropped black hair, spoke in stilted English. 'I am a colonel in the police,' he said. 'You must come with us.'

What Vine did *not* know was that the colonel was under the direct command of General Mao Sen – known as 'Bloody Mao' – chief of Chiang's Secret Intelligence Corps, now seconded as Police Commissioner for Shanghai. He was under orders from Chiang to 'clean up the city'. Mao had unlimited powers and was directly responsible for dozens of mysterious disappearances in Shanghai – and for the scores of bloated bodies washed up almost daily in the Yangtze.

Vine insisted on phoning his wife. He told her, 'I've been picked up by some people in the police,' and almost as an afterthought added, 'If I'm not home by five this evening get in touch with someone – the Consul or any of the boys who happen to be in the Press Club.'

He was bundled into an ancient American car. Until this moment he had regarded the 'arrest' as nothing more than an unfortunate but unimportant brush with the law for which he would probably receive a dressing-down. But then he noticed that the car was driven by a soldier in uniform. This, and the title 'Colonel', made him wonder whether he was dealing with ordinary police. Then he was squeezed in the back between two of the armed Chinese, while the colonel sat in front next to the driver. The car roared into action, with the motors revving ('Just like an American movie,' thought Vine), and set off along the Bund from where Vine expected it to turn off at the Hankow Road to the Central Police Station. As the car shot past the turning, Vine cried, 'Hey! This isn't the way to police head-quarters.'

The colonel twisted his head round. 'No, it is not', was all he said as the car turned into the avenue Edouard VII and headed at speed for the far end of the old French Concession. Within a few minutes the car drew up at a derelict, grim-looking house and

Vine was told curtly to get out. Then he was led into a room facing a bedraggled, unkempt garden. Behind a desk sat another colonel – Colonel Yeh – and another prisoner was brought in. It was Graham Jenkins.

Against a background of thugs, all armed with tommy guns, peering through the door and windows, Colonel Yeh in what seemed a never-ending harangue gave the two Westerners 'the biggest dressing-down I can ever remember'. He threatened 'serious reprisals' for breaking martial law. There was, he said, only one punishment – and that was the death sentence. Nodding in the direction of Jenkins, he said laconically, 'He has already been sentenced. It is mandatory.'

Vine could see that Jenkins was getting more and more angry. When the colonel finally drew breath, Jenkins put his hands on the desk, looked the smaller Chinese in the eye and in his belligerent Australian voice said, 'Have you quite done, Colonel? Now just you listen to me for a moment.'

He let the colonel know precisely what he thought of him. He warned him not to interfere with the freedom of the press; he told him not to meddle with the rights of foreigners. Then it was the colonel's turn to get furious. Until then he had been coldly official when berating them; but after Jenkins's harangue he was in danger of losing face in the eyes of his henchmen: they could not have mistaken Jenkins's threatening tone. When Jenkins made a move, perhaps to sit down or even to leave the room, Yeh barked, 'Stand where you are, and listen to me.' He then proceeded with some difficulty to read aloud the ten points of martial law imposed on Shanghai, together with the punishment – in each case the mandatory death sentence. 'You are guilty by your own admissions of spreading alarm and despondency – and for that the only punishment is execution – for both of you,' said the colonel.

Vine, realising that the colonel's face had to be saved, tried to mollify him, by talking of their joint struggle during the war against the hated Japanese. He discovered that the colonel had fought in Burma very close to Vine's own regiment. 'We were brothers-in-arms,' he remarked. Vine thought that he was winning the colonel over until the latter said, 'You are a very brave man, Mr Vine. You must have faced death many times?' Vine nodded, at which the colonel added, 'So you won't mind facing it again, will you?' After this they were taken into a small room in the cellar crammed with Chinese prisoners, and later taken upstairs to an attic under the roof. It was furnished with two trestle beds. The key turned in the lock. The window looked down on the garden – and a chilling sight.

'Look at that wall, Graham.' Vine pointed to a brick wall in which there were three whitish patches where the bricks or cement had been chipped away. 'Those white patches have been made by the cones of bullets. This, of course, is where the secret police hold their executions. You know,' added Vine, 'they only want someone's signature and we'll be up against that wall.'

Vine was not overdramatising the situation. He realised that it might well be in the interests of the Nationalists to execute a couple of unimportant foreigners for a proved serious breach of the law. Britain had made no protest over the Communist attacks on *Amethyst* and *London*. Such weakness, before the Communists, Vine reasoned, meant, in a roundabout way, a loss of face for the Nationalists. *They* had always had to do what the Western powers told them – that is, if they wanted aid. Yet the Communists had publicly humiliated the West and the West had done nothing about it. Therefore it might not be a bad idea for the Nationalists to show that they were not just lackeys of the imperialists, that they were as independent as the Communists. 'What scares me,' Vine told Jenkins, 'is that we are just pawns in a game of Chinese face-saving.'

It was now nearly 8 p.m. and Ellen Vine was beginning to panic. She had telephoned everywhere. The office boy at the *News* could only tell her what he had seen – that three men had taken her husband away. It was raining heavily. She couldn't find a pedicab so she had to cross the Garden Bridge on foot to reach the British Consulate. She arrived, bedraggled, wet and tearful, with muddy shoes, at the very moment that several dinner guests, the men in black ties, the women in long frocks, arrived for a dinner party. She had a feeling that the servants were eyeing her feet in case she muddied the clean carpets.

All she could say was, 'My husband has been taken away by the police.' In a restricted foreign community like that of Shanghai, the assistant editor of the city's oldest English-language newspaper was a well-known figure, but it seemed that the Consulate would prefer to wait till morning before doing anything, that it was not convenient to upset the seating arrangements for a formal party. Someone muttered that they had no curfew passes anyway. At last, one junior did get through to the Central Police Station and returned with news that he hoped would reassure Ellen. The police there *had* picked up two white men on a drunk charge, but had let them go. 'So,' said the Consulate, 'it looks as though it was all a false alarm.'

Of course it wasn't. The Consulate had not checked the names. The two drunks turned out to be a couple of White Russians. Ellen returned to Broadway Mansions and there she found Clyde Farnsworth, a newspaperman with a wide knowledge of China (at one time he had been PRO to Chennault's 'Flying Tigers'). Farnsworth knew where the headquarters of the secret police was. He even had their phone number and rang them up immediately. They confirmed that they were holding Vine and Jenkins, who had admitted their guilt. Farnsworth thought it better not to tell Ellen that they had already been sentenced to death.

Around midnight someone from the British Consulate-General did reach the secret police station – only to be ordered out at gunpoint. By now Jenkins and Vine were convinced they would be shot. Jenkins had already been roughly handled before Vine appeared on the scene, 'and I was quite convinced in the middle of that first night that they would execute me'.

They owed their lives to Farnsworth, whom Jenkins remembers as 'a dignified figure, responsible and with authority, very impressive to a youngster like me'. Farnsworth had a curfew pass, so he was able to move freely. He was not able to speak to the two newspapermen on his first visit, though they did receive two blankets he brought for them with a note – so at least they knew they had not been 'lost'. Then Clyde settled down to talk for the best part of thirty-six hours with Colonel Yeh and to force him to change his mind. The colonel finally agreed to release the two men after Farnsworth had warned him, 'It would be very unwise to execute these men. It's the sort of thing that would bring down the combined wrath of the Scripps-Howard newspapers and the King of England.' They had to give an undertaking not to divulge what had happened.

Though Jenkins and Vine had to spend a second night in the attic, Farnsworth was able to see them twice and report progress. The next day, after their release, when a press conference was held for them, they had in Jenkins's words to be 'pretty evasive in our answers'. Graham was whisked out of Shanghai almost immediately – partly because one American news agency had filed a story saying he had been shot; 'so Chancellor, the boss, ordered me out'.

Ellen thought that George was also in a dangerous position. 'Don't you think we ought to give up the job?' she asked him. In one way Vine knew that he should leave, yet he wanted to see the thing through – to see what life would be like under the Communists.

'But surely,' argued Ellen, 'if the Communists win – and they're going to win – you won't have any paper to print?'

George thought it through for a day or two, then, after talking to his editor, he rang up an old friend at Butterfield & Swires and told him, 'I'm going to pack it in. Have you got any boats leaving soon? Check around, will you, and get me a couple of berths.'

Vine and Jenkins never realised – certainly not at the time – what a narrow escape they had had, for 'Bloody Mao' had instigated a reign of brutality in a last-ditch attempt to rid the city of the fifth columnists, crooks and black marketeers who had always infested it. General Mao not only liked sentencing people to death after summary convictions, he also enjoyed carrying out the sentences with the pomp of a Roman arena.

A few days after Vine and Jenkins had been freed, Shanghai newspapers carried the news that three men had been found guilty of being members of a breakaway group in the Nationalist party. 'Bloody Mao' decided to sentence the men in public, in the steel and concrete inner compound of the Central Police Station. Stands were erected for hundreds of sightseers, from coolies to the wives of officials. The compound was overlooked by the Metropole Hotel, the City Hall and several other buildings, including Hamilton House, headquarters of the Filipino Consulate. Every window in every building was packed. A sickened Mariano Ezpeleta felt that 'it was a free show given by Mao Sen, a purger turned showman'.

The men arrived from their cells in a Black Maria, and each was given a chair and a desk in the compound so that he could write his will. Each was given the right to make a short farewell speech; and each passionately proclaimed he was not a traitor but a martyr to the true beliefs of Sun Yat-sen which had now been twisted out of recognition. True to tradition, an official using red ink wrote the order for their execution with sweeping strokes of a brush on large fan-shaped placards which were then thrown at the feet of the condemned men. Then – since hungry men are never executed – each man was given a glass of wine and a plate of hot noodles, after which they were bundled into trucks and taken to Chapei, where they kneeled before shallow graves and were shot in the back.

It has to be said that 'Bloody Mao' also caught a few of Shanghai's top criminals, including Siao Chang, at 30 the boss of a gang known as the 'Razor Clique'. Siao and his thugs had terrorised Shanghai for years, and he was executed in public before an appreciative crowd. The police wagon taking him to the execution spot was followed by three pedicabs, the first two carrying wailing women, the third carrying a young sobbing girl whose face was buried in the arms of an older woman. The first two pedicabs carried two of Siao's concubines, the third his last, his youngest and his favourite, who was being comforted in her distress by Siao's understanding wife.

While all these events were taking place, several rich and influential Chinese were busy hatching a plot to sell out the city to the Communists without a fight – as many Westerners had predicted they would do. Most of the diplomatic corps were given vague outlines, including Ezpeleta, who remembered later, 'A close Chinese friend of mine, a bank manager, came to see me and with a smile told me that negotiations were almost complete for Shanghai to give up without a fight. He outlined the negotiations, the number of gold bars needed, and the men working for it.' It would take a few days to complete the plan 'because necessary funds were still being raised to make the negotiations possible'.

The plan would certainly have gone through but for one event the plotters had not foreseen. Chiang Kai-shek came out of retirement (for a limited appearance), making an unexpected visit to Shanghai towards the end of April when he told the military leaders, 'Shanghai will fight to the end. There will be no surrender.' Any talk of compromise was treason, he said in a nation-wide radio appeal, in which he promised, 'I wish to pledge at this time of crisis that I shall share the sufferings of my fellow countrymen and that as long as I live I shall take part in our struggle against enslavement.'

Since Chiang went back into retirement shortly afterwards, Ezpeleta felt that he was only concerned about impressing the US. As he noted, 'The reason is plain. He was playing for bigger stakes. He wanted to show America that the Nationalists were still full of fight, in the hope of getting more arms from the United States.' After all, Madame Chiang was in America begging for help; so was Ambassador Koo. American aid had now been very much reduced but Ezpeleta felt that 'if he could put up a good show in Shanghai and prove that there was still some fight in him, then American aid might be forthcoming'.

It didn't work that way, and Chiang's speech had a disastrous effect on the city's economy which was almost grinding to a halt. The day before Chiang made his speech, 1 American dollar could buy 1.2 million Chinese dollars. When the speech was published, the rate dropped to 1.7 million, and the day after that it dropped to a staggering 3.75 million for 1 American dollar. Chinese money was now worth less than the cost of printing it.

The peace plan was hurriedly abandoned. The plotters suddenly vanished, and Ezpeleta heard of one man who hid in a hospital for the deaf and dumb. His bank manager came to see Ezpeleta, not in the Consulate but at home. 'He was plainly scared. Would I please forget our talk about negotiations?'

Now, more than ever, as troops prepared to defend the outskirts of Shanghai, workers refused to accept their wages; instead they demanded to be paid in kind. Tens of thousands started taking their 'salaries' in rubber boots, pots and pans, stepladders or buckets, rolls of Chinese cotton. They spread these things out on squares of brown paper (to be carefully folded each evening and used over and over again) on the pavements of the Bund, under the shadows of the great foreign trading houses.

Billy Hawkings was walking along the Bund to the Shanghai Club one morning when he saw his boy Lau Wu talking to a man squatting behind an array of rubber boots. He was Lau Wu's brother who worked for the Shanghai Rubber Corporation. As they talked, a scrawny farmer with two heavy baskets over his shoulders came up to them, and eventually they made exchanges. It was significant to Hawkings, because those rare farmers who had a surplus of food always refused to sell their produce for money; but they did want new boots. On his way back from lunch, Hawkings again passed Lau Wu's brother. The stock of boots had dwindled and he was discussing a different transaction with a fisherman. Later he would probably barter some of the goods he had bought for something else until in the end he had something to sell for silver dollars with which to buy rice.

By the first week in May the Chinese dollar had dropped to 35 million to the pound and notes had become so scarce that people were paying up to 50 per cent discount to get them. Even the silver dollars were in short supply and firms like Jardines who employed a large labour force were finding it almost impossible to get enough money to pay the men. The financial mess was exacerbated by the fact that all the directors of the Central Bank – the pivotal point of government – had fled, and the bank was being run by underlings. It was as though Bank of England employees were handling the world's sterling without any of the directors to guide them. David Middleditch, the young ex-Army officer who had joined Jardines, remembers being present one day when the company safe was opened. He could hardly believe what he saw. 'It was filled with gold and silver bars and every kind of currency.'

The next day he was detailed to go to the bank to get some money for the wages.

'How much?' he asked the head cashier.

'It's all arranged,' came the reply. 'Fifty thousand million dollars.'

So he took a five-ton truck, three armed coolies, and 'collected fifty thousand million grand!'

Yet that night Middleditch dined at Delmonico's, one of Shanghai's best restaurants. Dinner for two, with wine, cost £2.

9

Waiting for the Attack

May 1949

Chinese Nationalist troops had for years suffered from a shocking reputation which, though justified, was not entirely their fault. Many were simple young peasants plucked from lonely villages and pressed into army service against their will; once in uniform they were often abominably treated by corrupt officials who, from general down to corporal, took a cut on everything from the man's minuscule pay to his miserable rations. The wretched recruits were forced to walk up to 300 miles to the depot, each one haltered to the man in front by a neck rope. Sometimes 80 per cent died before reaching their destination.

Theodore H. White, the American author, who lived several years in China, tells how he and a visiting American general watched some Chinese marching along a road, almost every man tugging a dog on a makeshift lead. The general smiled as he said, 'Here they are! The GIs the world over – they all love dogs!' 'Teddy' White pointed out that the dogs had been stolen, but not as pets. 'When the soldiers run out of rice and other food,' he explained, 'the dogs go into the cooking pot.'

Inevitably the treatment they received affected the troops' behaviour. They stole, they begged, they looted. In the countryside they raided the peasants' crops. Given the right stimulus and the right leadership they were magnificent fighting men; General Stillwell had proved that to his own satisfaction. But now, disillusioned, with no fire in their hearts, no food in their bellies, they had become hated by everyone.

Until the Communists crossed the Yangtze, Shanghai had been spared the rigours of a large-scale military presence. Troops had been coming and going from the beginning of the year, even before, but it was not until the generals started proclaiming that Shanghai was China's Stalingrad and would 'fight to the last man', that brave words had to be matched with visible preparations.

Suddenly, during April and May – coincident with martial law, censorship, the refugees, the currency crash – troops poured into the city in their tens of thousands with nowhere to sleep and little food to eat. General Tang En-po, supreme commander of the Nanking–Shanghai sector, and General Chen Ta-chin, Shanghai garrison commander, had laid down certain egalitarian rules. Their troops could ride free on all public transport, they were entitled to free seats at cinemas and theatres when off duty. It might have been splendid in theory, but in practice it could never work, for Shanghai was not geared to be a garrison town.

Darrell Berrigan, the American writer, found that the 'demoralised, undisciplined troops have made themselves very unwelcome. Streetcars are tied up for hours in protest against soldiers demanding free rides on cars that will hold no more passengers without bursting their metal seams.' When he visited one cinema, a crowd was fighting for admission, with soldiers demanding the reserved seats for which civilians had paid in advance. One brawl only ended when an angry soldier pulled the pin out of a grenade and several civilians were killed. To prevent such 'disturbances' General Tang formed a Peace Preservation Unit, but its members reacted too brutally by executing a wounded soldier who had been fighting outside a theatre. Shanghai, as unpredictable as ever, took the side of the wounded soldier, and attacked the 'peace unit', killing three of its men.

The soldiers had, of course, to be quartered and the army commandeered every building it could lay its hands on – schools, private houses, factories, even temples. Wounded soldiers, many in rags, some on crutches, others with arms in slings, fought their way on to the few boats or trains still leaving the city, forcing out men, women and children who had sacrificed their last dollars for black-market tickets and were now left stranded on platform or quay. Berrigan saw

wounded and demoralised soldiers crowd the jetties waiting for southbound ships. Few have tickets or the money to buy them. But the combined efforts of the police, military and ships' crews cannot prevent them from clawing, butting and biting their way aboard the little ships, swarming up the gangplanks and through the portholes as some hunger-crazed animal pack might swarm over the helpless bulk of a stranded whale. To save itself the ship has to pull out into the river, shake off pursuing sampans and flee.

Soon it was war between the civilians and the soldiers – with most citizens praying for swift delivery by the Red Army, particularly when General Tang sent out troops to round up unemployed labour gangs to help throw up urgent defence works. Each man had to bring his own spade or other digging equipment, even his own food, though the rich paid starving coolies to take their places. To transport them Tang requisitioned trucks, buses and other vehicles from the big foreign firms who also had to supply drivers, petrol and spare tyres for 'temporary requisition'. Evasion was punished swiftly: the owner's licence was simply cancelled.

Shanghai businessmen were furious, for Tang had violated the basic creed which had served Shanghai through four wars in the past twenty-two years – that it considered itself above war or politics unless there was a profit to be made. Angry deputations visited the Mayor, who went to see Tang. In the end the general was forced to withdraw his press gangs and offer the same work at 'danger' wages to recognised compradores who supplied labour.

The Cathay Hotel, the Palace, Cavendish Court and other plush hotels or apartment blocks were soon filled with Nationalist troops, many of them boggle-eyed at the unaccustomed luxury in which they found themselves. George Vine happened to be in the lobby of the Cathay on his way to the cable office when he saw an officer walk in, followed by fifty or so soldiers. Politely but firmly, the officer announced that on the orders of the garrison commander, he had come to requisition a dozen rooms to install machine-gun posts overlooking the waterfront and other vital points. As George watched, soldiers carrying full packs and wearing German-type helmets clattered across the imposing lounge and reception area. They carried pots, pans, rice, vegetables, even firewood, and he heard one soldier ask innocently, 'Where can we billet our mules?'

The manager of the Cathay was able to persuade the young officer to give him time to remove items of valuable furniture and to transfer his few guests to other hotels. 'Guests don't have to leave the hotel,' said the officer blandly. 'We will wait here in the hall while you make arrangements.'

Guests were hurriedly moved (without their consent if they were not in their rooms) while the hotel staff set about saving the best furniture, mostly from the Tower nightclub on the hotel's upper floor. They wheeled out a grand piano, removed rugs, furniture, liquor, and pulled down hand-carved dragons, silk lanterns and other wall decorations. Soon only the gilded buddhas, smiling in their niches, remained.

Over the centuries wars in China had become as much a part of normal life as earthquakes in Japan or typhoons in Florida, and one would have thought that Shanghai was inured by the shadows of defeat which had lengthened year by year; yet this was not the case. The city had withstood most things – crime, corruption, poverty, plague, floods and famine – but it had never withstood a siege. Now it had difficulty in grasping the implications.

'What has never happened isn't going to happen now,' one Chinese told Billy Hawkings. 'We've never been under siege because we've no fortifications, no food, no arsenals. You can't change historical facts overnight.'

In an attempt to instil a 'siege mentality' the military had overreacted, and the people of Shanghai were confronted with the spectacle of more than a quarter of a million troops with little to do but stop vehicles, search passengers, snarl up traffic, and generally get in the way.

To Mariano Ezpeleta who toured the city, 'Shanghai looked like a battleground. Storekeepers boarded their windows and glass showcases, leaving only small apertures for occasional customers.' The latest 'Paris creations' always displayed at the Salon du Nord could now only be seen behind closed doors.

Ezpeleta found troops in full kit directing traffic from sandbagged enclosures at almost every intersection. Gun posts had been erected at the Garden Bridge, almost underneath the windows of the British Consulate; the small park between the Consulate and the river was bristling with guns manned day and night. Troops dug trenches in any vacant plots seemingly haphazardly – and strung up barbed wire at the entrances to all public buildings.

The City Hall and Central Police Station were both opposite the Philippine Consulate, so Ezpeleta could see how the entrances were protected by walls of sandbags five feet high with

Shanghai's famous Long Bar, more than a hundred feet, was generally agreed to be the longest bar in the world. It was certainly the showpiece of the exclusive Shanghai Club, whose imposing columned entrance is pictured below. *(Godfrey Moyne)*

Chiang Kai-shek promised to defend Shanghai "to the last man," but his troops hardly fought. Here a Nationalist officer chooses an unusual form of transport. *(Associated Press) Below:* Nationalist troops parading along the Bund. *(Associated Press)*

More than a million Red Army troops were involved in the crossing of the Yangtze. With bugles blowing, flags and banners flying, they swept ashore on the south bank virtually unopposed. (*Popperfoto*)

The Red Army used every conceivable type of river craft when their legions crossed the Yangtze *(Keystone Press Agency);* the civilians of Shanghai *(below)* were ordered to build moats and anti-tank ditches in the vain hope of defending the city. *(New York Times)*

Norman Watts, the Chinese scholar who had saved Chou En-lai's life, was arrested by the Communists as Shanghai fell. This photograph was taken in 1938. *(Norman Watts) Below:* From the roof of Broadway Mansions, Shanghai's press headquarters, Nationalist troops fire down on the Communists. *(Associated Press)*

Journalist George Vine was sentenced to death but later freed. While condemned, Vine looked down on one of several "execution gardens" in Shanghai. Three Chinese *(above)* are pictured at the exact moment of death. The bullet is just passing through the pullover of the man on the right, who has been rocked back on his heels by the force of the impact. *Below:* Vine is seen (third from left) in the Long Bar at the Shanghai Club. *(George Vine)*

"The Limit" was the home that Billy and Gladys Hawkings refused to leave when the Communists shelled the city. *Below:* Gladys Hawkings with her dog Timmy in April 1948. *(Gladys Hawkings Collection)*

Robert T. Bryan, an American lawyer, was jailed after the Communists took the city. *Above:* He is seen with his wife Gertrude just before the Communists arrested him. *Left:* Taken just after his release, this photograph shows the terrible change in his appearance. *(Mrs. Gertrude Bryan)*

machine-gun muzzles just visible. On the flat roof of the Messageries Maritimes Building, on the Bund facing Pootung, men had set up trench mortars.

Official Nationalist communiqués recited victory after victory, but Ezpeleta felt that 'the more battles Tang En-po won, the more worried and distressed his troops looked. The city was filled with men, women and children rushing about in dilapidated trucks or pedicabs, bringing with them their bedding and kitchen utensils – people with blank stares running around aimlessly for places of safety, but without knowing where to find them.'

Crazy new edicts followed one another without rhyme or reason. Suddenly General Tang levied a special emergency tax on every motor vehicle in the city. It was the equivalent of $50 US – a fortune to a small trader working with Chinese currency. The money, said an official proclamation, would be used 'to balance the budget'. The announcement was greeted with wry hilarity, for everyone knew that Shanghai had never balanced its budget since 'extrality' ended. In the same week, the army organised several parades designed, said the general, 'to impart to the residents the significance of the war against Communism'. Fifty requisitioned trucks, filled with men, women and children 'volunteers', paraded through the streets which had been dutifully decked out with bunting and portraits of Chiang while 'supporters' lined the streets or peered from windows.

All this was worse than nonsense; it was interfering with Shanghai's first priority – to make money, an urge that beat not only in the hearts of every taipan and compradore but also in the breasts of those stalwarts (if that is the right word) of Shanghai's night life, the dancing girls who decorated places like the Canidrome, Ciro's, the Majestic and the Paramount ballroom in Yu Yuan Road. These buildings had been commandeered to provide barracks, throwing 15,000 people out of work.

The girls were the first to protest against the 'siege conditions', which they argued were nonsense in a port they had helped to christen 'the city that never sleeps' but which was now turning out the lights at 9 p.m. Several hundred planned a demonstration, in which they would march in evening dresses from the start of the Bubbling Well Road all the way to the Bund. The first girls had hardly put their feet outside the Paramount before they were confronted with armoured cars manned by the secret police of 'Bloody Mao'. The first six, picked out at random, were whisked off to indefinite jail sentences without trial, and the others were abruptly given an alternative: march and be arrested under martial law, or go home and be spared. They went home.

Some places tried to beat the curfew and night patrols by staging tea dances from two to six, but somehow the nightbirds of Shanghai could not bring themselves to buy rolls of tickets for taxi dancers in daylight. The Palace Hotel even hired a hip-swinging troupe of hula dancers and a new swing band: the Park abolished its cover charge and advertised cut-price 'Early dinner under the moon' on its fourteenth-floor Sky Terrace; but no one wanted to dine at 6 p.m.

A few nightclubs did carry on, after heavily bribing the authorities. But even in these the atmosphere had changed. Ezpeleta remembered with nostalgia how, shortly after the war ended, he had visited Shanghai with a mission, and had 'as part of our social duties visited the ballrooms where old age was proscribed and solitude a crime'. Then he had found 'countless alluring girls, each one more alluring than the next'. In those days – all of three years before – there had been no vulgarity, everything had been done with decorum and politeness; he had found that a girl would measure a man up carefully before allowing any advances. Now, when he went to see the few places that remained open – the Metropole, the Eventail, the Merry Widow – all was changed. The girls were younger and less exotic, and 'the piquancy had gone; gone too was the measuring look; it was enough that you were there with a little ready cash. War, we told ourselves, was indeed a great leveller.'

Most Westerners refused to take the war seriously, especially the young ones, most of whom had fought in the World War and could only regard this one as something of a joke. When David Middleditch of Jardines went to Hungjao one day to make sure that the villas of his taipans were not being commandeered, he saw something of the Nationalist defences and noted in his diary, 'It's true that they are digging in a lot of guns at Hungjao, but as a number of them are pointed towards Shanghai rather than away from it, the theory is that they've already been sold to the Communists.'

Middleditch had no illusions about the future of Shanghai – or the ability of the Nationalists to fight for it. 'Having passed through all the stages of lunacy in government, trade, currency and everything else, Shanghai's about to blow up,' he wrote to his family. 'No one's going to stop the Communists or even try to.

The Nationalist forces round here haven't got a kick left in them. Meanwhile we all continue to go to the office, play golf at the weekends, and drink brandy after dinner, while waiting to see what will happen.'

Nor was he impressed by Shanghai's most extraordinary defence measure – a wooden stockade, thirty-five miles long, which had been hastily erected to guard the inner city. The entire project of the 'Shanghai Wall' was ludicrous. 'It surrounds the land side of the city,' wrote Middleditch, 'but I can only conceive that it is designed to keep the population in rather than the Communists out, as it could easily be breached by a resolute bullock.' Most people were convinced that the stockade had been erected to enable a local timber merchant to become a millionaire.

Shanghai had three airfields in general use. (A fourth at Dazang, north of the city, had not been active for some years.) The only commercial airport was Lunghwa, south of the city perimeter, and backing on to the river so that flying boats could use it. Kiangwin, a few miles to the north, and also near the river, was by far the best equipped. At the end of the war the US Air Force had taken it under control, installing new equipment, lengthening runways, turning it into one of the most modern airfields in the East. Protected by Nationalist naval vessels in the Whangpoo or the Yangtze, and the guns of Woosung forts at the confluence of the two rivers, it was easy to see why it had become the Nationalist military airbase.

Finally there was Hungjao airfield, to the south-west, bordering the perimeter of Shanghai and the villas of the rich. For some time it had been used by General Claire Chennault's Civil Air Transport, but had now assumed a new significance in the eyes of Nationalist troops who believed the Communists would use it and the surrounding area as their jumping-off place for the attack on Shanghai. The area was flat, the airfield mostly deserted, yet studded with buildings, and the country between the perimeter and the residential area was wooded. Since a Communist attack from the north was considered to be out of the question, it seemed obvious that the final Communist thrust would come from the direction of this airfield.

It was in Hungjao that a British family – the Hawkings – decided to make a stand, not against the Communists but against the Nationalists who were trying to ruin the house and gardens on which they had lavished so much care.

The Nationalist troops, with the mock-heroics of comic opera, were turning Hungjao into an impenetrable fortress, a last-ditch defence before Shanghai. To do so, they had seized any property that happened to be empty. Gladys Hawkings was on her way to church one Sunday morning when she was caught up in a two-way flood of human beings – on the one hand refugees pouring into the city, and, facing them, impressed labour, pushed and bullied by soldiers, going out into the countryside to dig defence works. Billy Hawkings had gone ahead and Gladys found the road leading to the Cathedral impassable. 'Suddenly I was convinced that I ought not to have left our home without any of us there,' she wrote later. She returned to find her garden alive with soldiers smashing down the fences, hacking away at trees. In fluent Chinese, Gladys managed to stop them, but this was only the beginning. Forty refugees were soon squatting on land behind the house. They had been ordered to erect pillboxes. The next day, after Hawkings had left for the office, Gladys, still in her dressing gown, was sitting sewing, when some soldiers demanded entry into the house to make sure there was a clear line of fire from the bedrooms to a village near the airport. Pointing his gun at the village, one soldier cried, 'The Communists are there. They want to shoot us. We must be sure we can shoot back.'

Sure enough there was a sudden burst of firing from the village, followed by the thud of mortar fire and puffs of smoke from the direction of the airfield. Gladys's first thought was that she had better get dressed, but as she wrote to her daughters, 'What does one wear to meet an oncoming Communist army? I put on my best skirt and the new walking shoes in case I might have to walk the ten miles into Shanghai.' In the end, it turned out that the firing in the village had been a mistake. Rumours had caused panic: the Nationalist soldiers had been firing at each other; there were, as yet, no Communists in sight.

Realising that they could be cut off from Shanghai, the Hawkings had laid in supplies – enough basic foods to last for several weeks, thirty tins of paraffin stored in an outhouse, not only for their own use 'but for a real emergency, as it can be exchanged for rice when money becomes impossible to find. All cash is so hard to get and even if Dad does bring money at night, it sometimes is only worth a quarter in value by the time we wake up the next morning.' They also had two five-gallon bottles of distilled water, for there was a real danger that the water would be cut off.

On the Hungjao Road, which led from The Limit to the city, troops were cutting down all the big trees and slashing the bamboo groves, turning the trees into 'tank traps' by laying them across the narrow road, then digging trenches on either side. In one place they dug up the Chinese cemetery, scattering the bones anywhere, while the country people arrived with cardboard boxes to try to retrieve the remains of their ancestors.

No Shanghailanders would have minded any destruction necessary to throw up defence works in the hope of making Shanghai fight to the end, but the puny efforts of isolated bands of soldiers hardly seemed to matter in comparison with the complete absence of *any* serious defensive measures in or around Shanghai. The mood was listless. The only questions everyone in Hungjao asked were – 'When? And what is going to happen afterwards?' No one – least of all the Nationalist troops – seemed disposed to fight. So why dig up people's graves, or ruin their gardens? 'It's a question of face,' Hawkings told a friend. 'They've got to be seen to be doing something – until the fighting starts, anyway.'

The Hawkingses became unwitting spectators of several incidents. When Nationalist troops camping behind their house made a routine search of a peasant, they found four passes in his pocket – and that surely meant he was a spy. They beat the man mercilessly before burying him up to his neck in a flower bed, leaving him there for several hours until finally he screamed that he would confess. Soldiers then dug him out and tied him to a tree for thirty-six hours without food or water, before dragging him away the next morning. The Hawkingses never did find out what happened to him.

Another day Nationalist troops caught a man stealing from the Hawkingses' coal shed which their commanding officer had promised to protect while his men were billeted in the grounds. The thief was tied to a tree in front of the house and men set about beating him brutally. When Mrs Hawkings protested the Chinese officer looked astonished.

'But I cannot stop,' he replied. 'I have lost face after telling you that I would look after your property.'

The Limit was so close to Hungjao airport, which both attackers and defenders regarded as a military prize, that it could not escape being in the line of crossfire if it came to a real battle. Yet the Hawkingses could not bear to leave it. They knew that

129

if they did so their property would be requisitioned. Much of their wealth was tied up in The Limit. Besides, having lived there for twenty-seven years, they could not bring themselves to desert their servants. Gladys summed it up as follows: 'They have stuck with us through all the bouts of trouble. Lau Wu has been with the family for forty-five years, amah, thirty-four, for they worked for my father before us. We don't think it fair to desert them in what might be their biggest trial.' In any case – 'It's good for British prestige to stay and carry on normally.'

Eventually an emergency meeting of the Shanghai consular corps was convened, to bring the 'ravaging' of Hungjao to the attention of General Tang; it was not a success. Tang told the consuls that nothing could be allowed to interfere with military operations. Ezpeleta, who was at the meeting, remembers one consul exclaiming, 'I have always asked myself whether the Nationalist troops are here to protect the civilians, or the civilians to protect them. Now I know the answer.'

The Hawkingses' ordeal soon brought them fame in the international press. Not only did they carry on, but they tamed the troops and earned from them genuine respect. Sidney Smith of the *Daily Express* cabled a story of the 'front line woman whose admirers can be counted in millions'. Gladys asked Smith to lunch – for roast mutton, homegrown vegetables and fresh strawberries, for which Smith thanked her with the words, 'The best mutton I've eaten since 1939'. In the middle of May five more correspondents arrived at The Limit, including Robert Doyle of *Time* magazine and *Life*. Doyle wrote: 'In front of the house a group of soldiers were wolfing down bowls of rice. When Mrs Hawkings appeared in her cardigan sweater and plaid skirt, the soldiers stopped eating and gazed at her with awe and affection. One young soldier started singing China's national anthem. "They're nice boys really," said the mistress of The Limit.'

Perhaps what impressed Doyle most was the way in which 'the soldiers, overwhelmed by her bearing and perfect Chinese', obeyed her in everything she said.

By now the Hawkingses had made a 'stronghold' out of a corridor linked to the pantry on the ground floor. It was protected from above, of course, and between the outside walls of the house and the pantry were two thick inner walls. Into this cell they crammed mattresses, sacks of rice, tin trunks, together with sandbags and baskets of earth. The walls were lined with rows of canned goods and bags of rice. Upstairs, they piled sacks of cement against the windows. Four baths were filled with water in case the supply was cut. Hawkings reckoned they could, if besieged, last out for three months.

During their first night in the stronghold, shells landed near the Chinese bungalow behind the house, wounding six soldiers out of thirty billeted in the grounds. Despite the shelling, Gladys phoned her doctor for instructions, then treated the wounded with disinfectant, lint, cottonwool and pain-killing tablets. Next morning she reported, 'It was a rough night. For the first time in my life I slept with my shoes on.'

Among regular visitors to The Limit was David Middleditch who was making periodic inspection tours of the company houses in Hungjao. Though in general he found it difficult to take the war seriously, he had nothing but admiration for women who refused to be ruffled; the more so because to outsiders Shanghai was often represented as an exotic city, where wives were pampered, surrounded by servants and with no cares beyond the next dinner party. He found that 'ladies take the dangers very calmly without a thought of quitting'. Back in his office one day he heard a director tell his wife that he couldn't return to their home in Hungjao that night, adding, 'There may be some stray machine-gun fire, so I think you had better take a carpet down to the boiler room and sleep there tonight.'

The exact date when Shanghai itself was invested by the Communists varies according to people's memories, but Middleditch is convinced that it was on Saturday, 14 May. That was the day when he heard his first clap of gunfire and there was a strong rumour that the Communists would take over the city within a few hours. He remembers the date particularly because it was warm and sunny and the Country Club opened its grass tennis courts for the summer season, serving strawberries and cream for dinner. Middleditch also remembers that – despite his artificial leg – 'I played ten sets and by the end of the day was finding the war most fatiguing'.

Though the Communists were now within a few miles of Shanghai the over-all military position was far from clear. The Red Army was making one thrust at Hungjao, another north of Shanghai, though the main armies were by-passing the city, heading along the Grand Canal towards Hangchow on the coast.

131

There were, of course, no foreign warships left in Shanghai. The British cruiser *Belfast* had reached Woosung, where the Whangpoo joins the Yangtze, to replace the damaged cruiser *London* as the flagship of Vice-Admiral A. C. G. Madden, second-in-command, Far Eastern Station. She was anchored with other British and American naval vessels. The US Navy had already warned that, once American vessels had moved to Woosung, 'no further facilities of any kind will be provided by American authorities for the protection of American citizens in Shanghai and they must be prepared to remain'.

There was nothing anyone could do about the poor *Amethyst*, by now a prisoner of the Communists. Any thought of immediate help from the RAF had been ruled out. The nearest effective British air support consisted of a fighter squadron in Singapore, 2250 miles away; there was no British carrier in the area. When questions were asked in the House, a Government spokesman replied: 'Any decision to send in planes might produce international complications.'

Communist envoys near *Amethyst* had advised the British Navy to leave the frigate where she was 'because of continued warlike activity both up and downstream'. The Navy had, for the moment, decided that discretion was the better part of valour.

If the British Navy was helpless, so was Acting President Li, to whom Chiang had made the hollow public promise, 'I am prepared in my private capacity to follow the lead of all my compatriots [and] to support Acting President Li in the prosecution of the war.'

Now, all Li, whose efforts had been so selfishly sabotaged by Chiang, could do was cable his apologies to President Truman, admitting, 'It is regrettable that, owing to the failure of our government to make judicious use of [American] aid and to bring about appropriate political, economic and military reforms, your assistance has not produced the desired effect. To this failure is attributable the present predicament in which our country finds itself.'

Honour, courage, unity were now debased words, as the consuls discovered when they tried to persuade the Mayor to declare Shanghai an open city.

General Chen Liang had recently been appointed Mayor in place of the previous incumbent who had fled to Taiwan. He was in his sixties and had inaugurated his term of office by proposing a 'Health Week', urging people to keep fit for the trials ahead. On the morning of the 18th the consular corps formed a committee of three to ask him to act. Mariano Ezpeleta was included 'because the Chinese would take me as a fellow Oriental and a friend', but the Mayor proved difficult to track down. Finally Ezpeleta was invited to dine with him at his home in Frenchtown.

Passing through the cordon of guards, he was ushered into 'a big living room opening on to a terrace and garden lit with Chinese lanterns hung in the trees. There was a pervading air of pleasantness, even victory in the gay atmosphere.' There was no sign of the Mayor, but several other guests were being served drinks from 'a large table, heavily stocked with bottles', and a gramophone was churning out the latest Shanghai ditty, in itself a barometer of the city's '*Maskee* syndrome'. It had originally been sung in Chinese, but now an English version had been recorded, and it went:

Me no worry
Me no care,
Me going to marry a millionaire;
And if he die,
Me no cry,
Me going to get another guy.

The Mayor's wife apologised for the fact that her husband had been delayed, but about 9.30 he finally arrived. He had, he said, been out on a morale-boosting tour, and was planning to leave again in a couple of hours for 'a night inspection'. Ezpeleta had no chance to ask the Mayor to consider the consular project of making Shanghai into an open city, but he did tie the Mayor down to an appointment the following morning.

'That's a promise,' said the Mayor. 'I'll have my secretary call your office to fix the time. Tomorrow morning – definitely.'

That was the last of the consular plan – and the last of Mayor Chen. The secretary did call Ezpeleta, to tell him that immediately after dinner the previous evening, Chen had flown off to Taiwan.

Randall Gould of the *Post* had the last word, in an editorial: 'Ex-Mayor Chen Liang was certainly sincere about Health Week. He found out what was best for his own health, and promptly did it.'

Ezpeleta was digesting the news of Mayor Chen's flight, and wondering how to break it to his consular colleagues, when his administrative officer, Conrado Uy, walked into the office as though in a daze. Ezpeleta asked what was troubling him.

'I can't believe it,' said Mr Uy. 'I didn't have time for breakfast this morning so I stopped for a cup of coffee. You know what it cost me? Three and a half million dollars! For one cup of lousy coffee! I was so fed up I threw in another half a million dollars as a tip!'

Then Mr Uy's face brightened. 'I suppose in my old age,' he said, 'I shall look back with pride on the day when I gave a working man whose name I didn't even know, half a million dollars as a tip. I challenge the Rockefellers and the Duponts to be as generous as that to a waiter!'

If the consuls (and the Mayor) knew the end was near, so did everyone else, and it was unexpected touches that signalled the approaching crisis. A few days before their departure, George and Ellen Vine held a farewell party at Broadway Mansions, and as the guests sipped their drinks on the balcony they looked down, as everyone always did, on the busy, ant-like life of Soochow Creek. The boats were so closely packed that Vine remembers one guest saying, 'Sardines in tins have nothing on the Creek.'

The next morning, Ellen called to George, 'Come and look – you'll never believe this!' He followed her on to the balcony. For the first time since they had come to Shanghai, they could see the whole length of Soochow Creek. Every single sampan – each with its cockle-shell family – had vanished. Vine never found out where they had gone to, but 'the Chinese grapevine had warned them when it was time to leave'.

Vine's party was one of the last to be held by correspondents in Broadway Mansions, for the newspapermen had decided to close their club. With a Communist fifth column now openly operating in Shanghai, there was a very real danger that journalists might suddenly find themselves unable to cable, might even be held hostage.

'It wasn't an exaggeration,' George Vine remembers. 'Many of the club servants had been thoroughly indoctrinated, and were already hinting that the "Imperialist aggressors" should hand over their furniture and effects – in other words that they should be expropriated. They did in fact establish a Broadway Mansions collective.'

Many reporters noticed that their boys had become more aggressive. The rents for apartments suddenly had to be paid into a 'collective account' instead of to the Nationalist landlords. Operators decided to close three out of the four elevators – so that only one man was needed to check the movements of news-papermen coming and going.

At the moment of crisis, no journalist dared risk being caught in a trap, for a few hours' 'voluntary detention' could mean missing the biggest Shanghai story since the end of the Second World War. So closure of the club became inevitable.

The club had assets. They included all the furniture – even a Hammond organ – and two cars which they had bought over the years and which were normally rented with drivers to visiting foreign correspondents. The assets were quietly sold for around $10,000 (American)* – a tidy sum in those days. The cheque was handed to George Vine to take to Hongkong.

While the families on Soochow Creek moved out, the diplomats moved in. It was essential for all consuls and senior executives to remain near their radio stations day and night. It was becoming increasingly hazardous to drive, even with CD number plates, yet most members of the consular corps lived in flats or villas that were often some distance from their offices. Urquhart, the British Consul-General, was luckier, for he and most of his senior staff lived in the compound with their offices next door.

Others were not so fortunate. John Cabot, the US Consul-General, lived in Frenchtown, so he now decided to move into the American Consulate-General and sleep on a camp bed; his wife had returned to America. He noted in his diary on 13 May, 'I still think a practical policy is better than an impractical straddle which only, I fear, result [sic] in falling between two stools.' Cabot, who admired his British counterpart, also noted that day, 'Urquhart is very apprehensive.'

The US Consulate-General had in fact recently moved from its headquarters in Hongkew, across the Garden Bridge, to the more modern Glen Line Building on the Bund at the corner of Peking Road, and adjacent to the British Consulate-General. Cabot had master-minded the difficult task of moving staff, files, codes, radio equipment (including over thirty high-powered

---

* The $10,000 was used to found the Foreign Correspondents Club in Hongkong.

transmitters) in three days without interrupting the daily routine. The new Consulate had originally been the head office of a famous British shipping firm but after the war had been taken over by the US Navy. When the Navy decided to close its office in Shanghai, Cabot lost no time moving in. It was a modern six-storey office building, very different from the British Consulate with its separate dwellings behind protective walls. But it was practical and the American Navy had spent a great deal of money modernising it. One floor had been turned into two excellent apartments for visiting VIPs. There was a cafeteria, even a small hospital. Since the US Consulate-General now had one of the largest staffs in the entire Foreign Service – largely because it helped to handle so many aid programmes – it had long since outgrown its original headquarters. The new building had one intriguing feature – a back door, kept locked on both sides – which led directly to the grounds of the British Consulate.

Cabot moved into the new Consulate just in time. By the third week in May, the Communists were poised for the final attacks, one to the south, the other against the Woosung forts. From the RAF Club in the dome of the Hongkong and Shanghai Bank, members could see long pillars of thick black smoke from the big oil depot about six miles down river. The industrial area of Pootung was filled with Mao's fifth columnists, and if the Communists could gain control of Pootung, they could fire across the half-mile-wide river directly on to the massive offices, hotels and apartment houses on the Bund, to say nothing of Lunghwa airfield.

Yet, incredibly, Lunghwa seemed oblivious to the fact that there was a war in progress. Normally an airfield is the first place to be taken over by troops, but as late as Saturday, 21 May, the Canadian Vice-Consul invited David Middleditch to drive out there with him. He was going to see some friends off. The airfield had been under shell fire on the Saturday and the radio had announced that the last plane had taken off. But 'this is merely one of those things one has to accept in Shanghai'. When Middleditch arrived he was astonished to see two planes landing and the airport buildings, though rather empty, still functioning. The airfield was bordered to the east by the river, and Middleditch was shocked to learn that the Communists on the opposite bank were firmly entrenched in a factory which overlooked the airfield. Yet while he was there ten planes landed and took off. The Communists could have shot up every single one.

Most of the incoming planes were empty, landing hurriedly to take off with refugees, for surely no one would want to *arrive* in Shanghai at a time like this. Yet a few did. As Middleditch watched, one plane landed and out stepped a heavy-set man with a bag and a satchel. Two minutes later the plane took off again, as Albert S. Browne, American Consul and Budget Officer, was taken to the reception area.

'This really is a comic-opera war,' Middleditch wrote home that night, 'and if I don't make it all very clear to the family, I shan't be surprised, as it couldn't be less clear to me.'

While Middleditch was at the airport, Dr A. Trivett, the Dean, was marrying a young couple at the British Cathedral – a few days earlier than they had planned. Harold Fabian and Sue Crouch had hurriedly put forward the date from June in case the Communists should prohibit a white church wedding on which Sue had set her heart. She was a pretty young Australian brunette from Sydney who worked with UNRRA. Harold was a partner in a flourishing business.

There had been a few problems in changing their wedding date. When Sue tried to cable her parents in Sydney, she found a huge backlog of cables; this meant that there would be a delay of several days. So she sent a message to a friend in Hongkong asking her to cable Sydney, then set about arranging all the details of a Cathedral wedding without her family's help. Somehow she managed to get a cake made, flowers ordered, 150 guests invited. Her wedding dress had to be made, so had a hat.

And then on the evening before the wedding, the Dean called the bride and groom to his study. Urquhart had been on the phone. 'The C-G says he's been advised that the Communists plan to take over the city tonight,' the Dean said. He offered to marry them there and then.

'But what about the guests?' cried Sue. 'Let's take a chance and wait until tomorrow.'

Sue had barely made the decision when the Shanghai correspondent of the *Sydney Sun*, hearing that she had refused to be evacuated with her UNRRA colleagues, said he was on his way to interview her.

Her wedding was a great success. There was no sign of the Communists. Indeed, Sue even heard news of her wedding on the radio, for the consuls had arranged to broadcast a midday bulletin on a consulate transmitter. 'It's a beautiful day,' said the announcer. 'Nothing serious is happening – except that Sue Crouch is getting married today.'

Mercifully Sue did not know at the time that the friend in Hongkong whom she had asked to cable her parents had never received the message; so her parents knew nothing of her wedding until they opened the *Sydney Sun*, and stared unbelievingly at the headline screaming across the front page:

SHANGHAI IN PANIC AS LAST PLANE GETS AWAY
SYDNEY GIRL STAYS TO GET MARRIED
WON'T LET WAR STOP WEDDING

The main story started:

Inside the city of 6,000,000 there is indescribable panic [*sic*] with business at a standstill, food scarce, and traffic hopelessly at a standstill.

At the last minute Miss Suzanne Crouch cancelled her seat on one of the consular planes to get married. Shells are falling on the city, but Miss Crouch insists, 'I prefer to face unknown dangers here with the man I love than fly off to a lonely security in Hongkong.'

Of course Sue had never said anything of the sort. Perhaps it was as well for the reporter that he left Shanghai the next day.

Everyone faced problems of one sort or another. John Cabot had to find half a million US dollars – in notes – after a leading American businessman phoned him, saying, 'I know you must be pressed, but we need half a million dollars – in cash – to tide us over and pay wages. Can you help?'

Cabot had no qualms about the collateral. He knew the government would be repaid by head offices in America if necessary. But as he said, 'We don't keep that kind of money in the consulate.'

'It's damned urgent.'

Cabot thought quickly. There was one way to get it – from Admiral Badger, C-in-C of the US Navy, near Woosung. The Navy always kept huge stocks of ready cash to pay its thousands of employees. 'Give me a couple of hours and I'll see what I can do,' he promised.

Admiral Badger was only too willing to oblige – against a

receipt, naturally – but there was one problem. 'I can send half a million by helicopter to Lunghwa airfield,' he agreed. 'But from the moment it lands you must accept total responsibility for the money.'

Lunghwa was at least five miles from the Consulate, and Cabot had visions of armed gangs overpowering the car that was carrying the money, for Shanghai's notorious gangsters were taking every advantage of the crisis, and violence had increased in a city that had always been a haven for sinister underworld characters. It was at this moment that Cabot remembered an old consular rule: 'In an emergency currency may be destroyed in the presence of three consular officers.'

'I'll accept responsibility from Lunghwa,' he told Badger, then summoned three young officers to his office. He told them they were to drive together to Lunghwa. They must never – 'repeat, never!' – leave each other's company. They were to use a Jeep in which would be placed a small but lethal explosive device.

'There shouldn't be any problems,' Cabot explained, 'but if there are pull the trigger and run like hell before the Jeep blows up with the money in it.'

Luckily the precautions proved unnecessary, and the American business community collected the loan at the consulate.

Other businessmen had different kinds of problems thrust upon them without warning. One of the oldest tea-broking firms in Shanghai suddenly found its offices and godowns invaded by its employees, their wives and children.

Robert Anderson & Company had been founded in the middle of the nineteenth century, and was now being run by the founder's grandson, twenty-four-year-old Philip Schlee, with a staff of about fifty. Schlee's father was in London, and had told Philip in 1947, 'The firm should always be headed by one of the family. You're my son – go out and run it.'

At first he had loved the good life, with a car, a comfortable flat in Craig Court, plenty of servants. But soon nothing could dispel the mounting anxieties of having to run a highly specialised business with the Communists on the doorstep. Paying the staff became a nightmare. If he sent someone with a suitcase to the bank to collect money for the wages, any unexpected delay, even a traffic jam, could mean the money might have lost 20 per cent in value by the time the workers were paid. His instincts were to close the business down at a time when everybody was still insisting that nothing serious could happen, but his father hated the idea – and told him so by cable. Philip even found that the older Chinese workers, many of them sons and grandsons of the original employees of Andersons, also had sublime faith in him and 'the company', and were convinced that 'everything would be all right'.

On Monday morning, 23 May, they expressed their faith in a singular manner. When Schlee arrived at his office near Soochow Creek, the first thing he saw was a big Union Jack draped from a godown window above his head. Then there were strange noises in the godowns over the office – kids laughing or crying, women shouting. Finally, as he walked through the front door, there was an overpowering smell of cooking.

'What the hell's happening?' he shouted to his head clerk.

'Communists come soon, master,' the clerk said, smiling, so everyone come here for protection.' They had indeed; everybody was there, with their cooking pots. 'It couldn't have been more crazy,' Philip Schlee remembered later. 'There couldn't have been a worse place to come for protection than to a firm belonging to the British. But when I saw them all – and that Union Jack – I must say I felt a bit of a lump in my throat that they could have so much faith in the old firm.'

Ezpeleta was greeted by a similar shock in Hamilton House, where the Consulate-General of the Philippines occupied the entire first floor, with emergency offices on the fifth floor. The rest of the building consisted of apartments occupied by foreigners, who had now been evacuated, leaving their servants behind.

When Ezpeleta walked into the office that morning he was 'greeted by a familiar yet unexpected smell coming from many of the apartments. It was curious because it reminded me of the Quiapo Market in Manila.' It transpired that the hurried departure of the owners had been the signal for their boys and amahs to give shelter to their country cousins, and now they were all preparing for a siege – by salting fish and hanging them up in the apartments to dry.

There were hundreds of empty apartments – and hundreds of boys or amahs with relatives in the city, who now flocked to take advantage of a roof over their heads and free gas or electricity in apartments where no one had had time to tell the utility companies to switch off supplies.

Some of the poorer Russian émigrés also gained a little unexpected respite. Their richer compatriots had got out and their apartments were quickly taken over. Chernov's magnificent restaurant, the St Petersburg, became a semi-official hostel for a month after the owner had departed for the Philippines. A 'gentleman' to the last, Chernov left behind all the non-perishable foods with instructions for them to be used by his fellow émigrés. Many a White Russian beggar had his first square meal for weeks as he waited for the Communists to arrive.

The western Europeans – the British, Danes, Dutch and so on – didn't face any real problems, other than their dismay at seeing a way of life they loved being swept aside. Most either worked for foreign firms who would look after them, or owned firms which had money abroad. And all had sublime, if misplaced, faith that the Communists would want to do business with them. The British artisan class, which played such a big part in running the utilities, faced no problems either; most lived in messes, their wives and children had been evacuated several months before, and all accounts indicate that they thoroughly enjoyed their bachelor life; the war was not their concern and they did not expect to be hurt by it.

In the back-street tenements, some of the Chinese gained unexpected windfalls as more and more Nationalist soldiers took advantage of the crowded city to get rid of their hated uniforms and desert. Since the conscripts had to wear *some* clothing, there was a rush to loot stores selling cheap Chinese clothes. No young Chinese, even in rags, would dare to accept a Nationalist uniform, but the women, and the frail old men who could never be mistaken for soldiers, gratefully made use of the cast-off clothes.

Very few of those remaining in the city wanted to be evacuated. Five RAF Sunderland flying boats did fly from Hongkong and land in the Whangpoo, taking off last-minute evacuees, most of them special cases – a few elderly Europeans, people who were ill, or a few who had valid passports but no money. Each flying boat took thirty people, and though baggage was limited, one British woman arrived at the seaplane base in a truck with her piano. When the RAF refused to load it, she refused to go. Among the last to leave by seaplane were a group of Sikhs – each carrying a tin trunk on his head. They were some of the old International Settlement police force who had elected to leave, though many others stayed on.

Some Americans also decided to leave at the last moment, so Captain Robert W. Cavenagh, commander of the US naval squadron anchored in the lower Yangtze, sent in a landing craft right up to the Bund. It took twenty Americans to the American destroyer *Tucker*. On the whole, though, people just carried on – like the American School, which was continuing with plans for its annual Commencement Day on 25 May.

By Monday morning – the 23rd – it was clear that a major attack was about to be mounted. The Red Army was pounding the suburbs; in the Woosung area plumes of smoke darkened the sky. Yet even at this hour the Nationalists continued with their madness and hypocrisy. For now they decided to mount a huge 'Victory Parade'. It took place the next day, after a night alive with heavy gunfire.

As Tuesday dawned, it was as though the noise of the night had been erased as easily as a nightmare. Promptly at nine o'clock Nationalist flags began to sprout from poles and windows in every street of Shanghai. The city was transformed with bunting. 'It was like a public holiday,' Middleditch remembers, 'only of course it wasn't a holiday at all.' Before long the morning echoed with the sounds of military bands, both Chinese and foreign-style. Drums rolled, cymbals clashed. A traditional Chinese dragon writhed through the streets. Children packed in trucks sang patriotic songs, others threw red and blue streamers into crowds attracted by this evidence of 'rejoicing'.

In his diary, John Cabot wrote, 'Streets all bedecked by order to celebrate "glorious victory". (Nationalist order!) Crowds waiting to see parade and general air of expectancy. Most shops open, police on job.' He also noted: 'setting up emergency transmitter in case of problems in Glen Line Building. To Empire Day meeting at Shanghai Club.'

This was a rather different kind of celebration, and being typically British, was more subdued. Since the Bund was closed for the parade, members were unable to gain access to the Club by the front entrance, so made their way through godowns and back streets until they arrived in time to unveil a memorial to members who had died in the Second World War. After that there was a reception to toast Empire Day, at which Mr Urquhart paid the expected tribute to the resourcefulness of Shanghai's British community.

'Optimism as commonly understood is hardly the word to explain our attitude to events,' he said. 'Given fair conditions we are confident we can serve the people of Shanghai and, indeed, of

China and develop trade to our mutual profit.'

As he was speaking, and as the bands blared out their martial music in the neighbouring streets, the Communists south-west of the city near the Hungjao airfield had breached the puny so-called 'main defences'; and the Nationalist Ministry of Foreign Affairs was warning the consular corps that it was moving out. No, its destination could not be disclosed. Director Cheng phoned everyone to express his regret at being unable to say goodbye personally. 'But,' as he told Ezpeleta, 'there is no need to worry. I believe everything will be all right.'

10

The 'Battle' for Shanghai
May 1949

No one can pretend that the 'battle for Shanghai' was in any sense a real battle. The Communists put on a massive show of strength and the Nationalists crumpled at the first whiff of gunpowder. The almost formal withdrawal of one side, followed by the equally precise advance of the other, reminded Howard Gill, the British Consulate security officer, of a typical take-over by Chinese warlords in the old days – a great deal of brandishing of weapons, a spate of fiery speeches filled with dire threats, all masking a prearranged peaceful transfer of power.

The people of Shanghai – foreigners as well as Chinese – were more intrigued than afraid, for the normal fears of being involved in a battle, of being killed or maimed or taken prisoner, were replaced by curiosity.

There was, of course, some fighting and the attack on the city was in fact launched from the Hawkingses' grounds at Hungjao, which had been under fire for three nights before the final Communist assault. The phone, electricity and water had all been cut off. From time to time heavy firing started up in the daytime, obviously from Communist positions near the airfield or golf course; when this happened Billy and Gladys retired to their bullet-proof redoubt and read by candlelight. Whenever it was time for the BBC world news, 'we went upstairs, sat on the floor in a corner of the drawing room waiting for the magic words, "This is London calling".' Then they would crawl back to the pantry.

The Communists had discovered that some Nationalists were hiding in the grounds of The Limit and without warning there was a lot of banging on the front door and shouts of 'Open up!' Lau Wu went to see what was happening, and came back looking terrified. 'The Communists gave me this, missee,' he said. It was a letter on rough paper headed 'The Advance Unit of the People's Liberation Army', warning the Hawkingses to move from the house, as the area would be shelled that night.

The shelling lasted for three hours. At times Hawkings could hear men moving about outside, but could see nothing. The Communists were, as he discovered later, digging trenches and gun emplacements within a hundred yards of the main house. Finally the Nationalists must have surrendered, for Hawkings could hear shouting and what seemed like the sound of men being marched away.

With firing liable to start at any moment, the Hawkingses were virtually trapped in their hide-out for three days and nights. They had a small paraffin stove to heat tins of soup and cups of tea to supplement the iron rations of corned beef and other tinned food. When the firing finally stopped – it had been quiet for three or four hours in the early hours of Wednesday the 25th – Hawkings went to the drawing room to look outside. At the last minute Gladys accompanied him. Just as well, for outside the window was a face silently staring in. Gladys almost shrieked, but in the dim light the Chinese smiled. He seemed friendly, and after a moment's hesitation she finally said to Billy, 'Let's go and see what he wants.'

Billy unbolted the heavy front door and opened it. Then he called out, and three Chinese in green uniforms came running round and bowed politely. When Gladys spoke to them in Chinese they beamed and smiled and insisted on shaking hands. No, they wanted nothing, they were just making sure no enemy troops were hiding. No, they did not intend to billet troops in the house. The Red Army, they said proudly, was not allowed to seize any property.

After that Billy and Gladys were able to go upstairs, even sit on the veranda and watch the Red Army troops move on to take Shanghai, thousands of them, often with mules or horses. The Hawkingses were not able to let their friends in Shanghai know they were well, and not until later did Billy realise that the main attack on Shanghai had been launched from the grounds of The Limit and that 'if that attack had met with a stubborn defence, nothing would have saved our house'.

*　*　*

In Shanghai, unknown to most of the sleeping population, a small advance guard of the Red Army secretly slipped into the city under cover of the curfew around midnight on Tuesday/Wednesday, 24/25 May. Few saw them, but one who did was Mariano Ezpeleta whose bedroom window overlooked their objectives.

Ezpeleta had decided to spend the night in the emergency bedroom suite of his consulate. His window looked out on the City Hall and Central Police Station and he was awakened by the noise of heavy army trucks in the street below. Peering out, he saw men loading them up with cabinets and boxes of papers. He could see that 'the papers must have been important because there were so many guards around'. Obviously the Nationalist officials were pulling out of the City Hall and Police HQ. The doors of the trucks were closed with a clang and the vehicles drove off in the direction of the Bund. Within an hour the din started all over again, but this time with different trucks and cars arriving below his window. Armed troops took up positions in front of the two public buildings. Some men came out, saluted – then the soldiers marched in. Troops mounted guard at every street corner. 'The Reds had taken the City Hall and Police headquarters. No shot was fired. Apparently, it was prearranged.'

A few hours later, in the early hours of Wednesday, the first troops of General Chen Yi, clad in their green uniforms, entered Shanghai proper from the south and south-west after breaching the wooden palisade that so ineffectually ringed the city. They marched two abreast down the avenue Edouard VII in Frenchtown, hugging the buildings, always ready to dart for the cover of doorways at the first sign of opposition. There was none. Curious spectators soon started to line the streets as though gaping at yet another procession, this time of the well-disciplined *palus*, as they were nicknamed. Most were armed with modern weapons, many of them American, and they handled their tommy-guns as though they knew how to use them. Yet many stared almost with disbelief at the imposing buildings, the broad avenues, the obvious opulence of the richest city in China, while shopkeepers hurriedly scraped anti-Communist graffiti and posters off walls and the police tore down the bunting and photographs and Nationalist victory banners which the day before had adorned the main streets.

As the soldiers led the way in the general direction of the river,

146

auxiliary troops followed close behind, slapping up posters telling the people to be calm, stringing telephone cables from public offices they had entered, and marking important street crossings with white arrows, fixing the routes into the city for the main force still waiting in the suburbs. From time to time, units moved away from the marching columns to take over police stations and local military centres, most of which had been abandoned. Despite occasional sounds of distant rifle fire, there were no incidents. Many municipal police eagerly welcomed the newcomers, showing their allegiance simply by slipping red armbands over their uniform sleeves. Others waited unarmed. At the City Hall they had even produced a huge sign reading 'Welcome, People's Liberation Army'. White flags soon started appearing all over the city, on municipal buildings, police stations and other strategic centres where sentries were posted to await the arrival of more troops. Church bells pealed and from somewhere a bugle sounded.

In the residential areas it was all over by 8 a.m. People who had gone to bed the previous night wondering when or if the attack would come, woke up to find the city under new management – with long rows of Communist troops sitting quietly along the roadside. By 9 a.m. shopkeepers in the side streets were even taking down their shutters and opening up for business.

Early on the Wednesday morning Ezpeleta was able to take his first look at the Communist soldiers. Remembering Hollywood war films, he said, 'I had half expected to see steel helmets at rakish angles, machine-guns under arms, pistols at the hips, grenades dangling from belts.' Instead he found slightly-built teenagers in coarse rice-green cotton uniforms which hardly fitted, no helmets, and tennis shoes in place of army boots. None wore any medals, decorations or campaign ribbons, and he noticed that 'they seemed almost mortified when anyone approached them'. He had the curious feeling that 'they were self-conscious and embarrassed. They wanted to be left alone, to be ignored.' He noticed too that they steadfastly refused to accept any gifts. He watched women street-sellers offer some of them rice cakes and tea. They refused with a smile and a bow.

The most noticeable factor among the thousands of people who turned out to watch their new masters was the almost complete absence of fear. Yet there must have been many pro-Nationalists desperately trying to hide evidence of past allegiance, which was not difficult if one could beg, borrow or steal some coolie clothes.

There is little reason to doubt the official Communist description of the early part of the take-over, for there *was* an almost embarrassing display of welcome by many people who cheered only because it was expedient to do so. The New China News Agency described how Shanghai citizens paraded the streets with banners inscribed 'Sunshine has come to Shanghai'. It added,

> When the advance guard of the People's Liberation Army advanced into the centre of the city, pavements and balconies were crowded with spectators, while columns of workers and students marched alongside the troops singing songs of welcome and performing Yangko dances. Some students presented Communist soldiers with flowers of victory. Posters were put up to salute the PLA and Mao Tse-tung.

When PLA soldiers rested at the South Station, 'this slum quarter became transformed into a place of festivities'. Workers and their families surrounded the troops and 'vied with each other to shake hands with the victors'. Another account said that many workers invited soldiers to their homes – though in view of the wretched housing conditions, one wonders if that was true. According to the News Agency, 'a special banner of welcome greeted troops from a house in the rue Albert which had previously been used by the Kuomintang for torture chambers'. Everybody remarked, said the NCNA, on the perfect discipline of the Red Army. Each man was carrying iron rations and was forbidden to buy anything before a proper exchange rate for local currency was proclaimed.

On the other hand, Communist-inspired reports in the NCNA news bulletin that Nationalist commanders in the Shanghai area had ordered their troops to carry out a systematic destruction of the city were nonsense. The Communists claimed that orders to that effect had been found in captured telegrams signed by General Tang. If such orders had been given, surely some of Shanghai's buildings would have been blown up.

The orderly progress in the suburbs leading towards the Bund gave way to sporadic fighting nearer the Whangpoo, where the Peking Road entered the far end of the Bund by the Garden Bridge which spanned the Soochow Creek. One of the busiest intersections in Shanghai, the bridge was overlooked by the

British and American consulates and the offices of Jardines on one side, with Broadway Mansions and the Post Office on the other bank. In front of the consulates a small park decorated the area between the Bund and the Whangpoo and this was now the scene of a brief but spirited display of firepower. The Nationalists had chosen the Garden Bridge – and the gardens in front – to stage a delaying action while they attempted to evacuate men and equipment by sea at Woosung. Already some Nationalist troops were boarding river craft at Woosung, while those from the city were hurrying to join them in a general exodus – often by rickshaw.

Every moment was precious, and it seemed that the Nationalists were prepared to fight for time if nothing else. The decision did have one consequence, for the Communists sealed off the area around the Bund so that those who had spent the night on the Hongkew side of the bridge had no hope of getting home. The worst hit were several hundred refugees who had swarmed into the Post Office for shelter, and about 200 foreigners trapped in Broadway Mansions. Their plight was made worse by the presence of a hundred Nationalist troops in Broadway Mansions – or on the roof – guarding the vital escape routes.

A lacy silhouette of humped iron, the Garden Bridge looked wildly improbable. Since the day of its opening it had been one of the sights of Shanghai, a magnet not only for visitors but also for beggars and children lying in wait for the next rickshaw or pedicab because the hump made it difficult for a puller to haul his load across. As a vehicle neared the centre, the beggars and children would surge forward, pushing cheerfully then clamouring for a few coins from the passenger.

Now, Nationalist troops with machine-guns operating from the roof of Broadway Mansions could rake the approaches to the bridge. Yet the Communist reaction was puzzling. They could easily have taken over some of the tall neighbouring buildings such as the Cathay Hotel and from there wiped out the defenders. Instead they seemed content with occasional sorties round the corners of nearby streets.

David Middleditch saw the entire 'battle', for he had spent the night in the office flat reserved for John Keswick, Jardines' taipan, whose main home was at Hungjao. Middleditch had slept on a sofa and woke stiff and sore, uncertain whether or not the Communists had arrived. The Bund seemed to be open, and though there was no traffic he could see a few cautious pedestrians. Some soldiers were digging defences in the small park on the waterfront, but 'since one Chinese soldier looked very much the same as another I couldn't be sure whether they were on the home or away side'. He watched for a few moments, then went to have breakfast with John Keswick and his wife Claire.

All seemed quiet at first. Then came news that the Mayor, the garrison commander and the Chief of Police had 'scooped up what remained in the municipal till and departed for more temperate zones, so all appeared to be over bar the shouting'. In the morning, though, came the 'sound of firing from the Garden Bridge. By midday it had increased considerably, and Middleditch found the situation ironic. 'We sat in a beautifully furnished room,' he wrote,

> complete with books, pictures, bowls of flowers and the dog asleep on the carpet while three Chinese boys in long white gowns served cocktails, followed by a meal consisting of roast beef and Yorkshire pudding and rhubarb pie. Not more than a hundred yards away a full orchestra of rifles and machine-guns and mortars was making so much noise that speech was frequently impossible.

The Nationalists in the park were firing from sandbag emplacements. A dead soldier lay in front. Middleditch went up to the roof and had 'one of the most remarkable views of a battle that one could wish for, as we could see what was going on on both sides'. The Communists were trying to work their way up the Bund, dodging from cover to cover, every now and again opening fire on the Nationalists in the gardens below the Jardine offices. Middleditch could see soldiers take a quick look down the street, fire a burst, then duck behind their sandbags. They also had a mortar that lobbed shells along the waterfront.

The battle lasted for two days. The Jardine 'war-watchers' became a little more cautious on the first afternoon when a couple of bullets whistled through the window of the room in which they were sitting. They moved down to John Keswick's office and ate their meals on office desks. What was really extraordinary was the way in which life had returned to normal just a few yards behind the Bund. Shops had opened; people walked the streets not 200 yards behind the waterfront.

Though no one could discover if the Hawkingses were safe –

because their telephone was still cut off – Middleditch found it incredible how the essential services were carrying on. From one window he could see up Peking Road and 'I could hardly believe my eyes when I saw a postman wandering down the street. John Keswick was able to send a wire to England (it read "Half way through the wringer but all well") and one of the men in the office telephoned a running commentary of the fighting on our doorstep to head office in Hongkong.'

Others had different tales to tell. The manager of the Jardine cotton mills, Jack Cheetham, was confronted by some Nationalist troops who wanted to use a godown on the waterfront for their mortars. All but one of the godowns were filled with inflammable material, but the empty one was not far from the line of fire, so Cheetham conducted the Nationalists by a circuitous route, stooping behind walls, peering carefully round corners. Eventually the party arrived, slightly breathless, on the roof of the empty godown and carefully looked over the parapet to see if there were enemy troops below. There were none. Instead, there was Mrs Cheetham with three friends playing tennis.

While Middleditch watched the battle from Jardines, Margaret Hampson in beleaguered Broadway Mansions was telephoning a running commentary on the fighting to her husband Fred, whose Associated Press offices were in Frenchtown. His wife was in the thick of the action, Fred was out of it – and could not get back. The Nationalists were firing not only from the rooftop of Broadway Mansions, but from neighbouring roofs clearly visible to Mrs Hampson. As she telephoned the story, incident by incident, to her husband at the other end of town, he repeated it word for word to a colleague who had an open line to Hongkong. The AP story of the 'Battle of Broadway Mansions' was actually on the tapes to newspapers within ninety seconds.

Fred was also able to scoop the world on the incredible terms for the final cease-fire at Broadway Mansions. The foreigners trapped there were terrified that the Communists would retaliate by shelling the building, and a deputation tried to persuade the Nationalists to surrender. At first it was unsuccessful, but when Chiang's troops learnt that the Communists had crossed the Soochow Creek further up river and outflanked them, they agreed to hoist a white flag – at a price. The foreigners must pay for a slap-up Chinese dinner for the hundred troops in the building. Broadway Mansions with its restaurant had an excellent chef and the troops sat down to a sumptuous meal, after which their officers handed each man a red armband to be worn when leaving the building.

From the top floor of Hamilton House, Ezpeleta also had 'first-row seats and enjoyed the sham battle'. He was convinced that the Communists could have cleaned up the area in an hour had they so wished, but 'apparently there had been prior arrangements, so both sides exchanged courteous, aimless fire. They made a lot of noise but, as intended, nobody was getting hurt.'

Everyone had his or her anecdote. Eldon Cook, who shared a house with Middleditch, worked for a small trading firm and decided he must reach his office. He got to the far end of the Bund when a burst of machine-gun fire split the air just behind him. Bullets stabbed into nearby walls. He could see the puffs made by disintegrating stone as firing raked the Bund. Young Cook dived for the nearest shelter – which happened to be the pillars flanking the entrance to the Shanghai Club, several of whose members were watching the scene from the Long Bar's bay window. One face at the window belonged to Cook's boss. As the crossfire showed no signs of abating, Cook continued to crouch until suddenly the massive door behind him was opened and there stood his boss.

'He didn't say anything,' Cook later told Middleditch, so Cook scrambled to his feet, expecting to be invited into the shelter of the Club; instead of which his boss barked, 'You can't come in *here*! You're not a member.'

Apparently he had second thoughts. 'Wait a moment,' he grunted and vanished inside to reappear with another elderly member. 'Come inside,' he beckoned Cook. 'I'll propose you and my friend will second you for temporary membership – so you can come in now.'

The few people – mostly Westerners – who saw the fighting near the Garden Bridge asked their Chinese employees afterwards whether they'd been in the firing line. The answer was invariably no, unless they had happened to be further down the Whangpoo. Once you had gone a few yards along Peking Road, you were in a different world. One of the Chinese members of the *North China Daily News* staff lived within walking distance of Broadway Mansions. He had no idea there had been a 'siege' until he turned up for work two days later. 'When I was told not to report for work,' he said, 'I spent most of the day playing with my

children in streets lined with cheerful, resting Red Army troops.'
A Chinese bookkeeper on the Jardine staff told Middleditch later
that he took his wife to a small restaurant 'which was open as
usual' where he 'celebrated having an unexpected day off'.

In retrospect the whole performance struck Middleditch as
macabre – 'watching the fight as though it were a game, going
away for a meal and a drink every now and then, and coming
back after the interval to see what the score was. Though troops
within a hundred yards of us were fighting for their lives, it was
hard for us to take in what was happening.'

Considering the size and density of population of Shanghai,
and the problems of logistics involved, the smoothness of the
take-over was remarkable. There was no panic, none of the
foreign consulates was besieged by anxious nationals. In the
American Consulate, which had a bird's-eye view of the fighting,
John Cabot noted in his diary on the Thursday, 'Firing starts again
beneath my window. I have moved my bed into the living room
for safety. By breakfast the going is getting a bit rough – a number
of grenades explode in front of us. Commies try to bring up
mortars but driven back. One member of the staff hit by flying
glass when bullet entered kitchen.'

During the fighting, Cabot watched Nationalist soldiers take
up positions in concrete urinals near the park, and remembered
later, 'Their main weapon of attack was a flame-thrower. The
Communists had a mortar. The Communists would steal up to
the corner of the US Consulate, pop the mortar round the corner,
fire, and retreat.' There was little danger to the onlookers
providing one kept away from windows. One man whose desk
was near a window did have a lucky escape. He left his office for
a few moments and when he returned found a bullet embedded
in the back of his office chair.

The British Consulate was also in the firing line, but its only
souvenir of the battle was one bullet embedded in the
mantelpiece of Robert Urquhart's office. Apart from that, the
Communist officers near the Consulate behaved with perfect
decorum. Commander John Proud happened to be on stand-by
duty during the fighting when a guard rushed into his office
crying, 'A Communist officer is at the gate. He demands to come
in.'

Proud refused to hurry, but strolled to the iron gates in his own
time and asked the Communist, 'What's the problem?'

In excellent English the officer explained, 'I need to set up a gunpost for crossfire. The Consulate would be perfect – it commands the bridge.'

'But you must realise that I can't allow you in here,' Proud protested. 'This is neutral territory.'

The officer saluted and replied, 'Of course – I quite understand.'

Hongkew, the other area of fighting, was packed with fleeing soldiers and deserters. One of the clerks in the Philippine Consulate who lived in Hongkew managed to reach the office on the third day, and told Ezpeleta that thousands of Nationalist soldiers had thrown away their uniforms and were offering all the money they had for any old civilian clothes. The streets were strewn with 'thousands of uniforms and blankets and relics of military equipment' for which the residents of Hongkew were scrambling in the hope of finding material they could use. Many Nationalist soldiers had thrown their weapons into the Creek or the Whangpoo. Evacuation to the safety of Taiwan was not uppermost in their minds. They wanted to go home. They had been pressed into military service against their will and had fought against their will. The clerk met one soldier, young and frightened, who had been conscripted on the day of his wedding and had never seen his wife again. 'They wanted to go home to their families, plant rice and raise children,' said the clerk. 'They would rather be peasants on the mainland than corporals in Taiwan.'

In Pootung, a few miles down river, the Nationalist General Wang Fu, who commanded an infantry division, had billeted several hundred of his men on the shipping wharf run by Norman Watts. These wharves had a long frontage on to the Whangpoo with berths for five or six vessels; behind them were houses, a football pitch, a pool, a club house and other recreation facilities.

Nationalist troops had used tens of thousands of bags of sugar (which were on the wharf awaiting shipment) to fortify their defence positions. Fifteen hundred Chinese civilians had crowded into the godowns for refuge, including thirteen women who gave birth to babies during the three days; Watts found himself having to act as midwife. General Wang used the company billiards room as his bedroom, sleeping on cushions arranged on the billiards table, which was large enough to accommodate two concubines he had brought along.

But General Wang was unaware that he had been betrayed. The Nationalist general further down river, guarding the river bank where the Whangpoo spilled into the Yangtze, had defected with all his men. Without a shot being fired the Communists had silently crossed the Yangtze from the north bank, landed, picked up their American arms from the Nationalists, and started to advance on the wharf area where General Wang was in theory ready to defend Shanghai. Wang knew nothing about this until he was awakened on his billiards table by bullets smashing the windows of his makeshift bedroom.

Within an hour Wang and his troops had bolted. Watts could do nothing against several hundred panic-stricken soldiers. He watched helplessly as they commandeered all the company launches, lighters, barges, sampans, and sailed off in the direction of Woosung – in ships flying the Red ensign.

When they had gone Watts decided to go to bed, though he kept his clothes on. The firing had ceased, but he was unaware that the Communists were almost outside the perimeter gates. He stationed the company guards near the barbed-wire fence 'and hoped for the best'.

About 3 a.m. the firing opened up again; this time it was uncomfortably close. In his first-floor room, Watts heard smashing glass, and the thud of bullets. The windows splintered around him, and machine-gun bullets ripped through the floor of his bedroom, tearing through the skirting boards. Others smashed into a stack of empty packing cases he had left outside on the veranda overlooking the countryside behind the wharf area. He was about to jump up when more bullets stuttered through the floor and 'I thought that perhaps the best place to stay was on top of the bed'.

Finally the firing stopped. Watts got up and looked ·out cautiously from the veranda. As he could see nothing he went back into his house and looked out over the wharf area. A lot of refugees were moving in the shadows, but nothing seemed to be happening. He decided to wait in his bedroom in case one of his staff telephoned him.

About 4 a.m. the nightwatchman guarding the back gate banged on his door, and shouted in Chinese, 'Red troops are coming!' Watts hurried to the back gate. He decided he had better go to the village of Yangching, where he was well known, and see what was happening. It was drizzling as he set off along the narrow path leading to the cobbled village street.

He had gone only a few steps when a voice out of the darkness cried, 'Stand still! Don't move!' Within a minute Watts made out half a dozen more shadowy figures, 'then as one shone a light I saw the stars on their hats and, I don't know why, noticed that they were carrying American weapons'.

One asked him how many Nationalist troops were still on the wharf, and Watts told him they had all fled. 'I had the feeling they didn't believe me,' he remembers, 'and they were also puzzled because I spoke to them in fluent Chinese.' A few minutes later the main body of troops came swarming down the village street, and Watts was ordered to take a party, led by an officer, on a tour of inspection round the entire wharf area. Only when the Communists were satisfied that no Nationalists remained was Watts taken back to his own house, and told that he was being placed under house arrest.

'You must stay in the house and you cannot leave without our permission,' he was told. 'We will bring you food.'

Watts remained a house prisoner for about a week, living on a diet of watery cabbage soup and rice. 'I'm convinced that at first the Communists believed I had helped the Nationalists by giving them all our boats.'

After a week, one of the Chinese staff from the office came to his house. Watts could see that he was agitated. In pidgin English he said, 'Master, big trouble.'

'What you mean, big trouble?' asked Watts.

'Big trouble for you. Everybody making plenty trouble because soldiers want to put you on trial.' Finally Watts understood that his presence was required in the main office on the wharf at ten o'clock the following morning. A guard escorted him there, and he remembers entering the big general office where he had spent so many years of his working life and thinking, 'Lo and behold!' The room was filled with familiar faces, all members of his staff.

The main office was a large airy room split in two by a dividing counter. One half contained Dickensian-type desks with brass rails, the other half ordinary flat-topped desks where the junior clerks normally worked. All the flat-topped desks had been placed close together, leaving a space for five 'judges' to sit. Among the 'witnesses' were two coolies Watts recognised 'who couldn't know the first thing about anything', but what really sickened him was that the presiding 'judge' was the company's most trustworthy ledger clerk who for years had worked personally for Watts. 'I would have trusted him with my life and my fortune. He was loyal, he wouldn't have hurt a fly, he was the sort of company man who did everything I asked, yet now I learned that for years he had been the leader of a Communist cell in our company.'

Watts pleaded guilty to remitting large profits to his company at home – there was no point in denying it as the 'judge' was also the chief witness for the prosecution – and he was sentenced to six months' corrective training, suspended provided he reported daily to the police and behaved himself. 'At least the "judge" didn't forget that we had been old friends, and didn't send me straight to prison,' said Watts.

General Wang and his concubines were among thousands of Nationalists who turned the approaches leading to Woosung into a Chinese Dunkirk, as they tried to reach the sea and safety. Many were diehards who faced execution if caught by the Communists, others might have preferred to desert but were forced along by their officers. Outside Woosung fires raged unchecked for nearly two miles along a column of tanks, artillery, ammunition, trucks, waiting three abreast to be loaded on to ships, which had finally been abandoned in the pell-mell rush to reach safety. Exploding ammunition set off new fires, some of which burned for days. Along some piers fires had a chain reaction, exploding more ammunition which in turn toppled war *matériel* worth hundreds of millions of dollars into the Whangpoo.

At one time it was almost impossible to advance along either of the two roads approaching the port. Mountains of wrecked vehicles blocked every path. At least a hundred municipal buses, burned-out hulks, some pock-marked with shellfire, lay along the roadway next to taxi cabs, amphibious vehicles, road-scrapers, even earth-moving equipment which the Nationalists had originally planned to take to Taiwan but had abandoned in their haste. One road junction was littered with thousands of life-jackets labelled 'United States Army', and on the outskirts of Woosung the words on the side of a smouldering van read: 'US Navy Fleet Post Office'.

By Friday the 27th it was all over. The first groups of Communist political officers were installed in Shanghai at the Golden Gate Hotel in what used to be the French Concession. The last sporadic shots had been fired and, though the fires at Woosung were still raging, foreigners were freed from buildings in which they had been trapped during the isolated pitched battles. The

British and American Consulates were 'liberated' – that is, the gates were reopened and the occupants allowed to go home. Urquhart and Cabot took a look at the damage. It was not serious, though Cabot found that the American Consulate had been hit at least twenty times by stray bullets. The British Consulate had suffered less because of the walls surrounding the compound.

'Now the real battle starts,' said one junior member of the British Consulate, 'doing all the paper work and filling in all the forms to squeeze money for repairs out of the Office of Works.'

Friday was hot and sunny and thousands of dog-tired Communist soldiers slept packed like sardines on the hard pavements. Middleditch remembers seeing solid ranks of them, sometimes several blocks long, their faces turned to the sun, oblivious to its strong rays. 'They were fast asleep sitting up.'

The army, it seems, was sticking to its policy of self-sufficiency. Along most roads leading into the city civilians of the service corps passed with baskets of army rations dangling from either end of their bamboo carrying rods. Going the other way were the stretcher-bearers carrying the few wounded towards the country where field hospitals had been established.

What struck Fred Hampson of the AP forcibly was the speed with which the city returned to normal. 'Peasants who had been forced into labour gangs by the Nationalists were pulling down pillboxes and putting the covering topsoil back on their gardens. All along the Hungjao Road they could be seen with their heavy tilling rakes pulling the soil off the pillboxes they had been forced to erect against their will.'

The peasants seemed eager to tell foreigners how they felt. One husky youngster told Hampson, 'I can work in peace now. Until today I was always afraid of being conscripted. We all used to hide when the Nationalist soldiers were around. In these,' and he pointed to one of the huge storage urns which dot the fields in so many parts of China.

During these hectic days no one had received news of the Hawkingses, nor did they themselves know what had happened until Friday, when, as Gladys wrote, 'We knew Shanghai had been taken because suddenly the countryside was crawling with hundreds of townspeople stealing everything they could lay their hands on.'

In twenty-four hours – before the Communists started arresting the vandals – they had stripped the Hungjao countryside bare, stealing the bean crops from evacuated smallholdings, even taking down the fences of the golf club to be used as firewood.

To Mariano Ezpeleta, the most noticeable immediate change was in the traffic – particularly among rickshaw pullers. Under the watchful eyes of Communist police, 'It was orderly, the rickshaw and pedicab pullers smiling at each other and at the police. Yet only the day before they had snarled and cursed each other and spat at the traffic officers.'

But then without doubt the police were far more courteous now. Before the take-over, a stall-holder who held up traffic would have been cursed and his cart kicked over by bullying police. Now Ezpeleta actually heard a Communist military policeman say, '*Tui pu chi!*' ('Sorry') and reason with a woman stall-holder, telling her, '*Chang tao li*' ('Talk reasonably').

To David Middleditch, the most fascinating difference was the almost instant end to corruption. 'On 24 May,' he wrote in his diary, 'you could bribe everyone in Shanghai. On 26 May you could bribe no one – for perhaps the first time in a hundred years.'

He finally knew the war was definitely over on the Friday morning when a friend phoned him and asked cheerfully, 'Are you free to play polo this afternoon?'

11

The Months of Illusion
June–July 1949

Victory in Shanghai became official and was celebrated by yet another gigantic parade, with the Communists using the same trucks and buses which only a few days previously had trundled through the streets to celebrate the 'victory' of the Nationalist armies. The same people, marshalled like extras for crowd scenes in a film, shouted slogans, waved flags, raised clenched fists, with everyone trying to demonstrate how pro-Communist they were. The city seemed, if one could believe the visual evidence, to be populated entirely with Mao Tse-tung's sympathisers. Postmen, dustmen, street-sweepers, bill-collectors for various Nationalist-controlled enterprises, who for years had extolled Chiang's virtues, suddenly appeared beaming in rice-green uniforms.

The transfer of power took place without a hitch. Telephone and cable offices remained open, though there were long delays. The Post Office continued to sell Nationalist stamps until the new ones arrived. Within two days the railway to Hangchow and to Nanking was reopened, and food supplies began to pour into the city. At the first hint of any hoarding or of price increases in meat, fish and vegetables, Communist officers visited offenders and politely 'asked' them to co-operate.

Diehard black marketeers who regarded themselves as a match for these country bumpkins from the north were visited a second time. If they were unwise enough to persist in profiteering they were taken to the race-course for the 'Watch Chiang' punishment.

A long pole, with a pulley at the top, had been set up on the race-course, and the wrongdoer was hoisted up on a rope. Once there, a Communist shouted, 'Can you see General Chiang?' Obviously the answer was always a faint 'No!' – at which the Communist released his hold of the rope and the prisoner crashed to the ground. If he did not die immediately, the process (and the question) was repeated. Since crowds were organised by police to watch this grisly execution, the news soon spread; all signs of black marketeering disappeared within days – and incredulous Shanghailanders suddenly found that prices had stabilised.

General Chen Yi,* hero of the attack across the Yangtze, was immediately named Mayor of Shanghai. At fifty, Chen Yi was one of the most colourful generals in the Red Army; he was short and stubby, and invariably sported a French beret pulled down until it almost covered his ears. Below a drooping moustache there always seemed to be a dangling cigarette, often unlit, so that he resembled a French peasant with the inevitable Gauloise jutting out of the corner of his mouth. Why not? Chen Yi had spent his formative years in France, taking a degree in electrical engineering after which he had taken a job on the shop floor in the Michelin plant at Clermont-Ferrand; only after this practical experience did he return to China in the late 1920s to join Mao.

Under Chen Yi, Shanghai became the administrative capital of central and south-east China, for as well as being Mayor, he was elected Chairman of the Shanghai Military Control Committee, and Vice-Chairman of the East China Military and Administrative Committee. From then on his was the dominant voice. He immediately opened a Political Department in the Bubbling Well Temple (which still had a poster over the door proclaiming 'Death to all Communist Traitors'). Nearer the Garden Bridge he established a Foreign Affairs Bureau under Chang Han-fu, an old Communist trouble-shooter, to deal with foreign nationals and their trading concerns. Chang quickly promised 'complete protection of all lives and property of foreign nationals in Shanghai' providing they obeyed four rules: not to break any laws imposed by the People's Government; to refrain from espionage or politics; to refuse help to war criminals; to remain neutral in 'the struggle of the Chinese people for self-expression'.

What particularly intrigued foreigners was the orderly manner

---

* Not to be confused with General Chen Yi, the Nationalist governor of Taiwan, who in 1947 ruthlessly suppressed the abortive bid of the Taiwanese for independence.

in which the city changed ideologies. Of course the foreigners were never 'invited' to watch executions at the race-course, but most had vaguely correlated Communism with the violence of civil war and had expected the streets to be filled with Chinese fleeing the batons of brutal oppressors. Even Mariano Ezpeleta was surprised at the peaceful nature of the transition, remembering how the Japanese had arrived in the Philippines preaching the doctrine of the Co-Prosperity Sphere while 'their bayonets were still dripping with blood'. This was entirely different.

Billy Hawkings had a fascinating glimpse of the way indoctrination worked. Outside his office windows a group of students gathered with placards beseeching everyone, 'Help to make China a better country.' Others distributed pamphlets to passers-by, with promises, 'A meal a day for everyone!' or 'The New China has been born!' Hawkings saw one man in a hurry brush aside the free tract, only to be politely stopped by a policeman who whispered a few words to him, then called to a student who re-offered the leaflet which the chastened citizen now accepted with a bow and profuse thanks. Near Hawkings's office was a small bookshop, one of dozens in the area which had for years done a thriving business selling cheap novels, often pornographic. Almost overnight the book-seller had donned an intellectual mantle, displaying the works of Mao Tse-tung, Lenin and Marx. But what intrigued Hawkings even more were the obligatory photographs in the window. The picture of Chiang Kai-shek had been replaced by one of Mao Tse-tung, but the other photograph that had always by tradition been displayed still remained. Sun Yat-sen beamed down on browsers as he had done for decades, left there by the Communists as though to proclaim that they were still faithful to the tenets of the original revolutionary whom his disciple Chiang Kai-shek had failed.

Many foreigners had expected the Communists to seize any foreign property they needed, in much the same way as the Nationalists had ruthlessly commandeered private houses. The Hawkingses, with memories of their struggle to prevent Chiang's troops from occupying The Limit still fresh in their minds, awaited Communist demands with trepidation. None came. The Hawkingses were left in peace – for the time being. Providing householders were not known to have been connected with the Nationalist cause, they were not disturbed.

No one was more astounded than the owner of two splendid apartment blocks in Frenchtown – the Picardie on the avenue

Pétain and the Gascoigne on the avenue Joffre - when Chen Yi asked if he could rent half the apartments in the Picardie and three storeys in the Gascoigne, and offered £3000 a month on the spot. The Frenchman could not believe his luck.*

The arrangement was, in fact, an outstanding example of Chen Yi's indoctrination programme for his troops. Eight hundred Chinese soldiers quickly occupied the apartments, jammed like sardines in a tin, yet fascinated by things they had never experienced before. Many who came from small villages in the north had never been in a skyscraper, let alone in a lift. When the recently-married Sue Fabian went to see a friend in the Picardie, not knowing that the apartments had been let to the Chinese, she saw men staring with disbelief at food cooking without a flame - on an electric hotplate. One man even put his hand on the plate to test it. Others spent hours riding up and down in the elevators. Some soldiers found the toilets ideal for washing their rice - until someone else pulled the chain. Since the apartments had been built originally for French residents, many of the bathrooms contained bidets - and to the Communist troops, these were the most inexplicable new 'toys' of all. They were particularly fascinated with those that incorporated a spray, which they turned on full blast to give them a kind of inverted face shower. Their experience was, however, short-lived, for, in a brilliant plan for disseminating propaganda, the troops were changed every two weeks, each batch being dispersed over the country, where they would be certain to tell their colleagues, 'Yes, comrade, we slept in the tall buildings in Shanghai, just as Chairman Mao promised we should.'

The immediate result of this low-keyed Communist approach, of the absence of forceful coercion, of promises not to interfere in the livelihood of foreigners, was an upsurge of false optimism among anxious foreigners, a collective cry by relieved businessmen, 'I told you everything would be better when the Commies took over.'

David Middleditch wrote in his diary, 'The idea of doing business with the Communists may seem a bit cynical to people at home, specially after they have just shot up three of our ships. We have, however, a tremendous amount of capital sunk in Shanghai.' Middleditch was still convinced that China would

---

* The fact that the apartment owner was taxed out of business within two years is a different matter.

need a foreign outlet and if they didn't get it from the British they would go straight into the arms of Russia.

The Americans suffered from the same illusions. On the day after the Communist take-over, the American Chamber of Commerce held a meeting which John Cabot in his capacity as Consul-General attended. He was horrified at the mood, bordering on euphoria, and remembered later, 'The rejoicing couldn't have been greater if the city had been liberated by American forces. American and British businessmen were convinced – I can't think why – that they would do better under the Communists.'

Members of the Chamber even drafted a long cable to President Truman eulogising the situation. This was too much for Cabot, who interrupted sternly: 'Listen! The Communists have been here only twenty-four hours. None of us knows what they're going to do. Be circumspect!'

His advice was given short shrift. 'I was the only one among the twenty or so Americans at that meeting who took a wait-and-see attitude. What really horrified me was that these men knew China much much better than I did.'

The new government's attitude to the dozens of diplomatic missions in Shanghai was equally unexpected. It did not officially carry on diplomatic relations with any of the numerous consulates, yet the missions were unmolested. The British Consulate-General kept its offices open, the CG flew the official flag on his car. Radio communication buzzed between Whitehall and Shanghai, the consuls issued visas or consular invoices; each consul paid a call at the Foreign Affairs Bureau where he was received with grave attention and politeness, but only in a private capacity. One British consul who admitted he was making an official query found his interview abruptly ended, and when the American head of UNRRA wrote a note of protest to the Military Government about the handling of stores, the note was returned to him, torn in small pieces, for the government did not admit that his mission existed.

Since it was now forbidden to listen to foreign radio broadcasts, Cabot became concerned about the US Consulate-General transmitters. On 1 June he noted in his diary, 'Slightly worried about continued use of radio since regulations indicate it's not permitted.' Two days later he noted, 'Gave orders to be prepared to destroy coding machines and confidential files – danger is particularly great in view of regulations re transmitter sets.' Yet, though it was forbidden to use the radio for foreign broadcasts, anyone could pick up the telephone and be connected immediately with New York, London or Hongkong.

The Communists not only regarded the foreign diplomats as non-existent, they were also totally uninterested – at least on the surface – in what they were doing, or whether they had the right to remain in Shanghai. They rarely visited any of the consulates to enquire into their business or to ask why they were flying national flags outside their buildings.

One man who did receive an official visit was Mariano Ezpeleta. He lived in a splendid mansion with eight bedrooms and six bathrooms set in two acres of grounds in Anfu Road in Frenchtown. He rented it for a token sum from Dr J. T. Wang, a Yale-educated doctor of law who had become Chief Justice of the Supreme Court in Nanking and was a close adviser to Chiang Kai-shek. Knowing when he fled to Taiwan that he would be branded as a 'Nationalist war criminal' whose property was liable to seizure, Wang had begged Ezpeleta to live in his house.

Before long Communist officials arrived at the house and asked for details of the renting arrangements. Ezpeleta had had the foresight to draw up a proper lease. It seemed to be in order and nothing happened. However, some weeks later when Ezpeleta had occasion to visit the Foreign Affairs Bureau, he was asked if he still occupied Dr Wang's house. Ezpeleta said that he did, whereupon the official said politely, 'That's quite in order. But as soon as you no longer need the property, please let me know. The house belongs to a war criminal, and should be turned over to the people.'

Ezpeleta was no doubt allowed to remain in the house because he was a diplomat. Others who had connections with Chiang, however tenuous, were not so fortunate, and any buildings owned by 'war criminals' were immediately seized, sometimes with tragic consequences. Before long the private life of Alec McShane, the Scots 'sardine' importer, was affected. The McShanes had always lived quietly. He was about forty-five, though his Russian wife Natasha was much younger – perhaps twenty-five – and generally regarded as the most beautiful foreign wife in Shanghai. McShane himself was a cheerful extrovert; he played a fine game of tennis and was almost unbeatable at volunteer snooker. Though by no means in a big way of business, he lived in a magnificent penthouse in the avenue Joffre, for which he paid a peppercorn rent to an old friend, Tai Tsin-wei, a high-ranking Nationalist official.

What no one knew at the time was that McShane and Tai were much more than good friends; though Nationalist officials were forbidden to dabble in business, the two men were highly successful partners, and Tai had become so rich that he in fact owned the apartment block containing McShane's penthouse. Shanghai would also have been astounded to learn that the two men had shared Natasha's favours.

One day towards the end of June, McShane burst into Mardens' offices and told Hawkings, 'The bloody Chinese have arrested Natasha!'

Tai had also been arrested the previous week, and Communist officials had seized the entire apartment block, including everything in McShane's penthouse – the furniture, they said, belonged to Tai who was 'a Nationalist war criminal'.

That was only the start of the story. It turned out that McShane and Natasha had never been married. In fact she had originally been the girlfriend of Tai, who had met her when she was a hostess at Delmonico's. At first she had refused to live with him and only moved in when Tai gave her the penthouse. McShane came on the scene, and fell madly in love with Natasha. No doubt Tai had other ladies in his life and, according to McShane, 'He didn't seem unduly worried.' Besides, he needed a foreign businessman with whom he could fix contracts with extra commissions being banked abroad. Since McShane's business was floundering the two men needed each other. Accordingly, Tai moved out of the apartment and McShane moved in, ostensibly as the husband of Natasha.

For one man, the days following the Communist take-over had a heady significance. With the new government firmly established, John Proud, secret agent, felt 'an enormous sense of relief, maybe we can do something now'. At last, he might be able to make contact with one of the leaders, for it needed no seer to realise that before too long the Communists would proclaim themselves rulers of all China, and when that time came it would be essential to recognise the new regime quickly.

Yet it seemed a task fraught with difficulties. At first Proud found it hard to believe the stories he heard: how the new masters of Shanghai refused point-blank to admit the existence of the British Consulate. But it was true enough as he discovered when he visited the Foreign Affairs Bureau.

He found a Chinese who could speak English, and then as a test asked him, 'Can you please direct me to the British Consulate?'

The Consulate-General was perhaps the best-known landmark in Shanghai, but with a perfectly straight face the Chinese official replied politely, 'I'm sorry, sir, I do not know of any British Consulate in Shanghai.'

Proud then asked a British friend to post a letter to him at the Consulate; the friend would write his own name and address legibly on the back of the envelope. The letter was returned marked 'Address unknown'.

All this time 'Charlie Chan' and other agents had been burrowing away for Proud, though they almost never met. One day, however, Chan asked for a meeting – clearly something was brewing. They arranged to lunch at Tachenko's, one of the best Russian restaurants in the city, for though many 'decadent' restaurants and virtually all the night-clubs had been closed, Russian restaurants still flourished.

Charlie Chan had exciting news. Chou En-lai was in Shanghai and had quietly installed himself in an apartment in Frenchtown – as befitted a man who had been educated at the Sorbonne. Chou was Mao's link between East and West; if any dedicated Communist could be said to favour the West and dislike the Russians it was Chou En-lai, a man from a good family with a brilliant educational pedigree whom Mao had early singled out as his most experienced negotiator for the future.* Proud's immediate thought was, 'Is there any chance of arranging a meeting with him?' Charlie Chan, who had met Chou once, replied that he thought it would be much easier for Chou to meet an Australian like Proud than a Briton. A 'secret' meeting between the two men was out of the question; on the other hand, Charlie Chan had a friend 'to whom Chou owes a debt of honour', and he might be able through this man to arrange a meeting. 'Give me a little time,' said Charlie Chan. 'I'll report back in a few days.'

* There is a story, probably apocryphal, that on one occasion much later when Kosygin was seeking a *rapprochement* with China, Kosygin, surrounded by the pomp and luxury of power, suggested to Chou En-lai that they had more in common than at issue. At which Chou asked, 'What was your father?' Kosygin proudly replied that his father had been a lowly labourer, at which Chou said, 'Well, mine was a mandarin, so you and I do have something in common. We have each betrayed our class.'

Inevitably there are always loose ends in stories of Intelligence work; nor is it always possible to divulge in detail methods used by agents making contacts in foreign countries. Apart from other considerations, agents working for the same master in the same country for the same objective rarely know each other's identity. Proud, for instance, had not the faintest idea who Charlie Chan's colleagues were.

It is, however, an astonishing fact that, though Proud had never met Chou En-lai, and though Charlie Chan knew him only slightly, there was in Shanghai at the time one Englishman to whom Chou had once made a promise, furtively whispered in the dark, 'One day I hope I can repay you!'

The man was Norman Watts, the Chinese scholar who had fought with the Communist guerrillas against the Japanese. Watts was no Communist; certainly he had never been connected, even remotely, with Intelligence. But in the course of his extraordinary career, he had played one role of enormous significance: years previously, long before the war, he had been directly instrumental in saving Chou En-lai's life.

At that time, the Communist Party was proscribed, and there was a price on the head of each of its leaders. The reward for Chou was probably higher than for any other. One night a friend who knew that Watts was in the shipping business asked him, 'Could you help me on an urgent matter?' It transpired that he had a Chinese friend for whom the police were looking. Could Watts get him out of Shanghai? The request hardly presented a problem to Watts. Many coastal steamers took 'human cargo' if the right man was properly tipped, and Watts was easily able to arrange with the Chinese bosun of a small ship to give the Chinese deck space to Hongkong. The fleeing Chinese was to come to a house in the avenue Haig with his friend and they would then drive to the berth. The Chinese arrived looking rather lean and hungry, and with a fringe of black beard. The friend introduced him casually: 'This is Mr Chou En-lai.'

Watts was flabbergasted, for there was a huge price on Chou's head. He remembers that night how 'when Chou looked at me, his black piercing eyes bored right into me'. They made their way to the Bund and as they quickly bundled Chou on board, he turned to Watts and whispered, 'You are a good friend. One day perhaps I may be able to help you.' Not for many years did Watts realise that his action that night might have changed the history of China.

168

Now years later Chou had returned with the victorious Communist government, and Watts (though himself in trouble with that government) was probably the first Englishman to meet him.[*] What exactly passed between the two men we may never know; but we do know that Watts shared with Proud a firm conviction that the only way to safeguard British interests in China was for Britain to recognise the Communist government as quickly as possible, and a few days later Charlie Chan arranged for Proud to meet Chou En-lai. It was to be in the company of several other people, and the understanding was that Proud would spend a little time alone with the Chinese leader.

Chan and Proud drove to Cathay Mansions, near the French Club, one of the most opulent apartment buildings in Shanghai. Proud's first impression as he entered the room was of a furnished flat with typical pseudo-French furniture and a large balcony with rattan chairs; his second impression was of a strictly business meeting: no attempt was being made to cloak it with the trappings of a social gathering, in the way that a cocktail party is sometimes arranged to bring certain people together. There were no 'softening up' drinks, no canapés to nibble. Chou seemed bored by the men whom he had agreed to see, all Chinese except Proud.

Charlie Chan introduced Proud to Chou who motioned him towards a corner. Proud felt that he was being allowed a limited time to state his case; but at least Chou spoke passable English, and Proud had long enough to emphasise Britain's 'neutral stand' and its desire to be in a position to recognise Mao's government when it assumed control. But this, he pointed out, could not be done unless Britain had some inkling of China's thoughts on the matter.

Chou En-lai listened impassively until Proud had finished. Then he said that he did not see any reason why Britain and China should not be friendly, adding, 'There will be conditions – and above all it must be on a basis of equality.' Indicating that the talk was ended and moving towards the centre of the room, he added politely, 'I will be in touch with our mutual friend.'

Ten minutes later Proud was on the way down to the street, tingling with elation. This was a triumph of the first order – the

---

[*] When they did meet, Chou En-lai told Watts how grateful he was, and also admitted that he had at first been afraid that he might be walking into a trap. 'But then,' Chou told Watts, 'I took one look at your face and I knew I was safe.'

break through an implacable wall of silence for which he and his team had been working patiently for months. And as they reached the sharp, bright sunlight of the rue Bourget, where Proud had parked his car, Charlie Chan said: 'We'll have to work fast. Chou En-lai told me that he expects the government to be proclaimed formally long before the end of the year.'

'I'm in your hands now,' said Proud briefly as he crossed the avenue Foch and drove past the race-course. 'Where can I drop you?' he asked Chan. 'I'm making for Sinza Road. I'm popping into the British Hospital for a check-up. For weeks I've been coughing my guts up.'

Proud was not exaggerating. He had been feeling very ill, and when he reached the British Hospital for what he hoped would be a bottle of cough mixture or a few tablets, he was told bluntly after a preliminary examination that he must go and collect his pyjamas and toothbrush and return for tests that would take two or three days.

Reluctantly he did so. Three days later Proud faced the worst moment of his life: he was suffering from advanced tuberculosis. One lung was already beyond cure. The other could only be saved by prolonged rest and treatment. He must move into hospital immediately. He could be allowed out occasionally for exercise but that was all.

John Proud was not only a very brave man, he was a realist. He went straight back to the Consulate and sent a detailed report of his meeting with Chou En-lai, including the all-important news of the tentative Communist date for announcing their government. He had by now an assistant in the Consulate who would be able to send coded messages to London if necessary. What he needed now – and what he could never achieve alone – were the details of Chinese terms for recognition. Chou En-lai had promised to do his best and Proud felt that he was sympathetic to the possibility of British recognition. Now all Proud could do was wait and plan. A few days later he moved into hospital – 'and from then on,' as he remembers, 'I ran the operation from my hospital bed.'

The impatient Proud was at least waiting among friends. Another batch of impatient Britons were waiting among enemies.

Much had happened to *Amethyst*, though it was not until 26 April – a Tuesday – that Kerans had been able to make any contact with the Communists who had crossed the river near him, occupying the south bank directly opposite where he was anchored. On that day, just after lunch, three Communist soldiers and two civilians waved to the ship from the shore and asked the officer in charge to row ashore for 'a conference'. It was to be the first of a series of painful, abortive meetings.

Kerans, knowing the importance of 'face', decided not to go himself, but to send a petty officer. On the other hand, knowing that the Chinese also disliked losing face, he dressed the petty officer in an officer's uniform. Together with an interpreter and a companion to keep him company, the man was rowed ashore in the whaler (with a stock of provisions and cigarettes in case the small party was prevented from returning).

The crux of the Chinese Communists' 'demands' at this first and all subsequent meetings was one to which Kerans could on no account agree. Safe-conduct back to Shanghai would be granted on three conditions: first, that *Amethyst* admitted it was guilty of infringement of Chinese sovereignty; secondly, that *Amethyst* accepted the onus of blame; and, thirdly, a guarantee that the British would pay compensation for damage and loss of life to the Communists. Kerans refused point-blank, and settled down to the prospect of a long siege.

Before long his main problem was a shortage of fresh food, especially vegetables, eggs and so on. Kerans, who was now going ashore regularly for the 'conferences', usually in a sampan which the Communists had provided, asked if it would be possible to 'buy' fresh vegetables from local traders. No objection was made, though there was one snag – no one was interested in money. So Kerans decided to try to barter, using his Chinese steward as interpreter. The bartering was long and intense, but *Amethyst* did at that time have plenty of some staple foods which the Chinese lacked. In the first 'trade' *Amethyst* exchanged forty-five pounds of sugar for ten dozen eggs. These were followed by supplies of vegetables which at least helped to vary the diet.

Spring dragged into summer; heat that was sometimes almost unbearable alternated with downpours of tropical rain. Power for the ventilators had to be rationed because of a shortage of oil and when this happened the frigate became a furnace. When the telegraphist who was in touch with Hongkong was working during these spells, another man, using an old pair of bellows, had to blow air on his hands to prevent them slipping from the keys. At times there was not even power to flush the toilets. Rats bred with abnormal speed and there were soon so many that it was forbidden to walk around without shoes. The ship was alive with

171

cockroaches.

The discussions with the Communists went on. At least the excursions ashore meant a little variety, for sometimes they would be held at Chinkiang, fifteen miles distant, where the Communists had one of their area headquarters. Kerans always took a different member of the crew with him. It gave the men an outing, and they enjoyed sitting round the formal table with servants pouring green tea and offering them biscuits and, inevitably, sugared almonds.

From time to time other events broke the monotony for those on board. Fearnley, the RAF doctor, found an ever-increasing number of 'private' patients coming out from shore – and paying for his services with all kinds of useful items, including some ducks which made a pleasant change from tinned meat.

One of the crew suggested using the ship's relay equipment to play request programmes from their stock of gramophone records. The ship also had seven feature films on board which they rationed to two showings a week. The star attraction, shown over and over again, was Gene Autry in *Twilight on the Rio Grande*.

But the greatest treat of all arrived on 24 June when three bulging bags of mail arrived from Shanghai. Kerans had been pressing the Chinese for permission to receive letters, but the formalities had taken weeks.

The Chinese take-over of Shanghai had, of course, hardly been noticed on *Amethyst*, and by July stores were so depleted that Kerans ordered the ship's complement to go on half-rations. Yet shortage of fuel posed as dangerous a problem as shortage of food, for if Kerans was unable to use power to operate the ventilator shafts, the risk of illness increased. At each meeting with the Communists, Kerans demanded the right to two things: mail and oil. The mail had come, but he never for a moment expected to get the oil. And yet the oil finally did arrive, early in July: British oil, brought up the Yangtze by the Communists themselves – 54 tons in 296 drums. By 10 July the last drum had been emptied in the *Amethyst*'s tanks.

It was incredible really that it ever arrived. Kerans, at times baffled by the attitude of the Chinese at their conferences, the harsh demands mingled with exquisite politeness, said wonderingly to one of the crew, 'I will never know why the Communists let us have it.'

*　*　*

Little of this was known to the British in Shanghai. If the Chinese newspapers occasionally made mention of *Amethyst* it was to renew demands for compensation by 'capitalist and imperialist brigands'. In London the incident had been quickly shelved as an embarrassing problem at a time when the Communists were sweeping south of Shanghai against virtually no Nationalist opposition. It was obvious – to Whitehall, to Shanghai, and no doubt to Commander Kerans on *Amethyst* – that the long and painful civil war in China was drawing to its end. Once the British Government had accepted that the Royal Navy could be publicly humiliated by 'a bunch of Commies' (as one man put it) and was powerless to retaliate, it also had to accept the fact that *Amethyst* and her crew were pawns of little account in the battle that loomed ahead to salvage British interests in China.

This was what really mattered to the people of Shanghai. The determination to carry on as usual became even more marked. It was this attitude of mind that encouraged the Amateur Dramatic Club to give a performance of *Gaslight* at the Lyceum, for which rehearsals had proceeded as though nothing had changed.

Many taipans were lucky in that they had money to fall back on. Nevertheless they were taking part – with more than six million other Shanghailanders – in a bloodless revolution that would have repercussions in the Far East, indeed across the world, for years to come. At the beginning, until the end of June, the astonishing thing was the discretion with which everything had changed in a city which had been the victim of atrocious misgovernment and had tolerated corruption on a scale unknown in any other city in the world.

Quietly the Communists were 'reforming' the inhabitants; though people hardly noticed the changes – until Norman Watts pointed out one day that the pavement black marketeers, with their jingling silver dollars, had disappeared. In fact 2200 of them, including the big inside operators, had been whisked off to jail or execution. The gambling casinos, even the clandestine opium dens, quietly closed their doors. Part of the race-course was turned into a barracks, the other half was used as a playground where the young could do calisthenics – surrounded by huge pictures of Mao and Chou En-lai, and to a background of Communist radio propaganda. Almost every dance hall had closed. The ladies of the town had been rounded up and sent to work in canning factories or textile mills. The Park Hotel's beautiful Sky Terrace, a ballroom on the top floor with a dizzy view of Shanghai's night lights, soon closed because of the curfew. So did the Park's tea room on the ground floor, and the coffee shop – a favourite meeting place for ladies – in the Cathay Hotel. It seemed impossible, but Shanghai was actually becoming dull. A city that had always laughed its way from crisis to crisis had even lost its sense of humour. When Billy Hawkings remarked on this, his friend answered sardonically 'Have you ever seen a caged bear laugh?'

When a young commissar made a routine visit to the French Catholic Mission, he asked Father Pierre if he was pro-Communist. The priest said he was not. Was he pro-American then? No, he was not, answered Father Pierre. Watching the puzzled look on the young commissar's face, the priest added gently, 'We all work for Christ.' The Commissar smiled thinly and answered, 'I don't know him, but I'll bet he's a capitalist.'

The puritanical attitudes of the new rulers hung over the people like a cloud. Re-education squads of enthusiastic 'new democrats' started monthly courses of political indoctrination 'to reform your thoughts and ideas by discussion'. Those who could not leave their offices or factories were dealt with at work by special squads consisting mostly of fanatical students whose lectures on the New China were followed by party songs.

Frank Moraes, the Indian author, who visited Shanghai at this time, felt that the first Communists to reach the city were little more than 'efficient robots. All their thoughts and impulses had been classified. They knew only mass emotions.' Their first concern was to classify the inhabitants, to build up dossiers on everyone. 'One copy was lodged with the police at the Public Security Station set up in one's immediate neighbourhood. Each station had one household officer who appointed street committees.'

Members of these committees were ordered to report on any 'suspicious activities' in their neighbourhood, particularly by servants working for foreigners, so that by July, Gladys Hawkings was writing to her daughters, 'There are spies everywhere and no one dares whisper a word even to a friend. How lucky we are to have servants we can trust.'

Before long the inevitable happened. Shanghai began to run down. Its new leaders, with a few exceptions, lacked experience. All the men who had run Shanghai for the Nationalists had left or been arrested, and their assistants now had to perform their duties under the scrutiny of commissars who had no idea how to run a big city. It had been one thing for the Communists to take over a small Chinese town where the inhabitants simply continued their trades or occupations under new masters. It was a very different matter to administer a city of six million people which had more foreign investment than London or New York; whose inhabitants spoke thirty different languages.

The commissars, unused to these problems, were terrified of making mistakes – so refused to make decisions without reference to higher authority. But even if they did receive guidance from above, their superiors deliberately couched directives in vague terms in case *their* superiors changed their minds. When Westerners criticised the Chinese for procrastination, they never properly understood that masterly inactivity was a powerful factor in the battle for survival among the Communists. There was endless doubt and suspicion among the leaders and the led.

The administrative anarchy was increased by the coldly correct attitude of the officials, in a country whose people were naturally gregarious, where for centuries people had conducted their business over large dinners, at drinking parties and on visits to sing-song girls. Now, with the ever-present stigma of suspicion, everyone might be called 'comrade' but no one was a friend.

Mariano Ezpeleta had a practical example of the change in people's attitudes when an old Chinese friend, Johnny Yang, head of an investment firm, told him that a school friend of his had been appointed to a key position in the Foreign Affairs Bureau. He asked Ezpeleta to join them for a meal because 'as a Filipino you could act as a bridge between the new China and the democratic West'. But the dinner date was cancelled. Yang told Ezpeleta angrily, 'He's a fool, a bloody fool! He refuses to lunch with us, even with me alone, because he says that social amenities are nothing but capitalistic subterfuges to corrupt people. In college I even used to pay for his women! Now he says he will only study any proposition I make providing it is in writing.'

Every day foreign bussinessmen faced new difficulties, some of them the result of the nationalistic aspirations of Communism. Even after the end of the International Settlement in 1945, all government decrees had been printed in English as well as Chinese. Now orders and decrees were issued only in Chinese; even when they affected the foreign population, there were no English translations. Ignorance of the law was no excuse, yet it was almost impossible to get exact translations, even to find translators in a city where many Chinese were afraid of being seen in the company of a white man.

When Ezpeleta had to visit the City Hall, an old friend who had remained as chief of a section came out to meet him at the front door and escorted him into his office. Sitting by his desk was 'a kindly bespectacled commissar in his rice-green uniform'. Ezpeleta remembered later how his friend 'introduced me to his companion in Chinese and asked if I had brought with me my Chinese secretary. When I said that it was not necessary because he himself spoke perfect English, he smiled and said that under the new regulations official business could only be transacted in the Chinese language. I had to call for my Chinese secretary before we could proceed.'

All cables in English had to be accompanied by a Chinese translation. Even the neon advertising signs in English were replaced with new ones bearing Chinese lettering. Cinemas, restaurants, public halls with foreign names had to change them. Street names were replaced with Chinese names, so that, as Ezpeleta put it, 'In the French Concession where the streets and boulevards were named after the French immortals, a litany of Communist saints was inexorably replacing them.'

Robert Bryan, the American lawyer, had no illusions. He told his wife, 'The Communists have a word for such idle talk. It's *Hua la hua la*. I have listened to the English *Hua la hua la* at the Shanghai Club, to the American *Hua la hua la* at the Columbia Country Club. I remember the chairman of the British Chamber of Commerce declaring that everything was going to be all right, telling me, "They need us, don't you know. We'll get along, old boy, we'll get along." It's nonsense!'

Bryan watched as the Communists gradually tightened the screws during 'an astonishing fiscal binge'. Clients told him how they were being taxed on the number of rooms in their homes, even the bathrooms. They cited cases of Communist tax inspectors invading houses during private parties, counting the guests – and the number of bottles – and slapping on an extra tax on the spot.

When the US government froze all Chinese accounts in America, so that no one living in China could touch funds lodged in the US, the Communists counterattacked by taking over all American businesses in Shanghai.

Bryan felt they would never bother to nationalise his small law firm, but from that day every client on his books was cut off from him, for his clients' firms were now being run by Communist controllers who had been ordered not to have any dealings with his American law firm. Bryan still went to the office every day, but there was nothing to do except read books, and there was no money coming in.

It was the same everywhere as the original Chinese smiles of 'tolerance' were quietly, almost unobtrusively, replaced by frowns of annoyance.

Soon dissatisfied workers found a novel form of harassment if their foreign employers ignored their demands for higher pay. They locked them in their offices at night, and then sat outside in relays banging tin cans to prevent them from sleeping.

Sue Fabian of UNRRA was horrified to find a Chinese worker reading a leaflet, 'Labour unrest and disputes must be used as a weapon against foreign imperialism.' Foreign imperialism! She was *helping* – UNRRA and its allied organisations were *giving*. Sue wrote home, 'It is amazing how quickly these threats have been carried out. From day to day one wonders who will be the next to be locked in their offices by the workers who will keep them there by force if they can until their unreasonable demands have been met.'

Innocent foreigners were often made victims of trumped-up charges. When a young accountant called Sanders refused to pay a trishaw-puller twice the agreed fare, the Chinese called the police and said that he had been insulted. Sanders was given the equivalent of a suspended sentence for his 'first offence' but only after he had agreed to print an abject apology in both the vernacular and the English press.

By July, factory wage increases and the new taxes were biting savagely, both in business and privately. Under the new laws the wages of Gladys Hawkings's servants (which a year previously had, at $40 million, cost her £13 a month) were raised to £1300 a year. Yet no one was allowed to cut back staff. If a servant was dismissed, he or she had to be paid up to a year's wages in compensation. Worse still, two servants who had been dismissed by the Hawkingses fifteen years previously – long before their Japanese internment – suddenly reappeared and demanded to be reinstated; otherwise they would claim back payment for fifteen years! Luckily for the Hawkingses they both had criminal records and their demands failed. But, as Gladys wrote, 'In almost every caxe the worker is right and the employer (especially if of our colour) is invariably wrong.' Other expenses had shot up alarmingly. The car tax had risen to £360 a year while new number plates cost £120. 'People just put on any tax they like and seize property if it isn't paid. An easy game!'

The Nationalist naval blockade posed another problem. Shanghai had always depended on maritime trade. Now the Chinese could not get raw materials – coal, oil, spare parts for machinery; nor could they sell abroad. For years Shanghai had exported everything from silk to ham, from vegetable oil to smoked duck. Now goods were rotting in the godowns because ships could not run the blockade which Chiang, with his small navy, had imposed on the mouth of the Yangtze, making it impossible for them to enter or leave the Whangpoo.

This also meant that most foreigners were locked in Shanghai – exit visas, anyway, were rarely granted in these first months – and that mail was held up. To the beleaguered foreigners, letters were the only real link with home, something they missed, perhaps, more than anything else. The Communists could easily have allowed the mail to be sent to Tientsin and then to Shanghai by rail; but no, it had to come by sea, so that if it did not arrive it was the fault of Chiang Kai-shek's blockade.

Occasionally Chiang relented and gave a ship permission to enter or leave. Then the Post Office would accept letters but no parcels. What pangs of homesickness the foreigners of Shanghai must have felt when a handful of civilians received permission to leave late in July in the *Anchises,* which had broken down earlier in the year and was finally allowed to leave under tow to Japan. Four businessmen received special exit visas to sail in her. Gladys Hawkings wrote, 'I should think everyone in Shanghai is envying those four men.' This pleasant woman, who had lived in China and loved the country for so long, added the anguished sentence: 'There's no more pleasure living here.'

The Communists had another annoying habit – what in the British armed forces used to be called 'dumb insolence'. They simply ignored problems facing foreign institutions when a word from a minor official could have solved them. No one faced a better example of this than John Cabot when in mid-July the US Consulate-General in the Glen Line building was for several days the scene of an extraordinary siege – not by the Communists, but by 200 Sikhs, traditionally employed as guards of houses, offices or warehouses in Shanghai. These men had been employed before the take-over to guard the extensive United States Navy shipyards until the Navy pulled out, and since then had nursed a grievance (with justification) that in the rush to leave, the American Navy had not paid them off properly.

When the Navy had gone there was no one to whom they could voice their grievances, but once the Communists took over and the Sikhs saw the ease with which workers were intimidating bosses, they decided to lay siege to the American Consulate. Hundreds of turbaned Sikhs, complete with bedding, cooking pots, firewood, stores of food, took up strategic positions, determined to remain there for weeks if necessary. They refused to allow any members of the Consulate staff to leave or enter – while Cabot refused to negotiate with them until they called off the siege.

The municipal government could have stopped the siege within ten minutes, but the police were thoroughly enjoying the discomfiture of the Americans. They also took up positions outside the US Consulate, but only to make sure that the Americans used no force against the Sikhs.

Cabot was furious at being landed with a problem which was not of his making, but he was not unduly worried. The Consulate boasted large stocks of food, the cafeteria functioned normally, and the one-time naval hospital was quickly transormed into make-shift dormitories. Besides, though the Sikhs were convinced that they had sealed every exit from the building, they didn't know of the 'secret' door linking the American building to the compound of the British Consulate. This was obligingly unlocked by the British, so that any American consular official who had appointments in Shanghai was able to slip through the door and then be driven into the city in the back seat of a British Consulate car.

In the end nature – in the shape of a savage typhoon – beat the Sikhs. With streets awash, the drenched besiegers broke ranks and bolted for the comparative safety of their homes. Once the siege was lifted, Cabot agreed to meet a delegation of leaders so that he could send recommendations to Washington.*

The great storm of July 1949 – known as Typhoon 'Gloria' – came at a time when frustrated men and women, living through the long, hot summer, were on the point of exploding. Not that they could have done anything effective to make life easier; by

---

* 'It was a very stupid show,' said Cabot later. 'The US Navy had in the end to pay much more than if they had agreed to the just claims at the start.'

the end of July people had begun to see how inexorable was the grip of the government under which they had to live.

Typhoon Gloria broke during the night of Monday, 25 July, and it passed right over Shanghai. Billy Hawkings woke up in the dark with an uncanny feeling of 'utter, desolate silence'. For a few seconds The Limit was caught in the eye of the typhoon, 'in an eerie calm, with not a tree or shrub rustling, not a sound of any sort'. Then the rain lashed down, driven by a 110-mile-an-hour wind, which smashed doors, even forced its way through locked windows. The Hawkings lost two dozen of their treasured trees, saved earlier that year from the Nationalist soldiers. A twenty-five-year-old deodar tree in front of the house just keeled over and collapsed with a crash.

By morning, the Bund was under four feet of water. It swirled knee-deep in Wing On's famous department store in Nanking Road. The Cathay Hotel was cut off for several hours, with water rushing past its imposing portals and straight across the Bund into the Whangpoo. Though the walls of the British Consulate-General withstood the onslaught, its people were marooned as though on an island for six hours. Telephones, water and electricity supplies were cut for twenty-four hours. No one in Shanghai had ever known a typhoon like Gloria.

The typhoon continued westwards, turning the Yangtze into a series of swollen, flooded reaches and swirling, twisting currents. And as John Cabot no doubt hailed this 'act of God' with relief, another man, more than a hundred miles away, was also blessing the savage storm. Lieutenant-Commander John Kerans knew that never again would he see the Yangtze in such flood. It was – literally – a heaven-sent chance to escape from the Communist grip. But he had to act quickly. It was now or never.

12

The Escape of the *Amethyst*
Summer 1949

Kerans had for some time been wondering whether he dared make a break-out, especially after one night early in July when *Amethyst* was nearly rammed by a Chinese ship going down river. Kerans remembers thinking to himself at the time, 'If the Chinese can navigate the Yangtze at night, why can't I?'

So, keeping his own counsel, he had started working on a plan – just in case. He decided to cut away sections of the frigate's superstructure – this would not only reduce top-weight for stability but change her silhouette, make her look less like a warship. To his petty officers he explained that work and routine were the only ways of keeping up the morale of the crew.

The idea of making a run for it really crystallised at the moment when Typhoon Gloria hit Shanghai, and then moved up the Yangtze, turning the river into a swirling torrent. At the same time melting snows in the Himalayas were pouring millions of tons of water into the river thousands of miles away, all of it rushing in a mighty flood to the open sea. Though Kerans knew he could never escape during the typhoon itself he realised that there would never be a better opportunity than in the floods and blinding rain that followed it. Apart from anything else, the heavy flooding might well have made Chinese gun emplacements near the bank untenable, for the force of the storm had torn thousands of tons of muddy earth from the river banks. Most river traffic had disappeared, including Communist patrol boats; this meant an added safety bonus in the dark, when he would have to navigate the swollen current, along which was sweeping a despairing panorama of Chinese life – animals perched on floating haystacks, pigs trying to swim, even houses, wrested from their foundations, roaring past the ship.

Another factor influenced Kerans. The Communists had made it clear they would blow *Amethyst* out of the water if she tried to escape; so what would happen if, because of the storm, the anchor cable parted? He cabled Fleet Headquarters in Hongkong, 'If cable parts will run for it and if wrecked and salvage impossible will blow up ship.'

These were the positive points which he mulled over. There were other considerations. For two weeks the ship's company had been on half-rations. There was almost no flour left. The yeast and sugar had gone bad. And because many of the farms on the river banks had been flooded, he doubted whether the Chinese would have any fresh food to barter in the near future. The food situation was bad, but the water problem was worse, for the engineers were having difficulty in keeping *Amethyst's* evaporator running. They could patch it up for a little while longer, but not indefinitely; and when that went, there would be no drinking water. In the ship's sick bay disinfectant was in short supply; medical supplies were running down. There was even a shortage of toilet paper. Worst of all, the oil was running out again. Kerans reckoned that if he did not make a dash for it within a few days, he wouldn't have enough oil to take *Amethyst* to the open sea; then, eventually, there would be no alternative but to surrender.

Still not sharing his secret hopes with anyone, he ordered the anchor cable to be lashed with bedding which had previously been soaked in soap and grease, for, as he remembered later, 'The vital point will be on slipping the cable and turning the ship without making a noise. One sudden sound and we'll be blown out of the water.'

The order was at first received 'with blank faces', so, determined to keep his thoughts to himself, Kerans added, quite out of character, 'Every time the ship swings at her moorings, the cable screeches. It's getting on my nerves.'

At three o'clock on the afternoon of 30 July, Kerans sent for Lieutenant G. B. Strain, the electrical officer, and told him, 'George, I'm going to break out tonight.' It was just a hundred days since the first Communist gun had fired on *Amethyst*. Quietly Kerans explained his reasons to the young (and slightly stunned) officer.

'Tonight will be the last for another month with the phase of the moon just right for a break-out,' he said. 'The moon is due to set at eleven o'clock. I've decided to slip away at ten, accepting one hour of the waning moon as an unavoidable handicap. We'll need every minute of time if we hope to get past the big guns at Woosung before dawn.

'The Yangtze is still very high because of Gloria but it's due to fall very soon. And, travelling by night without a river pilot, we'll need all the water we can to take us over the mud banks. Besides, food is getting short, and we probably won't get much in the way of fresh vegetables from now on. Then there is the element of surprise after all the months of standing still.'

Kerans did not let the ship's crew know of his decision until eight o'clock that evening, when he summoned seventeen petty officers and key ratings to his tiny cabin, and told them in a matter-of-fact voice, 'I'm going to break out tonight.'

Shortly before ten o'clock, while Kerans was waiting for the moon to disappear behind cloud, he heard the sound of a ship's motor, then saw the dark silhouette of a ship sailing down river. It was just what he needed – 'Something I can follow.'

Amethyst slipped her cable shortly after 10 p.m. without a sound, and for the first fifteen minutes followed the Chinese merchantman, the *Kiang Ling Liberation*. Then a flare lit up the night ahead of them. Obviously it was meant for the Chinese ship, which sounded her sirens. At the same time Kerans saw, by the light of the flare, a Communist naval patrol vessel. Another flare shot up – possibly intended for *Amethyst*. Kerans took no notice, but followed the *Kiang Ling Liberation*.

Without warning, tracer bullets started streaming across the Yangtze – but astonishingly, they were not aimed at *Amethyst*. For some reason, never explained, the captain of the patrol vessel had opened fire on the Communist shore batteries. Then the shore batteries replied – and shells *did* start falling uncomfortably near *Amethyst*. 'Make smoke!' Kerans ordered. Somehow, weaving, and hidden by clouds of filthy smoke, *Amethyst* managed to get past the *Kiang Ling Liberation,* and made for Rose Island – the danger spot where the river was hardly more than half a mile wide. Obviously her dash was no longer a secret, and now Kerans had to run for it with all the speed he could find in the badly smashed-up frigate. To make matters worse, she had been hit near the water line, and water was pouring in near the stern threatening the steering. The pumps were manned and managed to keep the water in check.

Just before 1 a.m. *Amethyst* faced her next hazard – a boom laid by the Communists across the river near Kiangyin, the river port where *Amethyst* had spent the night on the way up river. Kerans had received reports about the boom; apparently it was constructed out of a line of old ships, sunk just below the surface, with only one channel in the middle. Any vessel hitting the boom would tear off her bottom. Yet there was no way Kerans could know where the safe channel lay.

As he approached Kiangyin, the guns opened up. Ahead Kerans could see one light – only one, and he knew that it lit the boom. But on which side of the light did the safe channel lie? Only the Communists knew, and they would normally have guided their own merchant ships through the channel. Streaks of tracer bullets from a near-by patrol boat made it imperative that Kerans decide on the instant to take a gamble. It was a fifty-fifty chance, and he won it. He took *Amethyst* close to port of the light, and she went through 'without a scratch'.

By 3 a.m. *Amethyst* had only forty miles to go to reach the open sea; but before that she had one more adventure – this time with an unknown civilian vessel. About four o'clock, Kerans made out the shape of a junk ahead, sailing without lights. He was running straight for it – and there was no possibility of evasive action. *Amethyst* sliced the junk in two, shuddered, and steamed straight ahead.

Miraculously the guns at Woosung forts never opened up and, just as dawn broke, one of the crew spotted the shape of a destroyer. It was HMS *Concord*. Soon she was so close that crew members could see men waving excitedly to them, while Kerans dictated his last radio message to the C-in-C: 'Have rejoined the Fleet.'

On the morning of 1 August, the Shanghai newspapers shrieked the news – with vituperation and demands for compensation and retaliation. *Amethyst*, they insisted, had sunk the *Kiang Ling Liberation* (which had in fact been sunk by Chinese gunfire); but the threats soon faded away. Mariano Ezpeleta felt that though the Communists had gained enormous prestige when they captured *Amethyst*, 'they were more than willing to forget the incident. They were not desirous to have the world remember that British prestige in China had been regained, and at their cost too.'

Shortly afterwards Ezpeleta met the British Consul-General at a party at the French Club. Ezpeleta congratulated him on the skill and daring of the escape, at which 'with characteristic British understatement' Urquhart drawled, 'Yes, I think the lad did a bloody good job,' and ordered two more double Scotches and soda.

The news provided the British colony – now reduced to fewer than 2000 – with a much-needed fillip. Though the dramatic escape might not have done much to restore faith in a government which seemed (to the Shanghailanders anyway) unconcerned with people stranded in China, it did illustrate the power of individuals to overcome almost insuperable difficulties. The example put heart into people determined to carry on, despite the fact that their lives had been turned upside-down for the third time in less than ten years.

Everything *was* changing. The new street names were unrecognisable, and deliberately kept so by bland policemen; if you asked a policeman to direct you somewhere using the original British name, he would pretend not to know it, though always with the utmost courtesy. Old and friendly landmarks took on new and sinister aspects. Broadway Mansions, emptied now of its ebullient press corps, was used as an interrogation centre for petty offenders – people charged with currency offences, illegally storing petrol or breaking the curfew. Though the British-run Bubbling Well Chapel was still allowed to hold Sunday services, the Communists used it during the week as an indoctrination centre. During these sessions the altar was littered with ashtrays and a portrait of Mao Tse-tung hung over the cross.

New edicts seemed to make no sense. A Chinese friend of Gertrude Bryan was arrested after her boy had informed the police that she still played mah-jong, the centuries-old Chinese game which had inexplicably been banned by the Communists. To deaden the clatter, which is a feature of the game, the lady had strapped plaster on all the tiles, but her boy had let the police in by the back door. She was sentenced to attend the police station daily until all her tiles had been destroyed at the rate of one a day.

Spot-checks became the order of the day – and night – even in the Shanghai Club, whose staid members became very angry when eight policemen demanded entry around midnight and searched every room, hauling away two members who were not carrying proper identification. Similar search parties made regular checks in hotels all over the city.

The curfew was ruthlessly imposed. No cars were allowed on the streets after 9 p.m. without a special pass; offenders were taken straight to Broadway Mansions where they sometimes had to wait until dawn before being questioned.

One man did beat the curfew. Ezpeleta stayed late one night at a party, and did not start to drive home until one in the morning. He told Hung, his driver, to unfurl his car flag, but they were stopped in the avenue Joffre by a dozen soldiers. Hung jumped out and spoke to the officer in charge. To Ezpeleta, sitting in the back seat, 'it looked as though Hung was giving the Communist officer a lecture, pointing at the officer's face, then his own, and then at the car'. Finally Hung returned and was allowed to drive home.

When they reached his house Ezpeleta asked Hung what he had told the Chinese. His driver replied, 'I wanted the officer to know that the Filipino Consul-General is a fellow Oriental, whose face resembled the officer's and mine, and I told him that the People's government should at least have the decency to respect a brother Oriental.'

There seemed to be no rhyme or reason for many of the bewildering anomalies of this changed life. For centuries local craftsmen or small-town factories had provided an unending supply of that most necessary item of Chinese life – the spittoon. Making handsome (or just workaday) spittoons was an industry which kept thousands happily employed all the year round. Without warning the government asked Harold Fabian if they could rent one of his largest godowns to store a consignment of goods which was arriving overland. The rent was good and Fabian was delighted. Then he went to see the cargo.

'I couldn't believe my eyes,' he told his wife Sue. 'Every inch of the place was stacked with cheap enamel spittoons made in Czechoslovakia. The Commies can't be very bright if they let the Russians pull a fast one like this.'

If the commissars mixed up their priorities, so at times did the rank and file. With everyone forming new unions, the servants and gardeners working in the British Consulate compound decided that they too should have 'protection' and went to register 'The British Consulate Workers Union' with the authorities. To their chagrin, they were told to go away. It was impossible, said the Communists – for what seemed a logical reason: Mao Tse-tung and Britain had not yet opened diplomatic relations; this being so it was obvious to any well-informed Communist that there was no such place as the British Consulate in Shanghai.

Worst of all, though, was an undefinable atmosphere, 'Not exactly pessimism, not only frustration,' wrote Gladys Hawkings, 'but more, a feeling of dreariness.' The old cosmopolitan air which had been the proud hallmark of Shanghai was disappearing, being replaced by an imposed visual monotony which perhaps took its cue from the regulation uniforms which in theory made everyone equal but in fact only standardised them, so that soon a crowded street might as well have been peopled entirely by clones. The Chinese and White Russian women, who had once been the flowers decorating a sophisticated city, accentuated the dreariness for they quickly saw that the only way to keep out of trouble was to make themselves as inconspicuous as possible. The old finery vanished. The beautiful clothes, the elegant fashions, were replaced by the forerunners of unisex blouses and trousers.

It was not only the girls from the nightclubs who were understandably afraid of being whisked off to indoctrination camps. Everyone was apprehensive – if not of a Communist official, then of a neighbour or relative in a city where the informer was regarded as a model citizen. It all led to a standardised anonymity, as though, from the highest to the lowest, everyone had something to hide.

Even the leaders hid. True, a few sleek cars still slid along the Bund, but whereas in the past you might have caught sight of a celebrity – or even a friend – reclining on the back seat, the passengers were now invariably hidden by that international status symbol of the Communist official lucky enough to have a chauffeur, a set of blue curtains.

Day by day – and certainly night by night – the sense of drabness increased; and this was an awful burden to bear for the people of a city which had prided itself on its reputation as the brightest, hardest-working, most immoral, polyglot city in the world. Not only the street names, but even the old human landmarks had changed, swept away by cold, impersonal officials who had no time for failure. You missed the engaging White Russian beggars on the Bund; the suave, long-coated money-changers with their pockets full of jingling coins; the ladies of the town who (in the best parts, anyway) had finesse and delicacy in handling the financial transactions involved. Even the rickshaw and pedicab-pullers had altered their ways. In the old days they had shouted at each other, vied with one another. True, they had for years been treated shockingly, like beasts of burden, victimised mainly by the Chinese; yet somehow the scrawny, panting man, with a strip of rag around his sweat-soaked neck, had had a curious sense of fun, even of pride in beating his fellow sufferer pulling alongside. In its way it was an illustration of man's ability to get the best out of even the darkest life. Now they pulled their loads in silence, with the grim determination of robots.

The one thing that *nobody* – whatever his nationality, whatever his rank or station – could do was disobey the newly imposed laws. Retribution was instant, as Ernest Gottschalk, a German Jewish refugee, and two friends discovered. Gottschalk had been a friend of George and Ellen Vine and was typical of so many men in Shanghai who had spent half a lifetime escaping from tyranny and had finally become too tired to flee any more. He had managed to escape from Nazi Germany to Italy, leaving behind a family business. When Mussolini joined Hitler, he escaped to Tangier. When the Germans moved into North Africa he fled to Shanghai. George Vine had begged him to get out when he and Ellen left, but Gottschalk had replied, 'Don't worry – I'll be careful. I won't get into any trouble.'

Gottschalk, who was living in a room at the YMCA, heard a tap on the door. Two old friends had arrived, Chinese who had been recruited locally for the Reuters staff in better days. Reuters, of course, had closed down, but the two men had 'inherited' the office equipment, which included a powerful short-wave radio receiver and a duplicating machine.

However, the one thing in short supply was cash – and they had to live. So they had the ingenious notion of monitoring the thrice-daily BBC world news bulletin, then duplicating 3000 copies which they sold to the foreign business community. It was an instant success. As listening to the foreign radio was illegal, businessmen did not dare to tune into the BBC in case their servants informed on them. Now they could glance quickly through the forbidden sheet in their offices, then destroy the evidence. However, the two ex-Reuters men faced a problem. They needed a quiet place to run the duplicating machine – which was why they went to see Gottschalk who had done occasional work for Reuters.

Like a fool he agreed – for he too needed money. The machine was installed in his room and all went well for a few weeks until inevitably the secret was unmasked. All three were arrested and charged with espionage. The two Reuters men were executed without delay and Gottschalk was sentenced to twenty years in a Chinese prison where he shared a cell with five other men.*

Yet in contrast to the danger and the drabness – the latter perhaps exaggerated in the minds of people cut off from families, denied mail, feeling forgotten – there was an abundance of unexpected things, particularly goods which did not interest the Chinese. It was impossible to buy a car, for the Communists had snapped them all up; French fashions had disappeared from the shop windows. Yet Shanghai, as a truly international city, had long been a paradise for importers who had laid in huge stocks of luxury items ready to satisfy the whims of their most demanding customers. Rice might be short, servants might be spies, taxes might be iniquitous, but it would be years before Shanghai suffered from shortages of Scotch and gin. You could go to any one of a hundred shops and buy any sporting goods – from a gross of tennis balls to a skiff for the Rowing Club. Most things cost more, of course, but everything was available from seemingly inexhaustible stocks.

Indeed, foreigners were suddenly astonished to find a whole new range of goods on sale – imported from Russia or the Eastern bloc countries yet of no interest to Chinese people, so that Shanghai, city of paradoxes, suddenly produced the greatest paradox of all – petrol at a prohibitive £1.25 a gallon, but unlimited caviare on sale in every grocer's shop at the absurd price of what would now be 50p a pound.

Billy Hawkings, as a director of Mardens, was at this time involved in bitter, frustrating arguments with Chinese workers who were suing him for wrongful dismissal – though the fact that the plaintiffs had never worked for Mardens did not seem to matter. On the morning that the case was to be heard Hawkings appeared at the Labour Bureau promptly at nine o'clock. For nearly six hours he was kept waiting, standing in a corridor, while representatives of the two hundred workers who were suing Mardens lolled in armchairs in the 'witnesses' lounge'. The

* Gottschalk was freed after ten years and Vine saw him later in Germany. He had only been allowed to read Marxist books and so, as Vine remembers, 'Gottschalk was the only man I have ever met who had read all the works of Marx and Engels in their original language. He knew them by heart.'

workers had lodged a ridiculous protest against an affiliated company in Hongkong, and even if Hawkings had been in the wrong, there was nothing he could do about it. Yet the workers demanded compensation of £25,000 for wrongful dismissal three years previously.

The Bureau adjourned the case and Hawkings thankfully returned to his office. Any hopes he might have entertained for a respite were shattered. Fifty or so workers locked Hawkings in his office for two days and nights, pushing cheap Chinese meals through the door at regular intervals, and escorting him to the toilet every few hours. Fortunately he was able to telephone Hongkong and explain what was happening. But it was two days before he was able to return to The Limit.

Almost every foreign firm faced its labour problems. One day, a number of workers who had been dismissed by Jardines years previously managed to catch the company secretary as he returned from lunch, and demanded immediate reinstatement 'under the new government laws'. But the secretary decided not to go to his office, knowing that once inside they would probably refuse to let him out. So he sat on the stairs to see who would get tired first. He won – having sat on the stairs for nine hours before the workers finally left.

Godfrey Moyle, who worked in Jardines insurance department (with nothing to insure) arrived in the office one morning to find an extraordinary notice pinned up in the entrance hall, headed 'The Union of the People's Insurance Co. of China'. It accused Jardines of 'being indifferent to the union's opinion', and claimed that the union had asked Jardines a question to which the company had replied that it did not know the answer.

'"I don't know" is a perfunctory answer,' said the notice, which ended with the startling demand, 'We now request a precise definition of "I don't know".'

Together with these difficulties, businessmen also faced Chiang Kai-shek's naval blockade. Chiang might have been unable to fight, but he had dispatched warships to guard the Yangtze estuary and prevent any ships entering or leaving. Since the Nationalists were still the legal rulers of the country – the Communists had not yet proclaimed their government – it placed foreigners in a difficult position.

With the vital import–export trade at a standstill, foreign businessmen were digging deeper into their reserves every day, and since the Communists did not object to foreign vessels arriving, the British Navy was asked to provide armed escorts for freighters attempting to run the blockade. But the Navy was powerless unless the politicians agreed, and Ernest Bevin neatly side-stepped the issue in the Commons by saying, in effect, that the blockade didn't exist. 'The Chinese Nationalist government claim that measures taken by them do not constitute a blockade, but merely give effect to a domestic closure order,' he explained.

August was the month of triumph for John Proud's careful planning. He was still in hospital but the treatment was not rigorous and, using the excuse of 'exercise', he made regular visits into the city. It was on one of these trips that Charlie Chan finally handed Proud the Chinese terms for 'accepting recognition'. It was a tremendous moment for Proud. He made his way to the Consulate-General and, disobeying doctors' orders, stayed on there, coding the long message that would give the British Government the vital information it needed. Thus when the Communist victory was final, Britain could step in quickly. Proud remained in the Consulate all night, waiting for his message to be acknowledged from London.

But he was under no illusions about the implications of the Chinese demands. Apart from insisting on 'a basis of absolute equality in all negotiations', Chou En-lai was adamant on one point which Proud knew would cause much consternation at home: Chou insisted that on the day Britain recognized Communist China, she would have to sever all diplomatic relations with the Chiang Kai-shek government in Taiwan. And the gesture would have to be made publicly. Nothing less would satisfy the implacable Mao Tse-tung.

Proud could imagine the quandary in which this would place the Government in London. After all, Chiang had been Britain's wartime ally, one of the 'Big Four'. At one moment, when the Communists had suggested a federal union on American lines, with power-sharing, Chiang had stood on the threshold of greatness. Had he accepted the challenge, victory over Japan could have been followed by peace. But Chiang would not agree to share power with Mao Tse-tung, and so the moment of compromise had passed. Yet, whatever his faults, Chiang had played an important role in preventing the Japanese from taking all China, and his stand in Chunking had been heroic. Even so, Proud remembers wondering as he coded the message, had Britain any right to deny the existence of Mao Tse-tung, the *de facto* ruler of China? Could Bevin remain indifferent to the fate of British people and British fortunes in Shanghai? However distasteful, he would have to recognise the new regime if or when Mao Tse-tung proclaimed victory.

Chan had told Proud that the Communists were planning to establish their government on 1 October; so Britain would have the choice of giving rapid recognition to the new government when it was established. Proud had successfully bypassed all the preliminary discussions that would normally have dragged on for months before the two governments came together. Instant recognition would be a godsend to the hard-pressed British businessmen who were suffering from the exorbitant taxation and punitive labour laws. But much would depend on the speed with which Britain recognized the new government, for Proud knew how sensitive the Communists were. Whether or not one approved of them, Britain would have to act swiftly. Any delay would be regarded by the Communists as an insult.

Earlier Proud had cabled to London some details of his illness. He had had to let them know that he was in hospital; and London had immediately urged him to leave for Hongkong. This he had refused to do until his mission was completed. But now it had ended, and he felt it was time to go. He suggested to London that he would leave when some plane or ship was available and they agreed. He alerted Charlie Chan of his plans, then put in a routine request to the Chinese Foreign Bureau for an exit permit, normally granted immediately to diplomats.

Nothing happened for a couple of weeks, but Proud was not unduly concerned, putting the delay down to Chinese bureaucracy. However, after two weeks he decided to check and was told that his application was 'under consideration'. This seemed a trifle odd, so a week later Proud made a new application. Again he was told that his exit visa was being considered, and now he began to be slightly worried; finding any transport out of Shanghai was difficult, yet there was no point in even examining the possibilities of getting away until he had his exit visa.

Then the blow fell. Charlie Chan phoned, and in a perfectly normal voice, made some commonplace remark such as, 'It's going to rain.'

This is the moment that all agents fear. Proud realised why his exit visa was 'under consideration'. Charlie Chan was telling him, 'Our cover has been blown.' Proud was flabbergasted; he had done nothing but try to help both countries. Why on earth should anyone tip off the Chinese – and even if they did, why should the Chinese worry? He could appreciate that one government department might be working without the knowledge of another, but he was not so much a secret agent as a behind-the-scenes negotiator. The only explanation was that the Communists with their phobia about spying couldn't tell the difference.

The one thing that never entered John Proud's head at the time was that he had been unmasked by the Russians. Yet this is what had happened. Only years later, when Kim Philby defected, did Proud learn that Philby had given the Russians a list of all the men who had trained with him in London.*

Worse was to follow. Chinese agents working with Proud tried to contact Charlie Chan, only to be told by his tearful wife that he had left home one morning, promising to return for dinner, and had vanished. He has never been seen to this day.

---

* Some years later, but before Philby defected, Proud, Philby, and the author, who knew Philby's father well, lunched together in Beirut; ironically enough, Proud regarded Philby as a friend, without realizing that Philby knew the details of Proud's current assignment.

13

Recognition – and a New War
Autumn 1949–Spring 1951

One sparkling morning, a rare thrill of excitement rippled through Shanghai. Taipans with little or nothing to do except peer out of their office windows overlooking the Bund, were astonished to see a small, rusty old tramp steamer, proudly flying the Red ensign, sail calmly up the Whangpoo. Members of the RAF Association, meeting for pre-lunch drinks in the Dome, found a pair of binoculars and were able to make out the name: the *Edith Moller*. She could not have been more than 500 or 600 tons, small enough to slide into a jetty not far down river from the Bund. She was the first vessel to arrive since the take-over. Almost before the hawsers were secured, the sampans started fussing around her, and scores of wives all over Shanghai were answering the ring of telephones as husbands vied with each other to be first with the news.

The arrival of the vessel meant that some of their compatriots had shown the guts which most Shanghailanders felt the British Government lacked – they had cocked a snook at Chiang's naval blockade. The *Edith Moller* not only brought mail – more than a hundred sacks of it – but also a much-needed supply of drugs worth £125,000, some raw rubber, coconut oil and raw cotton. She had eluded the Nationalist gunboats by hugging the north coast of the Yangtze estuary. Eric Barry, the first officer, who came from Hessle, near Hull, told members of the Dome at a celebration lunch, 'We entered the Yangtze through a channel which has been closed and undredged for eighteen years, and sailed through without lights, finding a passage which wasn't on the charts.'

It was an exciting moment for Alec McShane. He had, after much searching, found Natasha in Broadway Mansions, where she had been taken, together with hundreds of other foreign girls, by the authorities. Natasha was not charged with any crime and was not strictly a prisoner, but was nevertheless about to be deported to Russia as her country of origin, unless she could show that she had somewhere else to go. McShane enlisted Billy Hawkings's help in the hope that he would know of a British ship that was planning to run the blockade. Hawkings told him that the *Leong Bee*, a small coastal vessel, was on her way

The *Edith Moller* was not the ship he had been expecting, but he promised McShane to do what he could and when the *Edith Moller* sailed, Natasha was aboard. Hawkings and McShane were down at the docks to see her off, and Gladys Hawkings described later how 'Mrs McShane was brought on board by two very polite Chinese civilians [presumably they were· escorting her from Broadway Mansions] and she and Alec were able to say goodbye and make arrangements to meet in Hongkong as soon as his exit visa comes through. I don't relish Mrs McShane the trip – there are no real cabins on the ship, only a deck-house, so she will sleep on the saloon sofa.'

In fact Natasha did not reach Hongkong for more than a month. Captain Robert Hall, the Dublin-born master, managed to take the *Edith Moller* over the dangerous sandbars in the shallow waters near the north coast of the estuary, and headed for the open sea. He was at least ten miles outside the three-mile limit which Chiang had imposed when a Nationalist destroyer fired two shots across the *Edith Moller*'s bows. The second was dangerously close, and Hall had no alternative but to stop. The *Edith Moller* was 'arrested' and taken into the Nationalist naval base at Tinghai, the landlocked harbour in the Chusan Islands, south of Shanghai.

Meanwhile, the *Leong Bee* had successfully run the blockade and reached Shanghai. Now another friend asked Hawkings for help – Sidney Smith, the *Daily Express* correspondent, who wanted to leave with his wife. There were three other passengers on the *Leong Bee*. The men would sleep on deck, Mrs Smith in the saloon, and they left expecting to reach Hongkong before the weekend.

But the *Leong Bee* never even reached the open sea before she was fired on by a Nationalist destroyer, the *Yung Chin*, which promptly escorted her to Tinghai. The *Leong Bee* and *Edith*

Moller remained there for two weeks or more, but finally the latter was given permission to leave – without her cargo; there seems no doubt that this decision was made because the vessel was registered with British owners. The Chinese-owned *Leong Bee,* however, was not so lucky. She and her 1100 tons of cargo were confiscated by the Nationalists. At the last moment the Smiths and the other passengers were allowed to transfer to the *Edith Moller,* and one might have supposed that now their adventures were over. There was, however, one final bizarre episode.

A Nationalist gunboat escorted them to the open sea, and Captain Hall set course for Hongkong. Without warning, a burst of gunfire shattered the silence, and plumes of water shot up in the sea around them. They were being fired on by *another* Nationalist gunboat and again there was nothing for it but to stop. As Sidney Smith wrote at the time, 'We anchored 200 yards from her. She was flying a signal, "In need of assistance".' In Pidgin English, the captain of the warship said that he had broken down, his radio was out of order, and he needed a tow to Tinghai; but, as Captain Hall growled to Smith, 'That's just a trick to get us back into territorial waters and confiscate the ship on a new trumped-up charge.' Prolonged exchanges took place, with Captain Hall playing for time. 'Once it's dark,' he told Smith, 'I'll be able to make a dash for it.'

It was a long, tense wait for the passengers, for the Nationalist vessel was so close that they could see her guns being loaded, and ammunition being stacked in a ready position. Though the Nationalist officer said that he had only fired to attract attention, it seemed clear that he was not going to let the *Edith Moller* go, even if he had to use his guns to prevent her.

At eleven o'clock that night, Captain Hall decided 'to do an *Amethyst*'. He ordered all passengers and crew below, and took the bridge by himself. Extinguishing all lights, he slipped his cable, and made a dash for it. Smith remembers that 'as the anchor came up we began to drift astern of the warship, when she opened fire'. For ten minutes she blazed away with pom-poms and machine-guns, but fortunately had no tracer bullets, and the *Edith Moller* got away without a scratch.

The warship which had fired on the *Edith Moller* must have been one of a dwindling band remaining loyal to Chiang, who was being deserted right and left as he prepared to set up his new government in Taiwan – a move for which preparations were all but complete. There is no doubt that those who did desert in the autumn of 1949 were those whose families had not been ordered to live in Taiwan, which made them hostages. Bribery no longer seemed to be the main incentive; self-preservation was more important. This and the hope that when finally the civil war ended, men would be able to return to their homes on the mainland rather than have to start a new life in Taiwan.

In the same week the *Edith Moller* was freed from the Chusan Islands, the flagship of the Nationalist squadron based there surrendered to the Communists. The largest vessel left in Chiang's navy, the *Chang Chih,* a former Japanese destroyer, defected after 20 mutineers seized the ship's arms, murdered 5 officers, locked up 200 of the crew who did not share their philosophy, and sailed for Woosung at the mouth of the Yangtze, where they handed the vessel over.

At about the same time, one of Chiang's most trusted advisers, General Tung Chi-wu, who had been rewarded for his loyalty with the governorship of a province, defected, together with thirty-eight other provincial leaders who addressed a manifesto to Mao Tse-tung swearing their loyalty to him.

All these desertions in the autumn of 1949 were, however, overshadowed by the defection of eleven passenger aircraft. The planes – mostly DC3s – had actually been sent with nine others to Hongkong for safekeeping under the watchful eye of Colonel C. L. Liu, for thirty years one of Chiang's most trusted officials and close friends. They belonged to the China National Aviation Company, of which Liu was managing director. CNAC had started in 1929 as China Airways, an American company with an exclusive contract to carry mail between several large Chinese cities. It had later been reorganised, with the Nationalist government taking 55 per cent of the stock, the Americans holding the balance.

Liu laid his plans carefully and did not act until he was certain that he had eleven pilots eager to defect. They were good pilots, frustrated at being grounded, fed up with Chiang, and it is hard to believe that they were real traitors in the sense that Liu, the trusted executive, was. Liu also recruited sympathetic engineers and other aircrew, all in secret. Most were ostensibly employed on routine maintenance, but were in fact tuning up the aircraft for instant departure. Few knew what was going on, for the secret was brilliantly kept. At the very last moment Liu, who was able to

197

use his authority as managing director, ordered the aviation fuel bowsers to fill the tanks of the eleven aircraft. They were, he explained, making routine flight tests and flight plans would be filed before take-off.

Then, when the moment arrived, the airline staff was given a day's holiday, for a 'get-together' which would culminate in a 'staff lunch' in a private room at a Chinese restaurant in downtown Hongkong. Those members of the staff ignorant of the plot cheerfully assembled there at midday – only to find no Mr Liu, and a restaurant mystified by the large influx of clients for a party of which they had no knowledge. If anyone at that moment suspected treachery, it was too late. The traitors had reached the airfield before dawn. Mechanics and engineers – and of course Liu – became 'passengers'. One after another the planes took off. Once airborne, flight plans which had been filed with Hongkong authorities were torn up and the planes headed for Peking.

Added to the desertions, which by the very nature of things were infectious, were the military setbacks. By the first day of October 1949 Mao Tse-tung in Peking formally proclaimed the existence of the People's Republic of China. His armies had after all marched 2000 miles in less than a year, southwards from Mukden, averaging more than six miles a day.

It was a moment to savour, with one titanic Chinese leader toppling another – a moment of triumph but also a moment hailed with a sigh of relief by everyone in China, for though the event did little more than formalise a situation that was apparent to all, it did mean, to hundreds of millions of Chinese, the virtual end of civil war,* and for that – though they knew not what the future would hold – they had cause to be truly thankful.

For the businessmen in Shanghai it signalled at last a fervent hope that Britain's government and the new government of China would officially agree that trade knows no ideological boundaries. After all each country needed the other, and the British were on the spot, experienced traders ready and waiting to open up their godowns and load the ships.

It seemed to John Proud that nothing could now stand in the way of the formal recognition of a government that was in power.

---

* There was still sporadic fighting in the south, but Canton fell on 16 October and Chungking less than a month later.

The British Government had been told secretly the terms of recognition, and even if the Labour Party did not approve of communism as a creed, at least Mao would be more likely to approve of them than of a Government led by 'that anti-Communist warmonger Churchill', as he had once described the Conservative leader.

In Whitehall, however, the mood was different. The Government was uneasy; not exactly divided, but waiting to see what others would do. Time and again Bevin was pressed by MPs on both sides of the House for a statement. Even in mid-November his answer was brief: 'No decision has been taken about the recognition as the government of China of the Communist Chinese government.'

Walter Fletcher, Conservative MP for Bury, who knew the East well, indirectly suggested a temporary compromise· by tabling the question on 16 November: 'In view of the serious and anomalous position in Shanghai and other parts of China, where British lives as well as British property are at stake, would the Minister consider establishing some form of communication by appointing an official to the Peking government if he does not want to tackle the major question just yet?'

Bevin had to confess that he had tried to communicate with Peking, 'but I have not had a reply'. It was left to Churchill, leader of the Opposition, to sum up what everyone felt. In one of his typical, brilliant flashes of succinct argument, he retorted, 'The reason for having diplomatic relations is not to confer a compliment but to secure a convenience.' Recognising a person was not necessarily an act of approval, he said, adding, 'One has to recognise lots of things and people in this world of sin and woe that one does not like. When a large and powerful mass of people are organised together and are masters of an immense area of great population, it may be necessary to have relations with them. One may even say that when relations are most difficult, that is the time when diplomacy is most needed.'

But for the moment no action was taken in England, though not even Churchill – let alone the British people or John Proud – could have had the faintest notion of the reason why Britain did not recognise the new regime immediately. Privately, Bevin was anxious to do so without delay for, as he told a senior colleague in the Foreign Office, 'I don't really care whether it's the right thing to do, but I want to do it now so I won't get the bloody blame if things go wrong later.' (Perhaps he had in mind Duff Cooper's remark* on 'the harm that has been done by the reluctance of men to accept readily what they know they will have to accept in the end'.)

Bevin's down-to-earth philosophy was thwarted by one man – of all people, Attlee. The Labour Prime Minister had a soft spot for India and Burma – after all it was he who had had (in his word) the 'inspiration' of sending Mountbatten to grant quick independence to the Indian subcontinent. And when the Burmese became an independent republic, their leaders had the ear of Attlee.

They heard that Britain was planning recognition. Frantically they begged Attlee to delay the move until Burma had agreed on recognition. Their argument was unsubtle but understandable: the country's political leaders, anxious to show their independence of Britain, felt that if they followed Britain in recognising Red China, their critics would say they were still swayed by Whitehall, whereas if they recognised Red China first, it would provide a striking demonstration of their ability as world statesmen. Attlee told Bevin to wait, and thus Burma became the very first non-Communist country to recognise Mao Tse-tung's regime.

In Shanghai, as the foreigners faced the prospect of their first Christmas under Communism, disillusionment had set in. 'The Communists are so bloody inefficient,' one businessman wailed. It was a defect fostered by an almost pathological fear of taking any decision. Under the Chiang regime, at least you could get things if you were prepared to pay the right man the right amount of cash. But those days had gone, and corruption had been replaced by procrastination.

All the same, Sue Fabian was able to write to her parents in Australia, 'For those who hold no responsible job, life goes on much the same. There may not be as many parties, and though the diplomats aren't recognised by the new authorities, that hasn't deterred them from entertaining on their national days.'

Everyone exercised their ingenuity to help keep people busy. Mrs Urquhart, who was a *cordon bleu* cook, gave lessons at the Consulate to five young brides and at the end of their 'course' they prepared a celebration dinner for their husbands and members of the Consulate-General staff.

---

* In *Old Men Forget* (1953).

For many, the Lyceum Theatre was the favourite place to while away long evenings, for it was much more than a British-built, British-owned theatre; to the Shanghailanders it was a tradition respected as much as the Shanghai Club. With 300 performances behind it before the Communists arrived, it had become a club in which discussions and rehearsals played as big a part in many people's lives as the productions themselves. Its Green Room, open the year round, and presided over by Wong, the barman, had dispensed drinks for longer than anyone cared to remember. Despite difficulties it carried on, even though on one occasion Wong was taken away for questioning and warned that he was being 'too loyal to foreigners'.

Finally the Chinese took over the Lyceum, though (to the surprise of many) agreed to make it available to the Amateur Dramatic Society for its regular productions. The only stipulation was that all publicity – tickets, advertising posters and so on – had to be displayed in Chinese as well as in English. This was no serious problem, as the Chinese offered to do the translating at the Ministry of Culture (where they would also delete anything offensive). There were many who wondered how the Chinese would translate the society's latest offering, an innocuous old Aldwych farce called *One Wild Oat*. The Chinese posters finally appeared with the title translated:

ONE EXPERIMENT IN FREE LOVE

In many ways it was the older residents who suffered most. Many mothers – women like Gertrude Bryan – had sent their children home, and they missed them dreadfully, the more so as they did not even have the consolation of regular letters. The husbands suffered too. Bob Bryan's law firm had been so effectively blacklisted that he could not even make a pretence of work, though he insisted on going to his office every day 'to try and keep up morale'. The taipans' office routine had changed. Gone were the heady days of manipulating big business deals. Now their work consisted of sending an endless stream of cables to head office asking for funds to keep them going and pay the wages of employees they were unable to sack.

At the annual meeting in November of the British Residents Association, Urquhart had to admit that recent months had been 'disappointing', and that the knowledge that letters with news of families were piling up in Hongkong 'just outside our grasp, has come nearer to giving us stomach ulcers than all the shouting and excitements of the actual battle of Shanghai'. Nor could the Consul-General hold out much hope for the future. 'It doesn't look promising at the moment,' he admitted. 'If recognition is granted, if the blockade fizzles out soon, we shall feel encouraged, but the essential problems will still remain.'

There was nothing for it but to carry on. The Shanghailanders held the most successful St Andrew's Day dinner and dance anyone could remember in the hallowed Shanghai Club. Three hundred and ninety-five people bought tickets even though they cost the equivalent of £2.50 each. The haggis was ceremoniously piped in (with the Communists a few blocks away). American guests were astonished at the menu – Scotch broth before the haggis which was doused in whisky, then saddle of mutton, trifle and coffee. Scottish reels were performed by the Shanghai Reel Club, which had been practising twice a week for three months.

Christmas and New Year were hardly out of the way before the news for which everyone had been waiting was announced: Britain had officially recognised Red China. She was ready to establish diplomatic relations 'On a basis of equality, mutual benefit, and mutual respect for territory and sovereignty'. Each country would appoint ambassadors, but in the meantime Whitehall nominated a chargé d'affaires in Peking.

On the very same day Hector McNeil of the Foreign Office had the distasteful task of summoning Dr Cheng Tien-hsi, the Nationalist Ambassador to St James's, and telling this representative of a great wartime ally to pack his bags. As Chou had insisted to John Proud, this had to be done, for in the Chinese civil war it was a case of winner take all; but one can sympathise with the howls of rage from Taiwan. The Nationalist Foreign Minister railed at 'the phenomenon of Great Britain rushing to offer recognition to the puppet Communist regime', while Madame Chiang Kai-shek bitterly scorned Britain for 'bartering her soul for thirty pieces of silver'. The Foreign Minister was wrong in his judgement, for Mao was no puppet. Madame Chiang was nearer the mark, for everyone, in Whitehall as well as in Shanghai, knew that British recognition was a major triumph for Mao and hoped that it would show a handsome profit when British trade in Shanghai returned to normal.

There was a compromise in the arrangement, not generally appreciated in Shanghai. Mao had insisted on Britain's cutting all ties with Chiang, and she had made a public gesture to that effect. But in fact Whitehall had persuaded him that Britain did need to retain at least a consul in Taiwan, and Mao had finally agreed.

The arrival of the *Elsie Moller* gave six men the chance to leave Shanghai, among them John Proud, whose exit permit had finally been granted. He was a bitter man when he sailed on the evening of 20 January. Not only had his cover been blown, which irked his professional pride, but far worse there had been no word from Charlie Chan – a disappearance that made him doubly angry, because all the work they had done, all the risks Charlie Chan had taken, seemed to have been in vain: Britain had taken months to recognise the new regime instead of stepping in first. To Proud the delay had been inexplicable in view of the urgency of his original mission in Shanghai.*

With the arrival of the *Elsie Moller* in Shanghai, John Proud's superiors started making plans for his departure, and Proud was given top priority to leave in her. There was, however, some danger. After all, the *Elsie Moller's* sister the *Edith Moller* had been captured by Chiang's navy, and since the *Elsie Moller* was also a blockade-runner, she could not expect friendly treatment if spotted by one of Chiang's gunboats. Besides, no one knew at the time who had betrayed Proud. Was it possible that his activities had become known to Chiang Kai-shek? What would Proud's fate be if he fell into Chiang's hands? It would be very easy for Chiang to argue that Proud had been working against the Nationalists.

The British Navy knew that a Nationalist gunboat was still lurking near the southern shores of the Yangtze estuary where the channel was deep enough for larger vessels to negotiate it, and even though the estuary was about twenty miles wide where it met the sea, and the *Elsie Moller* would take the northern channel, there was always the chance that the gunboat would spot her. With Proud aboard, precautions had to be taken against this possibility. An urgent signal was sent to Hongkong and HMS *Cossack* steamed northwards to wait just outside the limit imposed by Chiang, ready to dart inside and rescue the *Elsie Moller* if necessary.

Among the six passengers, all men, was Leo Callanan of the US

---

* Proud did not know the reason for the delay until it was explained to him by the author when they met years later in Australia.

Foreign Service. They boarded the *Elsie Moller* off the Bund late at night, and must have been taken a little aback when shown the only cabin. Callanan later described it* as follows:

> The six of us sat or sprawled, wedged among our baggage and bundles of bedding in our quarters. The room was aft of the upper deck, perched on the wartime gun platform just above the stern. Its six bunks hung in pairs by chains, two on each side and two opposite the door. A table was fastened to the deck in the centre. About 12 by 12 feet, the persons and luggage of six people crammed the room to such a degree that movement by more than two at a time was impossible.

As they prepared to sail, the captain, a huge man, appeared in the doorway, his bulk almost filling the space. 'Remember,' he warned them, 'this is a light wooden structure and would offer no protection against strafing. If you hear a plane, go below to the mess room, draw the iron covers on the ports and sit tight. The ship's sides and bulkheads will stop machine-gun bullets.'

Two Communist guards boarded the vessel in Shanghai and announced that they would stay on board until the *Elsie Moller* had dropped the Yangtze pilot. Proud remembers being astonished, not only by their politeness but by the fact that when they searched his luggage they allowed him to keep his revolver.

Somehow the six men slept, wriggling fully clothed in their bunks, and awoke to find the ship well past Woosung, in water calm as a mill pond. She was sailing straight for the shallow, unchartered north channel, and Callanan looked out. He saw:

> Miles behind us the mined main channel glistened calm and deserted. Beyond it, where the muddy Yangtze water first darkens, beginning to lose itself in the sea, the Nationalist navy patrolled the entrance to the main channel. No ocean-going vessel had entered those waters in over five weeks, but the *Elsie Moller,* because of the skill of her captain and the shallow draft of her hull, had been able to by-pass them. She was not attempting a return by the same route.

The northern waters of the estuary contained several shoals and sandbanks, particularly one dangerous sandbar which

---

* In the *US Foreign Service Journal.*

sometimes almost broke over the waves at low tide. This of course was the reason why the Nationalist gunboats rarely ventured so far north. To cross the sandbar, the *Elsie Moller* had to reach the estuary at high tide, around noon. Unfortunately she had slipped behind schedule, and by the time she reached the estuary the tide was going out – and quickly.

A sailor on the main forward deck was casting the lead steadily, and everyone shared with Callanan 'a definite impression that the ship was occasionally sliding over mudbanks'. Finally the captain decided that the only safe course was to return to the vicinity of Woosung, anchor for the night, and try again the following day when the tide was higher.

At that moment Proud saw the silhouettes of two vessels. Straight ahead was the waiting *Cossack*. On the starboard bow was the smaller, dark outline of a Nationalist gunboat – and she was racing towards them.

As the captain prepared to turn back, Proud felt that 'this was a time to pull rank'. He was after all a naval commander, so 'I persuaded the captain reluctantly to try once more to slide the *Elsie Moller* over the sandbar'.

It was touch and go. At one moment, Callanan wrote,

the ship actually went hard aground. The engines were stopped, reversed, then she backed off the mud to probe for deeper water. Several more times the stern wave, the first rise in the wake just over the stern, built up and up until its crest was three or four feet above the ship's low rail, a sign that the water was becoming even more shallow.

The ship touched bottom five times – the last time just as the Nationalist gunboat opened fire. 'She was miles off target,' Proud remembers, 'as we stuck on the sandbar for what seemed a hell of a long time. She was still firing wildly as she raced towards us.' At that moment the *Elsie Moller* gave one huge shudder, trembled, then almost toppled over the bank and into the deeper water on the other side.

As the Nationalist warship came closer, the boom of a heavier gun split the air. The *Cossack* had fired a warning shot across her bows, and that was the end of the engagement. Chiang's ship turned tail and was soon out of sight.

The *Elsie Moller* was in deep water now and, with an escort, ready to sail straight to Hongkong. Her captain, who had no knowledge of Proud's VIP status, and presumably thought the *Cossack* was there by chance, must have been surprised to receive a signal flashed from the British warship, 'Does Commander Proud want to come aboard?'

It is typical of Proud that he refused. 'I thought I ought to stay with the others,' he remembers, 'and we reached Hongkong without incident.'

In a rather naïve underestimation of the problems involved, many Shanghailanders felt that since Britain and Red China were now 'friends', business would automatically be conducted on a friendly basis. It might have been so, had the Korean War not broken out.

All through the spring months Shanghai had been filled with rumours of the deteriorating relations between North and South Korea; but most had been ignored by the foreigners in Shanghai, who tended to dismiss alarmist newspaper reports as government-inspired propaganda. Then, in June, just as it seemed that day-to-day distrust between the new government and the foreigners in Shanghai was beginning to evaporate, North Korea invaded South Korea. Overnight everything changed.

Formally annexed by Japan in 1910, Japanese rule in Korea had ended with defeat in 1945, when Korea was divided. The Russians occupied the zone north of the 38th parallel, the Americans the country south of it. It was a temporary arrangement until each part of the country got back on its feet, but by May 1948 North Korea had proclaimed herself the Korean People's Republic under the aegis of Soviet Russia. Two months later South Korea became the Republic of Korea, under the protection of the United Nations.

Conflict was inevitable. On 25 June 1950, North Korean troops crossed the 38th parallel in a surprise invasion. Within hours the UN Security Council called for a cease-fire. North Korea spurned the order, and two days later President Truman moved US air and sea forces in support of South Korea. It was not only his decision to use American forces that angered the Chinese, but the blunt assertion to the world that Communists were engaged in an all-out bid to intimidate and take over smaller, defenceless nations.

'The attack upon Korea', Truman declared, 'makes it plain beyond all doubt that Communism has passed beyond the use of subversion . . . and will now use armed invasion and war.' He warned Mao Tse-tung to leave Taiwan alone. Any attempt to occupy the island would be 'a direct threat to the security of the Pacific area and . . . I have ordered the Seventh Fleet to prevent any attack on Formosa.'

Truman also warned Chiang Kai-shek, with whom he was thoroughly disillusioned, not to exacerbate a delicate situation by continued attacks on Communist China. They had to stop, he said, and so, with a certain irony, the American President whom many had denigrated before his astonishing election victory in November 1948, gave direct help to British businessmen in Shanghai. For whereas the British Navy had, on orders from Whitehall, timidly allowed Chiang's navy to stop British ships reaching Shanghai, even arrest them, Truman now told Chiang Kai-shek flatly to cease all air and sea operations against mainland China.

In one bold stroke Truman lifted the blockade which had harassed British trade for a year. And just in case Chiang did not realise that the United States now had a tough, down-to-earth President, Truman warned him that unless all ships were allowed free passage to China, 'the Seventh Fleet will see this is done.'

So started the war in Korea. Within three days British naval units had joined the UN forces. Within a week American troops had landed in South Korea. Before the end of the year, 200,000 Chinese troops would cross into North Korea.

With the war, relations between the Chinese and the foreigners in Shanghai worsened swiftly. Businessmen could only exist on remittances from head offices abroad. Any attempts to close down were greeted by a refusal of the Communists to issue an exit visa, and it was pointless to try to explain to the government's Foreign Bureau that there was no money left. The Chinese official almost invariably produced the latest balance sheet of the head office and pointed out that there were plenty of available funds. If one worked for a big shipping or trading firm with world-wide interests, many branches showing a profit, there was nothing one could say.

More and more families were being evicted from homes in which they had lived for years. The houses were, said the government, too big for married couples who had sent their children home to Europe or America; they were needed for schools or hostels – any excuse served, though most people believed the tougher attitude towards foreigners was directly caused by the American and United Nations determination to fight in Korea against what was, in effect, a Chinese Communist army.

The Hawkingses were particularly vulnerable, and one by one their neighbours were evicted – all, of course, with bland assurances that the moves were only temporary. In all fourteen European families living between The Limit and the city had been forced to leave their houses, each family being given only twenty-four hours to pack everything they owned. Yet nothing could lessen the shock when at 7 a.m. on Monday, 17 July 1950, the Hawkingses were told that The Limit was being requisitioned 'as a military necessity', and the house would have to be cleared of everything by seven o'clock the following morning. Anything left would be requisitioned.

This was less than two weeks before Gladys's sixtieth birthday and arrangements had been made for the biggest party The Limit had ever seen. Hawkings decided to appeal to the Mayor, General Chen Yi, whom he had met, knowing that the Chinese have a great respect for this particular occasion. On the Wednesday, 19 July, sitting tight under their eviction notice, they received a notification from the Foreign Office that Comrade Tong and three of his colleagues would arrive at The Limit at 6 p.m. that evening.

Tong proved to be a little man in a shabby uniform who spoke perfect English, but refused to discuss the matter except in Chinese; however, Chen Yi had obviously used his influence, for the Hawkingses were allowed to stay for Gladys's party on the 30th and then given a day to clean up so that the army could take over on 1 August.

Among the hundred guests at the birthday party were Bob and Gertrude Bryan, and Gertrude felt that 'in a way the party marked the end of an era. It was not only the last time any of us would see The Limit, but who in future would be able to invite friends to a sports day in their own grounds?'

So, to a background of bitter fighting in Korea, the year ran its course, with the foreign community in Shanghai making valiant efforts to 'carry on as usual'. The Rotarians held their annual Ladies' Day on 19 October. The Shanghai Royal Naval Association celebrated Trafalgar Day three days later, followed before the end of the month by a gardening tour (and a lecture on fertilisers) organised by the British Women's Association. The

British Council still functioned in its offices in Peking Road West, the highlight of October being a concert (piano solos and songs, entrance free), while early in November the Consulate-General arranged for a reading of T. S. Eliot's *The Cocktail Party* (the printed invitation adding archly, '*Real* cocktails will be served after the reading!'). In the third week of November Shanghai's Amateur Dramatic Society produced *The Man Who Came to Dinner* at the Lyceum Theatre.

Perhaps all these home-produced attractions helped to pass evenings that might otherwise have been spent at the cinema, for in November Shanghai's forty cinemas overnight stopped showing American films, which until 1949 had attracted an average monthly audience of a million Chinese. The decision, said an official announcement, 'is due to the political awakening of the masses who now see the reactionary nature of Hollywood products'.

Though the British community had dropped in two years from more than 4000 to 1200, everyone prepared to make the best of their second Christmas under Communism, by practising for the tableaux and carols to be sung at the Country Club, and for the pantomime *Dick Whittington*.

The Hawkingses invited Bob and Gertrude Bryan to spend Christmas Day with them in their new home, a house in Shanghai. It was a quiet party, with only a few close friends. Gladys wrote to her daughters, 'I shall always be eternally thankful that we invited Bob and Gertrude, for we never saw Bob again, and we did feel that at least he enjoyed his Christmas with us.'

14

The Death Cell
1951–1953

One Monday morning in February 1951, Bob and Gertrude Bryan were still in their pyjamas when Ah Ling, their number one boy, rushed up the stairs crying, 'Police here, master! Come to get you!' Within seconds they heard the clatter of heavy boots on the stairs. The door of their bedroom was thrust open and four armed police of the Public Security Bureau, dressed in blue padded uniforms, burst into the room. One hurled Gertrude on to a chair, another seized Bryan by the throat, a third rammed a pistol into his stomach, then threw him on the bed as all four started screaming abuse and curses at him, 'You're a spy – don't deny it! You're in the hire of the United States Navy as an Intelligence officer!'

A bewildered – and very frightened – Bryan, now fifty-eight, tried to shout back. He had never been in the Navy. He had never even been to sea in a warship. One man waved a card which said he *was* a spy. Another shouted that he spoke perfect Chinese and had used this knowledge against the Chinese people.

Bryan was powerless to struggle, but he still protested his innocence, even when one of them 'made me wish that I didn't know Chinese quite as well as I did'. He snarled that Bryan was being arrested and added, 'Your sentence has already been arranged. You will suffer the death of a thousand cuts.' This was one of the oldest (and at one time favourite) tortures, which had been practised for centuries in China. It consisted of inflicting 999 cuts on a man's body, over a period of time, each one more painful than the last, but none fatal – until the 1000th, which pierced the heart.

Gertrude had been taken into the next room, and Bob yelled to her that he was being arrested for espionage, that the charge was ridiculous. 'Will you please take it easy!' he shouted to her. Gertrude remembers shouting back, 'Be sure to dress warmly, Bob. I'll have Ah Ling get your winter woollen underwear.' At this, one guard pinpointed the real reason for his arrest – revenge. 'You are a filthy lawyer,' he shouted. 'You sent our comrades to death. You sent our comrades away to the Ward Road Jail.'

It was the moment when Bryan realised this was no routine arrest. Ah Ling rushed into the room with a bundle of bedding which the guard let Bob carry. They handcuffed him, prodded him down the stairs, pushed him into the back seat of an American car, and set off down Fah Wah Road to the centre of Shanghai.

When they crossed Soochow Creek, Bryan knew where they were going – to the Ward Road Jail which he had inspected once a month for fourteen years. Once there, he was taken up six flights and pushed into a cell. The guards took away his glasses, his watch, shoelaces, belt, even the string round his blankets, then clanged the steel door shut.

As he stood there alone, hands in pockets to hold up his trousers, Bryan realised that he had seen the cell before, because the walls, ceiling, floor, were all lined with cork. On his inspection tours in the past, the Chinese had always referred to it as 'the rubber room', and now, at this awful moment, he remembered one jailer explaining to him that it was 'suicide proof' because any prisoner who tried to bash his head against a wall would bounce back uninjured.

It was, in fact, the death cell.

Gertrude Bryan was a fighter – 'or I thought I was until I tried to take on the Communists' – and once the shock of that violent morning had been replaced by numbed acceptance, she became determined to free her husband. She went first to see Gladys Hawkings. A few days later they made their way to the Public Security Bureau, with Gladys acting as translator. It was the first time either of them had been to the functional building near the Soochow Creek, and Gertrude remembers being ushered into a small room with dull yellowish walls; a huge portrait of Mao Tse-tung hung on one wall. The only furniture consisted of two cane chairs facing an old, cheap desk behind which sat a young officer. People in green uniforms scurried in and out with papers, while Gladys, on behalf of Gertrude, explained politely who Gertrude was, what had happened, and asked for news of Bob Bryan.

The Chinese official looked at her blankly, and said, 'We have no record of any American in our prisons. Why should we imprison Americans?'

'But I saw the police arrest him,' Gertrude cried when the reply was translated. 'They dragged him out of the house! I *saw* them do it!'

The man gave both of them the kind of look that meant, 'I haven't time to waste on two hysterical old women.' However, he did relent sufficiently to explain that anyone with a genuine complaint must present it in writing. There was an office outside for this purpose, he added, and rang for a soldier to take them there.

There *was* a room – but there was no paper, and when Gladys asked an official for some she was told coldly that people making complaints had to provide their own writing paper. They returned home, wrote the complaint and presented it the following day.

Three weeks passed. Nothing happened. Gertrude decided to seek help on the consular level, though this was not easy, for with the return of John Cabot to America some months previously, the already tenuous diplomatic relations between the US and Communist China had ceased to exist. The British Consulate was handling American affairs, but was unable to make any headway on behalf of the citizen of a country with which China now considered herself virtually at war in Korea.

Gertrude decided to return to the Public Security Bureau, and this time she saw a different official, who took her and Gladys to meet his superior officer. Hardly had the two women entered the room before the Chinese asked harshly, 'You are Mrs Bryan?' Gladys pointed to Gertrude, at which the Chinese stabbed a finger in her direction and screamed, 'Your husband is a very bad man! He should be killed!' He waved them out of the room, shouting again, 'He should be killed – he is a spy!'

Shocked though Gertrude was, 'I felt a real surge of excitement' – for the phrase '*should* be killed' was the first hint that her husband was still alive. Confirmation soon reached her in another, equally sinister way. Three men in blue uniforms arrived at the Bryans' house in Columbia Circle and one, clearly the spokesman, told her the government understood she had asked the British to help her to find her husband. This was 'not permitted', he warned her. Any attempts to contact her husband would have disastrous consequences for her – and for him. 'It will prejudice his chances of a fair trial as a spy,' said the man, adding the stock accusation, 'Your husband is a very bad man. He should be killed.'

In vain Gertrude begged the man for news, to be allowed to write to him, to send him a parcel with some warm clothing or food. 'Chinese prisoners are not allowed to receive parcels,' the man replied. 'So why should foreign spies be treated differently?' With that, they left. The other two men had never spoken, but Gertrude realised they were acting as witnesses to a 'comrade's' behaviour. After some hesitation she did report the incident to the British Consulate; and there can be little doubt that the Chinese quickly discovered what she had done – or certainly that she had been in contact with the British. The reprisals were swift and brutal.

At seven o'clock one morning about a week later, two Communist officials banged on the door, refused to give Gertrude time to dress, and after she had hurriedly put on a robe, presented her with a printed form. It was a slip of paper similar to that which had been handed to the Hawkingses, and announced flatly that her house had been requisitioned for military purposes, and that she must quit the premises within twenty-four hours. She could take the furniture if she wished; any that was still in the house after seven the following morning would be seized.

The Hawkingses had been able to argue, but now in the hardening atmosphere there was no reprieve. Gertrude managed to borrow a small truck on to which she loaded some of the most treasured possessions that she and Bob had collected over the years. Billy Hawkings promised to store them in a godown belonging to Mardens, but everything else – beds, much of the furniture, all had to be left.

Bob's arrest had been a shattering moment in Gertrude's life, 'but this one came very close. We had built up our home, everything in it, with love, centring round a united family, and in some undefinable way I felt that while I was living in the house, I was keeping a home for him to come to. It was a symbol that stopped me giving up hope. But when I closed the door behind me for the last time, I was at my lowest ebb.'

Now Gertrude was not only homeless, she was penniless. Not a cent came in from Bob's old practice; even money owing to him had been frozen by the Communists. Luckily she had good friends; and her skill as a teacher had long been a byword in Shanghai, so that after spending a few days with the Hawkingses, she found a job. There was no salary, for the British School, its pupils reduced to a handful, had hardly a penny to spare, but Gertrude was offered a 'bed-sit' and board in return for general duties; she would help out with any problems that arose in these difficult times – anything from cooking if the Chinese staff were summoned to an indoctrination session to taking a class in maths if the regular teacher was ill.

The weeks dragged into months without a word about Bob, or from him, and it was becoming more difficult for his friends not to believe that he had joined the ever-increasing list of people whose arrest was followed by an unexplained silence never to be broken.

Then at the end of July, her phone rang at the School. A silky voice announced that this was the Public Security Bureau. In a maddeningly slow, polite voice – all the more sinister because it seemed to mask some hidden threat – the voice asked if that was Mrs Bryan, 'Mrs *Gertrude* Bryan?' Hands shaking, terrified by the matter-of-fact voice at the other end of the phone, Gertrude's first instinctive fear was that it would tell her Bob was dead. 'I steeled myself for the worst,' she remembers, 'and then I suddenly realised it might *not* be bad news.'

The bland voice, as though in ignorance that it was addressing a woman in an agony of suffering, announced without any pream-ble, as though arranging for the delivery of some groceries, that her husband would be very pleased to receive a food parcel – adding with appalling, unintended irony, 'That is, if you would like to send him one.'

Carefully the voice explained where the parcel should be delivered, but then as Gertrude begged for news, it said, with exquisite politeness, 'I'm sorry, I have just been told to deliver the message,' then courteously bid her good afternoon and hung up.

It was not the end of Gertrude's agony – that would last for many more months – but at least she had received a sign, something to sustain, even stimulate, her profound belief that one day Bob would come home. Happily for her, she had no idea how near to death her husband was.

For the first five months Bryan had been kept in solitary confine-ment. Only twice had his loneliness been interrupted briefly – on the occasions when he was arraigned before Communist judges demanding that he confess to being an American spy. Each time Bryan refused, and was thrown back into his cell.

The monotony was endless. Each morning before dawn a guard passed a straw broom through the bars of his door. After Bryan had swept the floor he handed the broom back and the guard then handed him his toothbrush and a small mug of hot water. Then came the daily ration of rice and pickled cabbage. As Bryan wrote later, 'I never had a wash, let alone a bath, I smelled foul. Sometimes I tried to collect a little water from my meals to wash myself.'

On one occasion the guard saw Bryan washing with an old towel; he rushed in and seized the towel, crying, 'Bathing is against the rules. Prisoners don't bathe any more than animals.' When Bryan weakly protested, the guard explained that monkeys had hair like human beings and they never bathed, therefore prisoners could live without bathing.

Bryan was not only denied facilities for washing, his captives refused to return his glasses, which caused him blinding headaches. Every time he asked for his glasses he was told curtly, 'Chinese prisoners don't wear glasses.' The one thing he was allowed, under careful scrutiny, was an unending supply of yellow toilet paper on which to write letters to the authorities pleading his case or his 'confession'. These – and messages to Gertrude his wife – he had to write standing at arm's length from the paper because he had no glasses and could hardly see. None of the letters ever reached its destination.

His health was deteriorating and he began to recognise the frightening symptoms of beriberi, the dietary disease which by now was crippling his legs. When all his pleas for a hearing failed, he determined on one last ploy – the threat of suicide. He had been thinking about it for some weeks ('not with any intention of doing myself in') because he realised that to a Chinese suicide had always meant enormous loss of face. He remembered a case in which a Chinese had wronged a friend and the friend had committed suicide on the other man's doorstep, thus causing the person to lose face. He, too, was in a way in someone else's house, and he had noticed his guards' deep concern for his survival. He decided to stage a hunger strike, which wouldn't be too painful for the daily ration of rice and cabbage revolted him and he had lost so much weight that he had to tie a knot in his trousers to hold them up. 'And I realised', he remembered afterwards, 'that I'd probably have starved to death anyway unless I took some action.'

On the morning of 12 July, five months to the day after his

arrest, he started his fast. When the guard pushed his rice and cabbage through the bars, Bryan told him, 'Take it away. I'm not going to eat that garbage.'

The uproar among the guards was immediate and it increased after Bryan refused all food on the second day. Some guards threatened him with torture, but for the most part they begged him to eat, tried to cajole him, and when they saw that he was adamant, Bryan realised that his guards were actually frightened; they had obviously been given the strictest orders to see that on no account must he be allowed to die. Finally, a Communist official came to see him, and Bryan presented his case, asking the Communist what *he* thought of a government which didn't even answer a prisoner's letters, which held him for months in solitary confinement without preferring any charges, which gave him such bad food that his legs were swollen with beriberi? What did *he* think of a government which asked a prisoner to write a confession, yet took away his glasses? And what about his wife? He had never heard from her, nor was he allowed any parcels.

The man went away, returning two hours later. 'If I arrange a hearing for you, will you eat?' he asked.

'No!' Bryan answered defiantly. 'I don't want a hearing now. I want to die.' Finally after much bargaining he agreed to eat providing he was given a hearing immediately.

Alas, the hearing for which Bryan had fought so doggedly was a disaster, for the Communists, with their perverse delight in humiliating others, forced Bryan to stand before the court judges and make his plea clad only in his filthy underclothes which had not been properly washed for five months. Bryan had laid out his only suit on the wooden platform which served as his bed, but when the jailers came to take him for his hearing, he was quickly handcuffed and not allowed to put his clothes on. 'Imperialists don't need clothes,' one jailer shouted. Bryan had planned to make a fighting defence as his own attorney, but as he ruefully remembered later, 'I found it impossible to be very convincing in my underwear'.

At a second hearing, however, he was asked, 'If we allow your wife to send in a food parcel will you promise to behave?'

This was Bryan's first inkling that Gertrude was still in Shanghai, that she must be trying to get him released. He agreed, and shortly afterward the parcel arrived. 'I remembered it, as a child remembers a Christmas present.' It was wrapped in brown paper, addressed in Gertrude's writing. Ravenously Bob explored its contents – some boiled ham, ten hard-boiled eggs, a tin of powdered milk, a tin of cheese, two packets of fruit-drops, a bottle of vitamin pills and some fruit – peaches, apples and bananas. For all his determination to ration his precious hoard, Bryan was much too hungry to control his impatience, and the parcel went quickly, with consequent attacks of violent stomach-ache in a body unused to good food. After a week he was back on rice and cabbage.

But at least his solitary confinement now ended. He was moved from time to time, from one cell to another, including one which even had the luxury of a flush toilet, instead of the usual bucket, so that he and his fellow prisoners were able to wash their clothes and themselves in the lavatory pan. It was at this time that he started on a long course of political indoctrination which he was warned would last for weeks, as a prelude to writing 'a new and better confession'. During all those months not one message from Gertrude reached him, so that Bryan never knew that towards the end of November 1951 Gertrude was finally given an exit permit to leave Shanghai.

She was torn by the cruel dilemma, but all her friends begged her to leave. She could never fight the Communists while in Shanghai, for every approach was met by a blank silence. So Gertrude left – by train to Canton, thence from Hongkong to Washington where she got a job as librarian in a girls' school.

Bryan was probably the only white man in the sprawling, sinister Ward Road Jail, but now that he was being shunted from one cell to another, mixing with different prisoners, he could not fail to learn that the building was bursting with new arrivals. Victims apparently of a huge purge, they poured in. Often they were bewildered, luckless Chinese destined to languish there while awaiting a trial that would never be held; they told terrifying tales of being arrested on trumped-up charges, often falsely accused by men who were paying off old scores. Others were pitiful innocents gathered into police nets spread indiscriminately over an entire neighbourhood.

Ward Road housed political prisoners. Those accused of 'normal' crimes were either executed or packed off to labour camps in the far north. These were often black-marketeers who were gradually starting to operate again, though more discreetly than previously, and dealing only in minor rackets such as digging up the graveyards in Frenchtown or on the Bubbling Well Road.

After throwing away the bones, they sold the coffins for firewood; these were much in demand because the resin in the wood made it burn easily.

But activities of this kind hardly interested the Communists. They had more significant problems, for as China became more deeply involved in the Korean War, Mao Tse-tung began to realise that some of his 'loyal' subjects were being assailed with doubts about the new regime. They were not yet serious enough to constitute a counter-revolution, but men who had been promised an end to war now found themselves being drafted to fight in Korea – and did not relish the prospect. Fathers who had welcomed their sons back to till the land suddenly found their family helpers snatched away again. City workers who had been granted shorter hours and higher wages were suddenly greeted at their factories or mills with notices ordering them to tackle 'Shock Attack Overtime' – for which there was no overtime pay. They were worse off than before, and if they failed to reach their norm, overseers draped black flags over their machines.

Chen Yi, the Mayor of Shanghai, believed that there were deeper reaons behind the vague undercurrent of unrest. It was caused by the speed of the take-over. Even people who *wanted* to like the new government found it difficult to cope with new ideological propaganda which assailed them at every street corner. For centuries they had learned Chinese ideographs which could condense a whole line of thought into a one-word picture. Now they were confronted at their weekly indoctrination meetings with 'portmanteau phrases' – spoken slogans like 'Beat Down the Big Feudal Exploiting Landlords!' and 'Stamp Out the Vicious Imperialistic Capitalists!' These slogans had to be learned by heart and later chanted in unison, under the watchful direction of professional cheer leaders. It was all too much to absorb so quickly.

And above everything else, the ordinary people of Shanghai, whose lives revolved round the family, could not understand a creed which praised a son or daughter for informing on a father or mother. It was unthinkable in a race where filial piety and family relationships had for 2000 years been an ingrained precept of the great sage Confucius. As a result, the warm friendships, the natural flow of cheerful life which even in adversity had for centuries been one of China's most endearing and graceful characteristics, was replaced by furtiveness, by stealth, by a lonely existence behind closed doors that no family dared to open.

People did not want to rebel against the new government – most of them certainly preferred it to the corrupt Chiang Kai-shek regime – but it was too big for them to ingest, particularly the fact that under Communism there was no private escape from the 'group mind', for now there was no greater term of abuse than to be called 'a democratic individualist'.

Mao Tse-tung had a rare instinct for sniffing trouble, and he decided to act quickly. No one can really pin-point the exact dates of the purges before and during 1953. However, Mao told Chen Yi to prepare for a swoop on classified 'enemies of the people', and Chen Yi delegated the operation to Lo Jui-ching, the chief of the Public Security Bureau, a tall, middle-aged man with pale, expressionless eyes, and a sinister twist to his mouth caused by a wound in his cheek. He controlled thousands of special police in Shanghai, many of them graduates of the indoctrination schools set up in the north years previously to teach 'basic thought-control methods'.

No attempt was made to keep the purges secret, though the small number of foreign residents hardly realised what was happening because reports only appeared in the Chinese newspapers. The almost automatic screams of rage preceded a swoop. The *People's Liberation Daily* shrieked, 'Shanghai is a nest of spies!' The headline was followed by 'official details' of 'secret-service organisations and special agents'.

It was the signal of fear for hundreds of thousands in a city which Mao had always distrusted. Confession was the only hope of escaping the dragnet; yet the graduates from the north seemed to have an uncanny instinct for assessing the true worth of a confession, and the slightest suspicion or doubt meant a swift ride to execution or jail. Black open lorries screamed through the streets, crowded with prisoners – men, women, children, roped together as they sped to the execution grounds. These were the unlucky ones to whom *'T'an pai!'* 'Confess' – had come too late, and who were now faced with crowds jeering, *'Champi!'* – 'To be shot'.

Tens of thousands had no trial; others faced a so-called public trial, in which a mass of herded coolies repeated screaming slogans over loudspeakers as the tightly-roped 'villains', on their knees in the dust, were held down by soldiers armed with tommy-guns. Frank Moraes, visiting Shanghai, was astonished to find that 'there was no attempt to conceal the terror'; Shanghai readers of the Party papers were kept informed of the numbers of

219

executions and arrests.* There were two kinds of execution, the one swift and merciful, the other more prolonged; the latter, Moraes was told, was called officially, 'Suppression of counter-revolutionaries with fanfare'.

A fanfare execution was preceded by a Mass Accusation Meeting which was often broadcast before the terror-stricken citizen was, in Communist jargon, 'deprived of existence'. Moraes studied official reports, in which the judge demanded, 'Comrades, what should we do with these criminals, bandits, secret agents, evil landlords, reactionaries?' From the crowd came a roar, 'Shoot them!' 'Should we have mercy on them?' asked the judge. Back came the expected roar, 'No!' followed by cries of 'Sha! Sha!' – 'Kill! Kill!'

One Communist told Moraes 'We had to stir people up', a philosophy echoed by Mao Tse-tung himself years later when he tried to explain away the Shanghai purges. 'To put it bluntly, it was necessary to bring about a brief reign of terror. Wrong cannot be righted unless proper limits are exceeded'.

Even if people were forewarned they had little chance of escape, for by now every person's life was controlled by the police. Everyone had an identity card, and a person could not spend a single night away from his dwelling-place without police permission. The police made regular swoops, often in the middle of the night, visiting every house in an area to check on the residents. Anyone found staying there without permission would spend the rest of the night in the police station after which he would have to publish a public apology in the newspaper.

Apologies filled columns of the Party newspapers. At the slightest sign of trouble – in a school, a factory, even in a family – the problem would be ventilated in 'frank' letters to the editor, criticising the actions of the schoolmaster, the foreman or the parent. After a suitable airing these were inevitably followed by a grovelling letter of apology from the offending person.

Often there seemed to be no motive behind the arrests or execution, as Alec McShane discovered. 'They just seemed to pick the names out of a hat.' McShane was waiting patiently for an exit visa, and realised that he must 'behave' or the permit

---

* Moraes wrote later that when he asked how many people had been killed, 'it was freely estimated that in all China some 15 million Chinese had been killed one way or another in the first five years of the regime'.

would be refused. Though there was little business for him to do, he kept on his modest staff and became increasingly bewildered by what was happening.

A 'resident commissar' arrived one day – 'a modestly educated man in a shabby uniform' – and said he would like to see how the workers were getting on. He would live on the premises. McShane eagerly offered him two rooms, but the man refused them, saying that he only wanted an iron bedstead and a straw mattress; he would provide his own food. He settled in and seemed particularly interested in three men on the staff.

The first was T. T. Chen, a Harvard-educated Chinese in his sixties who had invested a little capital in the business and was personal adviser to McShane. During all the hullabaloo for workers' rights, and the formation of a 'People's Workers Union' (with McShane at times locked in his own office), Chen faced all demands for wages and increased benefits politely but firmly. He gave way when he had to, but he refused to be bullied. McShane was concerned for Chen's safety, because the firm had dealt with Chiang Kai-shek, and sure enough, after months of labour troubles, Chen was taken away one moring for 'mass criticism'. McShane admits, 'I never expected to see him again.' But two weeks later Chen was back, smiling, affable, and ready to carry on work. 'They didn't treat me badly,' he told McShane, who never found out why he had been spared. 'I can only think the Communists realised that he was honest,' he wrote later, 'and that he didn't really exert any influence on the small Chinese staff, but was in fact a stabilising factor at a time when labour demands were getting out of hand.'

Lei Pi-wu was a very different kind of man, by profession a production manager who had risen from the shop floor, and had joined McShane after the factory for which he worked cut production. He had dealt with the compradores, allocated jobs according to aptitude, handled personnel problems and security. 'He was no angel,' McShane remembered, 'and there was a suspicion that he had fiddled a lot when the Japanese occupied Shanghai. But I liked him – and so did the workers.' Lei had a charming little old wife, a countrywoman addicted to burning incense before her household gods, and a son who was a bit of a work-shy wastrel, but quite harmless.

Lei acted as interpreter between the workers and McShane – as McShane thought, very successfully. Suddenly it all changed. McShane could only think that 'the faceless ones in the government suddenly became worried about anarchists or dissidents in the Shanghai labour corps, and had to make a stand. Maybe they were afraid that as a worker Lei possessed too much influence and leadership.'

Workers from neighbouring godowns and offices joined in mass meetings denouncing Lei. Walls were spattered with streamers attacking his honesty. Fresh denunciations followed daily. Then walls were defaced with a new kind of placard denouncing Lei as a rapist. Union chiefs from the factory where he had once worked produced a stream of elderly women who swore that in this factory they had only been able to hold down their jobs 'by submitting to the vile embraces of the lascivious Lei'.

The build-up continued. Lei was arrested 'by the unanimous demand of the neighbouring staffs and workers' and sent to jail. Then his idol-worshipping wife was arrested, so was the ne'er-do-well son. Workers from nearby offices and godowns paraded with banners and gongs and marched to a former greyhound racing stadium. The McShane workers who knew and liked Lei had to attend together with workers from the factory where Lei had once worked. The family was brought out, hands bound behind their backs, their legs haltered. 'The trial' by 'popular vote' was brief and noisy. The three were forced to kneel, then shot in the back of the head.

It was sickening – yet to McShane the fate of the third man was the most macabre of all. He was 'vocal and uncouth, an uneducated demagogue who delighted in wielding power'; it was he who had been initially responsible for starting the campaign against Lei and his family and indeed had cheered and laughed as they died. He seemed to be a perfect rallying point for Communist workers, yet within a week he too was arrested and banished to the north. The American-educated Chen told McShane, 'He had served his purpose, he was getting too big for his boots.'

The haphazard choice of 'guilty men' was no doubt due partly to the need of all totalitarian regimes to institute purges from time to time – not necessarily to weed out reactionaries, but as grim reminders to the rank and file to behave properly. This was what happened at Soochow University when one brilliant student, who had been foolish enough to comment on some Communist action, was picked out for trial. He was on the point of graduating; he had welcomed the new regime publicly and wholeheartedly. Yet for two days he was mercilessly interrogated, then had to face the entire student body and staff and listen for five hours to speeches denouncing him as a reactionary.

None who were compelled to attend, none who knew him well – masters as well as fellow students – dared do anything other than listen in silence. The boy was not executed but in the end he was publicly expelled. That was enough. His life was ruined, he knew that he would never be able to get a job. Broken in spirit, he said to a European friend, 'I'll believe anything, I'll do anything if only they'll let me alone.'*

Suicides soon became so frequent that Godfrey Moyle of Jardines used to walk in the gutter along the Bund to avoid the corpses. The Bund had many tall buildings and people intending to commit suicide could take the lift then jump. Godfrey Moyle remembers, 'I saw at least thirty die in this way in a matter of days.'

The police tried to stop the suicides by erecting nets which jutted out from first-floor windows over the pavement, in the hope of breaking a suicide's leap, but this only made them more determined. Instead of jumping from windows, they took running jumps from the roofs of tall buildings, so they would land in the street beyond the range of the netting. One man who jumped off a roof hit a rickshaw, killing himself, the puller and his passenger.

When it became increasingly difficult to jump from tall buildings guarded by Communist soldiers or police, many harassed Chinese drowned themselves in the Whangpoo or the Yangtze. Dozens of corpses were fished out of the river daily, giving rise to a macabre saying: 'He has passed his entrance exam for the Yangtze University.'

Poison also became more and more popular. The official veterinary surgeon to the British Consulate-General, a gentle old Chinese who had for months tended the Urquharts' pet poodle, was warned of impending arrest and quietly injected himself with the drug he normally used to put down sick animals.

The terror was brought home to the foreigners when it involved people they knew. Every woman in Shanghai knew Lau Kai Fook, who ran the silk shop in Nanking Road where Ellen Vine had bought her rolls of silk. He was a respected, honest man,

---

* This man, who told his story to a *Manchester Guardian* correspondent, must remain nameless as he eventually escaped to Hongkong, but has a family in China.

though a tough bargainer. He was forced to sign a confession apologising for his 'misdeeds', perhaps (no one really knows) because as a good shopkeeper he had been seen smiling once too often to a white customer. He threw himself from the top of a building.

Lau's neighbour Chen Wang Yu, who also kept a highly popular silk shop in the Nanking Road, was forced to confess, after being denounced by members of his own staff as 'the friend of the Imperialist Aggressors'. Poor Chen, who was in his sixties, not only had a fine shop with a staff of thirty, but until the Communists arrived had never had the slightest trouble with his workers. They loved him. He had been like a father to many of them, giving them an annual Chinese banquet in his home, offering jobs to the sons and daughters of his employees when the time came for them to earn a living.

With the arrival of the Communists, everything changed. A trouble-making minority insisted on forming a union, and none of Chen's friends dared to oppose the move in case *they* were denounced. The union then demanded that the shop be run as a workers' co-operative. Chen had no option but to agree. The union then 'ordered' him to prove that he bore them no ill-feeling by giving his workers the usual banquet. Again he agreed.

On the appointed evening, thirty-nine men and women sat down to a sumptuous sixteen-course Chinese dinner – all the workers and all the members of Chen's family. Not one of them survived the night. Chen had long since decided to take his life, and the lives of his family – and so he planned an exquisite revenge on those who had brought disgrace on his name. The food was poisoned.

As the terror continued, so the pressures on the foreign community increased. Sometimes it was blatant, sometimes incomprehensible, especially for the men and women waiting for exit permits – men and women to whom Shanghai was home but whose love of China had been replaced by an urgent desire to cut every bond, to sacrifice any business interests, just to get out as quickly as possible. 'I hate the place now and I never want to see it again,' wrote Billy Hawkings, who for decades had loved Shanghai. Both he and Gladys had applied for exit permits after Mardens had promised to send a replacement to run the office. By the middle of 1951 the permit had not been granted. Gladys wrote to her daughters in June:

Last week there were two lists within five days in the *North China Daily News,* but we were not on either of the lists. Now we just sit and smile while everyone says, 'Hard luck, but you're *sure* to be on the next list.' There is no rule about such things. I really don't care for myself, the delay postpones breaking up my last home in China and leaving our old servants, but it is for Dad's sake I want to get out. He is in a highly nervous condition, and badly needs a change. Yesterday he looked at some pictures of England and said, 'Fancy being a free man in a free city! Free to come and go as you like and say what you like!'

Any successful applicant for a permit celebrated with one last fling. Frank Moraes visited one of the few 'controlled' nightclubs, filled with 'a few thoughtful Chinese businessmen and their sad-eyed women'. In one corner some Europeans were dining, and it was evident that this was a farewell party for someone who had been granted an exit visa, for suddenly the band, which had been playing a selection of dreary Chinese tunes, made a roll on the drums and announced in English, 'Let's bid our foreign guests Godspeed!' The band broke into 'Auld Lang Syne'. Moraes found the occasion 'Ruritanian and unreal'.

One of the first to be lucky in the lottery of exit visas was Alec McShane who many thought might be refused a permit because of his friendship with Lei and others. One day McShane rang up Hawkings and announced, overjoyed, that his name was on one of the lists. The other names included that of Godfrey Moyle, whose insurance department at Jardines was virtually closed. For months he had been trying to get an exit visa.

The two men, who had apparently never met, were booked to leave on the same train on 26 June 1951. Seats and sleepers had been reserved in advance. They arrived at the famous North Station, packed with troops, milling crowds of Chinese clutching cardboard suitcases or whimpering children, perhaps lucky families being allowed to return to their ancestral villages. In one corner stood a huge group of resigned men and women dressed in blue cotton, guarded by soldiers, who herded them on to the platform from which the Tientsin train was due to leave. The long snake of carriages ended with a dozen or so cattle trucks into which the docile prisoners were unceremoniously bundled. The doors were bolted on the outside. There could be little doubt that the wretches were on their way to some indoctrination or labour camp in the far north.

McShane settled himself in his seat and one can imagine his feelings of excitement as he waited for the train to pull out. Further along, Godfrey Moyle said a last farewell to Chang, his boy, who had come to see him off. Then, as Moyle remembers, 'I had actually got one foot on the step of the train and was starting to climb in when I heard my name being called on a loud hailer. Would I please go to the stationmaster's office?'

Without any foreboding – imagining that at worst his passport required to be stamped – Moyle pushed his way through the jostling crowds until he finally found the small room at the end of the platform. Inside an official in a blue cotton uniform was obviously awaiting his arrival.

There were no preliminary courtesies. Once Moyle had explained who he was, the official demanded abruptly, 'Show me your exit permit.'

Moyle produced it. Without any explanation the official took it, read it slowly, reread it, looked at Moyle, and then without a word tore the precious document into shreds and threw the pieces into a wastepaper basket. After waiting all these months for his visa, poor Moyle was 'absolutely speechless, literally. I couldn't get one word out, not a word would come.'

At last, almost in tears, Moyle demanded an explanation. The official looked at him and shouted one word, 'Cancelled!' Then he strutted out of the room.

Moyle never did discover why his visa had been revoked. It took him more than two years to get another one and he was stuck in Shanghai until October 1953 – without any winter clothing which he had sent on ahead to Hongkong.

Though nine out of ten foreign businessmen dreamed only of the day when they would be permitted to leave, many faced daily insults by workers who knew perfectly well that their bosses were only staying under duress. On the office door of one taipan his workers painted a grotesque picture of a capitalist wearing a shirt made out of a Union Jack, being killed by a worker who had thrust a dripping bayonet into his stomach. It greeted the taipan every morning when he entered his office.

Another man was lampooned by workers who had enlarged a photograph of their employer and stuck it on a poster of nude dancing girls, giving the impression that their boss spent his time drinking champagne surrounded by nude prostitutes in nightclubs. Frank Moraes found himself thinking of 'the curious

226

resilient character of the British who were adapting themselves to the new order of things. To have your employees lampoon you openly in your own office was by any standard a novel experience, but the old China hand appeared to be taking it in his stride.' All this particular employer said to Moraes was, 'They've even got me on their placards!'

Some foreigners attempted to *give* their businesses to the Communists to save taxes and exorbitant running costs. For two years the owners of the prestigious Cathay Hotel tried in vain to abandon their property and hand it over to the state. They offered to give it to the Chinese for nothing, but the offer was rejected. For two years the manager tried to agree on the hotel's 'liabilities', during which time the liabilities increased day by day. In the end the owners actually had to pay the government a huge lump sum for the privilege of giving them a splendid hotel in excellent running order. Not until the final agreement was signed was the manager granted an exit permit.

The Cathay, like all foreign-owned concerns, had been compelled to pay taxes based on pre-take-over figures. Current profits and turnover did not come into the matter. Revaluation of assets and stocks, depreciation and turnover were still calculated on book values in August 1949, conveniently ignoring the fact that the Shanghai dollar had since then risen astronomically. It led to situations which would have been ludicrous had they not been so tragic. One British company of piano-importers received a demand in 1951 to pay the same taxes they had remitted in 1949, though the company had not sold one single piano since that date. Worse, taxes were due on the date a company received the demand, with interest charged at one per cent for every date of default.

One man did manage to make a killing out of the Communists and get away with it – just once. Young Philip Schlee, who had kept the family tea business of Andersons running single-handed, was ordered by Communist officials to produce his books and files for examination. The Communists were horrified to discover that Schlee had been sending cables to clients forecasting the size of the tea crop. He was accused of economic espionage, but was able to explain that forecasting was an important price-regulator and a normal part of any commodity business.

Fortunately Schlee knew the tea business thoroughly and the Communists didn't. 'They just hadn't a clue where or how to sell the crop,' Schlee remembers. This resourceful young man was able to persuade the Communist government to let him handle the sale (to his old customers) of Chinese green tea, which was grown mostly in the Nanking area. Schlee sold 100,000 cases of tea – a third of the entire crop – to North Africa. Financially it was a highly successful operation for Schlee, but he was convinced that the Communists regarded his commission as a reasonable price to pay for teaching them how to operate the tea market. For once they had learned the art and had discovered the names of his biggest clients, they started sending samples of tea behind his back and Andersons were cut right out of the market. At this stage Schlee had no difficulty in getting an exit permit.

At the end of 1951, those two stalwart old Shanghailanders, Billy and Gladys Hawkings, finally left – celebrating the 'freedom' for which Billy had pined with a trip round the world to see their daughters. But the manner of their going depended on a wild game of bluff by one man against an all-powerful government; even more extraordinary, Hawkings actually enlisted as allies the very workers who had been locking him in his own office.

Billy had almost given up hope of leaving because of the pig-headed attitude of one particular official in dealing with a problem simple enough to be solved by any intelligent five-year-old. Mardens had agreed to keep the business running in Shanghai under a new manager who would replace Hawkings and who was due for retirement anyway. Since Hawkings could not get an exit permit until the replacement received his entry visa, Mardens cabled from Hongkong giving the name of the man, all details of his work, and of course applied in Hongkong for the visa. For months nothing happened. Finally Hawkings hit on a plan. It was a long shot but he reckoned it might work.

Though there seemed to be no logic in the way exit or entry permits were granted, he had noticed the increasing influence of workers, particularly when they realised that a foreign business was in real danger of closing down. This would probably mean not only loss of jobs, but much worse, the grim possibility that workers would be uprooted and sent to distant communes.

With this in mind Hawkings telephoned Hongkong and quietly suggested to a baffled head office that they send a long cable authorising Hawkings to close down the business entirely. After some doubts, Hongkong agreed. The cable arrived. Hawkings called in the head of the union, the man who had locked him up in his office, and showed him the cable. He brought in a translator to help the man to understand it. The effect was instantaneous. The union leader went at once to the official whom Hawkings had been visiting without success week after week for nearly a year. Two days later Hawkings was told that an entry visa had been granted in Hongkong for his replacement and that exit permits would be ready within a week for himself and Gladys.

The couple left on the next available ship. Hawkings could not disguise his relief at escaping from 'this prison without walls'. Gladys, however, left with mixed feelings. 'All that we have had to go through during the last few years has been too much for Dad at his age,' she wrote. 'I hadn't come up against problems in the same way that men do, and anyway, I love China so much that perhaps I gloss over things.'

It was becoming easier now for more to leave, especially when it became obvious to the Chinese government that foreign businesses had finally been bled white. By April 1952 the assets of the Shell Company were requisitioned, together with those of British-American Tobacco, which gave up its entire business in China after two years of negotiations. Within a few months the Communists requisitioned the two chief British-owned dockyards – the Shanghai Dockyards Ltd which owned four large drydocks, and Mollers Shipbuilding and Engineering Works Ltd which controlled large wharf spaces, workshops and shipways. In November, after the Korean War's biggest bombing raid along the Yalu River, the Communists struck at the very heart of enterprises which the British had built up in Shanghai, seizing the British-owned water, gas and tram companies.

During all these months Robert Bryan was still lost to the world. He had now decided that it was useless to fight his interrogators on legal grounds. Browbeaten, sick and half-starved, he had decided that his only chance of life lay in some form of co-operation, so he begged for the privilege of indoctrination. But his final act had to be convincing, for he knew that his life depended on it. Never by nature a yes-man, his last remaining line of defence was '*Shih! Shih! Shih!*' – 'Yes, sir! Yes, sir! Yes, sir!'

There followed months of indoctrination by different Communist specialists, starting with the first who told him gravely, 'You are most fortunate. Your hands are stained with the blood of our comrades whom you have sent to prison and death. Shooting is too good for you, but the People's Government is merciful.'

'*Shih, shih, shih,*' said Bryan fervently, though he felt at something of a disadvantage as a 'convert', for by now 'my ankles were knotted with beriberi and my matted beard was five inches long. I hadn't bathed in ten months and I had that lingering pungent smell that comes from an endless diet of rice and cabbage.' Sometimes Bryan was allowed to sit during the 'lessons'. At other times he was forced to stand, handcuffed. From time to time during the preliminary sessions, a rubber truncheon was used.

For week after week 'experts' taught him the error of his imperialistic ways, feeding him with the most ridiculous lies, with which he had to agree. At a time when trade was stagnant, one specialist in economics explained to him patiently, 'The People's Government has industralised the whole of China and is entirely self-sufficient. China needs nothing from any other country. Embargoes by America would be absolutely ineffective. Do you understand that?'

'Yes, sir,' Bryan replied. 'Yes, sir.' At a time when the Americans were ferociously bombing targets in North Korea, a military expert solemnly lectured him on the might of the Chinese army. 'The People's Army, Navy and Air Force are invincible and could easily defeat the United States forces,' he said. 'Do you understand that?'

Once again Bryan answered, with all the enthusiasm he could muster, 'Yes, sir. Yes, sir.' His cell guard, at least, seemed delighted with Bryan's progress, and told him, 'You are learning the truth at last.' 'Yes,' replied Bryan. 'I am changing my thinking.'

By mid-March 1952 months of intensive indoctrination had ended and he had written his confession. He was then arraigned before three 'judges', one of whom told him scornfully that it was no real confession because he had not admitted to being a spy.

Desperately Bryan told his judge, 'I cannot confess to that. I am not a spy. I have changed my thinking, but I have never been a spy. I have always been a friend of the Chinese people.'

The judge made a gesture to the guards. Suddenly Bryan was blindfolded and carried to another building, where he was thrown face downwards on a table. As he was held down, his tattered trousers were ripped off and someone jabbed a hypodermic needle into his spine. Then he was left in a nearby room.

'After a few minutes,' he remembered later, 'I seemed to lose all power of thought, I felt as if I were sitting in a chair at a table but suspended high in the air. Below me I could hear a voice chanting, "You must be truthful. You must make a true confession. Write the truth."'

Bryan heard the voice drifting off before he blacked out, awakening the next morning on the floor of his own cell 'with a monster headache'. The following day he was taken before the judge and shown a complete confession of his spying activities, and his signature at the bottom. He asked permission to read the document.

'Don't be stupid,' said the judge almost kindly. 'You've told the truth all right. Everyone tells the truth finally. That's why we gave you *cheng yen yao* – the "true words medicine" – and you have now told us the truth.'

At last, hoped Bryan, he might be released. He had been indoctrinated, he had apologised, he had, he was certain, even signed a confession that he had been a spy. Was there any more reason to keep him a prisoner? Apparently so. He went back to solitary confinement.

For more than two months after making his confession, Bryan was kept in solitary confinement. But he had noticed that he was being more carefully looked after. The monotonous diet of rice and pickled cabbage never changed, but officials paid him regular visits, enquiring solicitously after his health. Though he could hardly walk because his legs were so swollen with beriberi, guards even helped him to exercise in his cell.

Then on 24 June two guards entered his cell with a bucket of hot water and a pan. 'Take a bath,' one of them told him, and Bryan tried as best he could to sponge himself down with his dirty face-towel. 'I looked like a skeleton,' he remembered thinking when he stripped. (He had in fact lost forty-six pounds in sixteen months in jail.) Another guard came in, this time with cold water, clippers and a Chinese razor. They clipped all his hair off, softened his beard and then shaved it off roughly.

Two days later another guard came to his cell and ordered him to 'pack your things'. Quickly Bryan gathered up his old shirts, underwear, mouldy blankets, and was ordered to say farewell to the official who had master-minded his political indoctrination and who, presumably, had decided that Bryan was now a suitable convert to return to the United States and preach the Communist gospel. He *must* have thought so, for after detailing Bryan's past 'crimes' and outlining his miraculous conversion, he extracted one last extraordinary promise from the bedraggled prisoner.

As Bryan stood there, the Communist solemnly told him, 'I want you to swear to tell the truth about the People's Government when you are released.'

As Bryan remembered later, 'I promised enthusiastically.' Three days later, on 29 June 1952, after his guards had taken him by train to the frontier, he stumbled across the narrow bridge that led to Hongkong and freedom. Then he set off by sea for San Francisco where Gertrude was waiting for him.

Bob Bryan had been brutally treated, but at least he was now reunited with Gertrude in free America. Others were not so lucky, even if they did not go to jail.

One Briton, Wilbert Mellor, had actually been on leave in Hongkong with his wife Dora when the Communists took Shanghai, and insisted on returning. He never saw his wife again.

'Bill' Mellor – as he was known to everyone – was fifty-two at the time, and one of the most popular men in the British community. He was not only managing director of A. R. Burkill & Sons Ltd, the reputable real estate agents, but chairman of the Waterworks Board and director of several other companies. But he was more than that. Very much in the Hawkings mould, he played a leading role in the cultural, sporting, financial life of the foreign community. It was this as much as the affairs of business that made him return, despite the doubts of his wife. 'There are things I must attend to,' he told her, but insisted that she should go to England where their two daughters were on the point of leaving school. 'They need their mother at this time,' said Bill Mellor.

He did not expect to remain long in Shanghai, for he was convinced the Communists would expropriate foreign firms, but the authorities decided to treat him virtually as a hostage. All demands for an exit permit were refused. True, he was not in jail, but he was in a kind of prison just the same, for early in 1953 doctors warned him that he was suffering from cancer, with no hope of a cure.

When his wife in London was told the news, she tried desperately to return to Shanghai so that they could be together; in Shanghai every attempt was made to persuade the Chinese to grant him an exit permit. 'In the end,' she said, 'there was nothing I could do except to wait, ready to fly at a moment's notice to Hongkong and meet Bill there if the Communists relented.'

They did not relent until, with a brutality that is hard to beat, they granted Bill Mellor an exit permit on the day he died.

Postscript

The callous way in which Bill Mellor was treated seemed to mark the end of an era in the history of Shanghai, for he was one of the last in a long line of men and women from every corner of the globe who had been drawn to live in this international metropolis, and to die in a Communist city.

Many different reasons had impelled men like Mellor to come here – the prospect of riches in such a profitable emporium, the hope of asylum, and most of all over the years, the heady lure of adventure. Many had prospered, many had died, the men sometimes violently, the women and children sickening of diseases for which their doctors at first could find no cure. Yet one has the feeling that, of the millions who passed that way, none regretted the life they had chosen, the part they played in creating out of nothing the greatest city Asia has ever known. It had been a unique experience – good, yes; bad, yes; but never indifferent.

Yet now, in a rebuilt city, its satellite suburbs depressingly reflecting the Soviet architectural influence, its people in their identical uniforms padding through the streets like sexless ghosts, the past seems strangely unreal, a dream conjured up out of the fanciful memories of a raconteur given to hyperbole.

Did it ever exist, that exotic city? Was it really built on mud? Or was it – to those who lived there – a city built on the foundations of happy memories which have the magical quality of lining every cloud with silver? A wanderer returned – an old China hand back on a package tour organised by the China Travel Agency – searching for landmarks to reinforce memories, might well wonder if the past had all been a dream.

If you want to rest near the corner of the Bund and the Soochow Creek, there are now two concrete benches where once the Nationalists and the Communists fought their brief, staged battle from the shelter of a urinal. Sitting there, you can see the British Consulate-General opposite, the flag still flying, its spacious lawns as trim as ever, though its long corridors are peopled mostly with echoes and the turbaned Sikh watchmen at the gates are missing; the jetty where Urquhart moored his consular launch is now used for boat tours. To your right the pedicabs still ply across the Garden Bridge, that improbable exercise in ironmongery, but the Bund now is quiet, half empty, its traffic no longer harsh and shrill.

The famous buildings of the past still stand, a haunting skyline. The handsome columns still frame the stout double doors of the Shanghai Club, only now it is a seamen's hostel, and the Long Bar, that monument of Edwardian splendour, is flanked with huge pictures of Mao Tse-tung and other Chinese leaders. The grandiose Hongkong and Shanghai Bank has become the City Council offices, though the two British lions which for decades sat majestically outside are still there, and superstitious Chinese still touch their paws as they pass, in the forlorn hope that the gesture will bring them good joss in a city where the only luck is bad.

Was it really here that a ship berthed in the dead of night and George Vine, in his office at the now defunct *North China Daily News*, watched coolies pad across the Bund with dangling loads of gold bullion? And was it to this bank that young David Middleditch drove up in a truck to collect $50,000 million with which to pay the wages? And if you return to the old Cathay – now renamed the Peace Hotel – to rest before a guide whisks you off to another collective farm or model school, carefully illustrated with smiling faces, you may wonder if in truth this rather tatty lounge was ever really filled with glamorous White Russians or Chinese girls twittering like starlings as the Filipino band struck up the latest foxtrot.

Venture out towards the suburbs and the past might never have been. Gone are the apartment blocks in Frenchtown where Norman Watts met Chou En-lai and smuggled him out of the city, and where later John Proud met the Chinese leader. Many have been razed to make way for the wide, dreary avenues so necessary for the endless military parades. The old race-course is a 'People's Square', the old golf-course a zoo, the Country Club a school. And if you venture further afield towards Hungjao, where the rice once grew in flat fields criss-crossed by irrigation canals, where are the grounds of The Limit? A satellite town has long since sprouted there, and the bright flowers tended so lovingly by Gladys Hawkings have been replaced by the strident colours of laundry jutting out on poles from every high-rise building, each cubby-hole in each soulless tenement a tiny refuge for people beset with tensions and miseries, seduced by slogans and promises they know to be lies, but which none dare denounce.

No one can deny that the old Shanghai was an aggravating anachronism, a boil which had to be lanced in the revolution that swept across not only China but all Asia; but in place of the old Shanghai with its wickedness, a different wickedness now prevails, 'an evil throwback', as Bob Bryan wrote after his release, 'in which people have never been cheaper in the history of China'.

Everything that drew men and women to Shanghai – drew even the penniless Chinese who preferred starvation inside its protective walls to degradation without – has been wrenched out, as though madmen had torn the heart out of a living being. The once-colourful streets are a mindless concrete wilderness. The walls shriek with 'Factory Emulation' posters, exhorting the masses to work harder. Once a week they rest from their labours – on different days, for there is no Sunday as we know it – and then they queue for hours outside the cinemas which open at 8 a.m. for the first of five daily showings.

There is nothing else to do, and that is the worst thing of all: the spectre of cultural emptiness in a great city whose citizens' drab existence is on a par with the security and working conditions of a domestic animal, and whose freedom is restricted to the length of a leash on a captive mongrel.

Today the United States and Communist China are officially 'friends', and the regime in Taiwan has been abandoned. Few can doubt that this political turnabout can do anything but good, and that it was futile for the Americans to pretend for so long that the regime governing the most highly populated nation on earth did not officially exist. It was of course easier for Britain to recognise the Communist regime quickly, and the steadily accelerating volume of British trade with China has done much to break down political barriers.

For centuries America has been obsessed with 'the Chinese dream'. Its businessmen see the country as a vast reservoir where American surplus grain and consumer goods can be sold in immense quantities. Its evangelists see yet another opportunity to convert hundreds of millions of people. Its Sinophile scholars are anxious to bury themselves *sur place* in one of the world's greatest cultures, and hope to persuade China's rulers not to eradicate its noble past from every history book in the country.

Let us hope they will succeed. It would be unfair not to remember that the present regime has ruled for only three decades in the long history of China, and unfair not to hope that good will come out of evil. All creeds change given time, many of them (but not all) for the better. Communists protecting their 'religion' are behaving no more wickedly than the Spanish Inquisition.

Change can only come slowly, but as the frontiers are opened up, perhaps the age-old virtues of China will again prevail, and then, as far as Shanghai is concerned, the city that started out as a dream, that touched the dizzy heights of splendid reality, will awaken from the nightmare into which it has sunk.

What Happened to Them?

Robert Bryan died some years ago, but his widow Gertrude now lives in Arlington, Virginia.

John Cabot and his wife live in Washington, DC. He has retired from the US Foreign Service.

Mariano Ezpeleta had a distinguished career, becoming ambassador to several countries before leaving the diplomatic service in 1971.

Sue Fabian (*née* Crouch) now lives near Woking. Her husband Harold died some years ago.

Billy and Gladys Hawkings are both dead. Most of their letters and papers were left in the safe hands of one of their daughters who lives in Kent.

Graham Jenkins, who so narrowly escaped execution, rose to the top of his profession, and is now owner and editor-in-chief of *The Star,* Hongkong.

John Kerans, who was awarded the DSO after the dramatic escape of *Amethyst,* stood for Parliament after leaving the Royal Navy. He is now a civil servant and lives in a South London suburb.

Alec and Natasha McShane finally married and settled in the south of France, where McShane became an advertising agent working with the author when he was the editor of a newspaper in France. Both McShane and his wife are now dead.

David Middleditch is now a director of Matheson & Co. Ltd in London, and lives in Winchester.

Godfrey Moyle lives in retirement in Hongkong.

John Proud has retired and lives with his wife in Melbourne, Australia.

Philip Schlee runs his own business in Hongkong.

Sidney Smith was for many years one of the top correspondents of the *Daily Express.* He now lives in France.

Robert Urquhart was knighted and now lives in retirement in Edinburgh.

George and Ellen Vine live in Bonn, West Germany, where George is the extremely energetic manager of the Reuters bureau and its chief political correspondent.

Norman Watts married after he left Shanghai and now lives with his wife and young daughter in the romantically-named Galloping Hall, near Diss, Norfolk.

Principal Dates in Sino-Western Relations

The rise of Chiang Kai-shek and Mao Tse-tung culminated in a lasting hatred between the two men. It led both leaders into actions which less bitter men might not have taken, and which turned Chiang from a man who had flirted with the Soviet Union into a rabid anti-Communist. This intransigence made successive British and American diplomatic missions foredoomed to failure. Though the history is well known, this brief chronology may be of interest to readers anxious to pinpoint dates before 1948 when the narrative of this book starts.

1842 Treaty of Nanking follows defeat of China by Britain in the Opium Wars. Under it China cedes Hongkong to Britain, and allows foreign settlements in Shanghai and other ports, thus giving birth to the International Settlement in Shanghai.

1866 Sun Yat-sen is born.

1887 Chiang Kai-shek is born.

1893 Mao Tse-tung is born.

1912 Dr Sun Yat-sen becomes Provisional President of the Republic of China following the fall of the Manchu dynasty. Chiang returns from military training in Japan to join him.

1921 Chinese Communist Party founded.

1923 Soviet Russia pledges aid to Sun Yat-sen while officially recognising that 'Communism and the Soviet system are incompatible with China's needs at this time'. Chiang Kai-shek visits Moscow, sees Stalin and Trotsky (long before Mao ever dreamed of an alliance with Russia). Within two years a thousand Soviet military and political advisers are helping China.

1924 Chiang Kai-shek opens (and becomes director of) Whampoa Military Academy, China's first professional military school. Sun thanks Russia for 'the lessons of the revolutions that have led us to inaugurate this academy'. Ironically, Whampoa's policy is to train young officers along Leninist lines.

1925 Sun Yat-sen dies in Peking.

1926 As Communists gather more recruits, Chiang becomes disillusioned – and afraid of – Russian infiltration in Whampoa and the Army, bans all Chinese Communist Party members from top army posts, removes all Soviet advisers from executive posts. It is this stand against Soviet infiltration into China that encourages Mao to form his own breakaway Army of Liberation which will one day defeat Chiang.

1927 Chiang feels strong enough to attack Communists in their stronghold of Shanghai. He cannot touch the International Settlement, but launches a ferocious massacre of Communists. Hundreds of thousands slaughtered in Shanghai and Canton purges.
Chiang Kai-shek severs diplomatic relations with Soviet Russia.

1931 The 'Mukden Incident' gives Japan an excuse to strike at this Manchurian city as part of a plan to take over all Manchuria. Mao establishes the first Chinese Soviet Republic.

1932 Mao Tse-tung declares war on Japan.
Japan establishes puppet state of Manchukuo in Manchuria.

1932 Japanese troops thrust southwards towards Peking and Tientsin.

1934 Mao begins his historic 'Long March' in which he and 20,000 survivors reach Yenan in Shensi Province during 1935.

1937 Nationalist and Communist parties create United Front to fight Japanese.

Marco Polo 'incident' near Peking marks official start of Sino-Japanese war.
Japanese take Peking, Tientsin, Shanghai (but not the International Settlement) and Nationalists retreat inland.

1938 Nationalists lose Yangtze valley, Hankow, Canton, establish their capital in Chungking.

1941 Japanese attack Hongkong, Singapore, Pearl Harbor in December, followed by declaration of war by Western powers. All foreigners in Shanghai's International Settlement are interned.

1942 General Stillwell ordered to Chungking to serve under supreme command of Chiang.
US loan of $500 million to China authorised.

1943 Unknown to foreigners interned in Shanghai, Western powers agree to renounce all extraterritorial rights in China, which means that when the war ends the International Settlement in Shanghai will cease to function, and it will become a Chinese city.

1944 Roosevelt appoints General Patrick J. Hurley his personal representative to China. General Stillwell recalled.

1945 Yalta Agreement signed in February by Churchill, Roosevelt and Stalin.
VE-Day, 8 May.
Japan surrenders on 14 August. Mao flies to Chungking to see Chiang.
General Hurley resigns in November. In a bitter resignation letter tells President Truman, 'It is no secret that the American policy in China did not have the support of all the career men in the State Department. The professional Foreign Service men sided with the Chinese Communist armed party . . . our professional diplomats continuously advised the Communists that my efforts in preventing the collapse of the Nationalist government did not represent the policy of the United States.'
General George C. Marshall becomes President Truman's

special representative to China with instructions to attempt to maintain peace between Nationalists and Communists.

1946 Full-scale war erupts between Nationalists and Communists. Nationalists move capital from Chungking to Nanking in May.

1947 General Marshall's recall announced. He becomes Secretary of State.

Notes on Further Reading

I have read many books while researching this one, and though a bibliography may be of value to the scholar, it has to be said that for the general reader many of the books are heavy going. Consequently I am suggesting only the names of a few books which I *enjoyed* reading.

My 'bible' has been the 1000-page *United States Relations with China, with special reference to the period 1944–1945* (1949), a masterly array of diplomatic dispatches, and notes of conversations between American and Chinese leaders, published by the US Department of State. Equally fascinating is Barbara W. Tuchman's *Sand Against the Wind: Stillwell and the American Experience in China* (1970). Theodore H. White's *Thunder out of China* (1946), written in collaboration with Annalee Jacoby, a newspaper colleague in China, is far and away the most exciting eyewitness story of the events leading up to the revolution.

The Role of the Chinese Army (1967) by John Gittings and *The Red Army of China* (1962) by Edgar O'Ballance show how Mao Tse-tung built up and employed his forces to achieve that revolution, while *Chinese Shadows* by Simon Leys (the pseudonym of a noted Belgian scholar) is a superb if heart-rending assessment of its impact on the Chinese people.

Yellow Creek (1962) by J. V. Davidson-Houston is an agreeable history of Shanghai from its earliest days, while for those who would like a fuller account of the adventures of HMS *Amethyst*. I can recommend *Escape of the 'Amethyst'* (1957) by G. E. Lucas-Phillips and *Yangtze Incident* (1949) by Lawrence Earl, an excellent book which provided me with much of the background for this naval epic.

I also derived a great deal of enjoyment when tracking down, with the aid of my translator, the Chinese Communist magazines and part-works of the period, many of which I found at the School of Oriental and African Studies, London.

Index

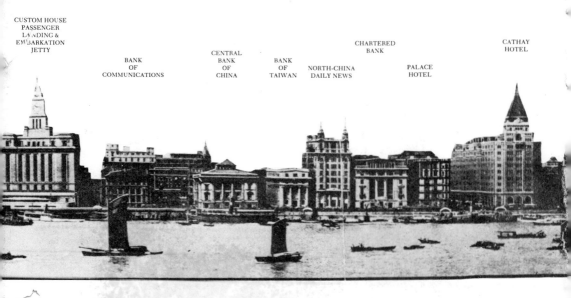

CUSTOM HOUSE
PASSENGER
LANDING &
EMBARKATION
JETTY

BANK
OF
COMMUNICATIONS

CENTRAL
BANK
OF
CHINA

BANK
OF
TAIWAN

NORTH-CHINA
DAILY NEWS

CHARTERED
BANK

PALACE
HOTEL

CATHAY
HOTEL

A PANORAMIC VIEW OF THE